C-3170   CAREER EXAMINATION SERIES

This is your
PASSBOOK for...

Building Construction Engineer

Test Preparation Study Guide
Questions & Answers

COPYRIGHT NOTICE

This book is SOLELY intended for, is sold ONLY to, and its use is RESTRICTED to individual, bona fide applicants or candidates who qualify by virtue of having seriously filed applications for appropriate license, certificate, professional and/or promotional advancement, higher school matriculation, scholarship, or other legitimate requirements of education and/or governmental authorities.

This book is NOT intended for use, class instruction, tutoring, training, duplication, copying, reprinting, excerption, or adaptation, etc., by:

1) Other publishers
2) Proprietors and/or Instructors of "Coaching" and/or Preparatory Courses
3) Personnel and/or Training Divisions of commercial, industrial, and governmental organizations
4) Schools, colleges, or universities and/or their departments and staffs, including teachers and other personnel
5) Testing Agencies or Bureaus
6) Study groups which seek by the purchase of a single volume to copy and/or duplicate and/or adapt this material for use by the group as a whole without having purchased individual volumes for each of the members of the group
7) Et al.

Such persons would be in violation of appropriate Federal and State statutes.

PROVISION OF LICENSING AGREEMENTS – Recognized educational, commercial, industrial, and governmental institutions and organizations, and others legitimately engaged in educational pursuits, including training, testing, and measurement activities, may address request for a licensing agreement to the copyright owners, who will determine whether, and under what conditions, including fees and charges, the materials in this book may be used them. In other words, a licensing facility exists for the legitimate use of the material in this book on other than an individual basis. However, it is asseverated and affirmed here that the material in this book CANNOT be used without the receipt of the express permission of such a licensing agreement from the Publishers. Inquiries re licensing should be addressed to the company, attention rights and permissions department.

All rights reserved, including the right of reproduction in whole or in part, in any form or by any means, electronic or mechanical, including photocopying, recording, or by any information storage and retrieval system, without permission in writing from the Publisher.

Copyright © 2025 by
National Learning Corporation

212 Michael Drive, Syosset, NY 11791
(516) 921-8888 • www.passbooks.com
E-mail: info@passbooks.com

PASSBOOK® SERIES

THE *PASSBOOK® SERIES* has been created to prepare applicants and candidates for the ultimate academic battlefield – the examination room.

At some time in our lives, each and every one of us may be required to take an examination – for validation, matriculation, admission, qualification, registration, certification, or licensure.

Based on the assumption that every applicant or candidate has met the basic formal educational standards, has taken the required number of courses, and read the necessary texts, the *PASSBOOK® SERIES* furnishes the one special preparation which may assure passing with confidence, instead of failing with insecurity. Examination questions – together with answers – are furnished as the basic vehicle for study so that the mysteries of the examination and its compounding difficulties may be eliminated or diminished by a sure method.

This book is meant to help you pass your examination provided that you qualify and are serious in your objective.

The entire field is reviewed through the huge store of content information which is succinctly presented through a provocative and challenging approach – the question-and-answer method.

A climate of success is established by furnishing the correct answers at the end of each test.

You soon learn to recognize types of questions, forms of questions, and patterns of questioning. You may even begin to anticipate expected outcomes.

You perceive that many questions are repeated or adapted so that you can gain acute insights, which may enable you to score many sure points.

You learn how to confront new questions, or types of questions, and to attack them confidently and work out the correct answers.

You note objectives and emphases, and recognize pitfalls and dangers, so that you may make positive educational adjustments.

Moreover, you are kept fully informed in relation to new concepts, methods, practices, and directions in the field.

You discover that you are actually taking the examination all the time: you are preparing for the examination by "taking" an examination, not by reading extraneous and/or supererogatory textbooks.

In short, this PASSBOOK®, used directedly, should be an important factor in helping you to pass your test.

BUILDING CONSTRUCTION ENGINEER

DUTIES:
Coordinate the operations of contractors and ensure conformity to specifications and standards. Determine and report rate of progress and prepare or approve periodic and final estimates. You would recommend contract change orders and would interpret plans and specifications, and would supervise assistants.

SCOPE OF THE EXAMINATION:
The written test will be designed to test for knowledge, skills, and/or abilities in such areas as:
1. Principles and practices of building construction;
2. Building construction materials and standards, and their application;
3. Drawings, specifications, and contract documents;
4. Structural components of buildings;
5. Coordination of multiple contract projects;
6. Inspection and supervision of building construction projects;
7. Understanding and interpreting written material; and
8. Preparing written material.

HOW TO TAKE A TEST

I. YOU MUST PASS AN EXAMINATION

A. *WHAT EVERY CANDIDATE SHOULD KNOW*

Examination applicants often ask us for help in preparing for the written test. What can I study in advance? What kinds of questions will be asked? How will the test be given? How will the papers be graded?

As an applicant for a civil service examination, you may be wondering about some of these things. Our purpose here is to suggest effective methods of advance study and to describe civil service examinations.

Your chances for success on this examination can be increased if you know how to prepare. Those "pre-examination jitters" can be reduced if you know what to expect. You can even experience an adventure in good citizenship if you know why civil service exams are given.

B. *WHY ARE CIVIL SERVICE EXAMINATIONS GIVEN?*

Civil service examinations are important to you in two ways. As a citizen, you want public jobs filled by employees who know how to do their work. As a job seeker, you want a fair chance to compete for that job on an equal footing with other candidates. The best-known means of accomplishing this two-fold goal is the competitive examination.

Exams are widely publicized throughout the nation. They may be administered for jobs in federal, state, city, municipal, town or village governments or agencies.

Any citizen may apply, with some limitations, such as the age or residence of applicants. Your experience and education may be reviewed to see whether you meet the requirements for the particular examination. When these requirements exist, they are reasonable and applied consistently to all applicants. Thus, a competitive examination may cause you some uneasiness now, but it is your privilege and safeguard.

C. *HOW ARE CIVIL SERVICE EXAMS DEVELOPED?*

Examinations are carefully written by trained technicians who are specialists in the field known as "psychological measurement," in consultation with recognized authorities in the field of work that the test will cover. These experts recommend the subject matter areas or skills to be tested; only those knowledges or skills important to your success on the job are included. The most reliable books and source materials available are used as references. Together, the experts and technicians judge the difficulty level of the questions.

Test technicians know how to phrase questions so that the problem is clearly stated. Their ethics do not permit "trick" or "catch" questions. Questions may have been tried out on sample groups, or subjected to statistical analysis, to determine their usefulness.

Written tests are often used in combination with performance tests, ratings of training and experience, and oral interviews. All of these measures combine to form the best-known means of finding the right person for the right job.

II. HOW TO PASS THE WRITTEN TEST

A. NATURE OF THE EXAMINATION

To prepare intelligently for civil service examinations, you should know how they differ from school examinations you have taken. In school you were assigned certain definite pages to read or subjects to cover. The examination questions were quite detailed and usually emphasized memory. Civil service exams, on the other hand, try to discover your present ability to perform the duties of a position, plus your potentiality to learn these duties. In other words, a civil service exam attempts to predict how successful you will be. Questions cover such a broad area that they cannot be as minute and detailed as school exam questions.

In the public service similar kinds of work, or positions, are grouped together in one "class." This process is known as *position-classification*. All the positions in a class are paid according to the salary range for that class. One class title covers all of these positions, and they are all tested by the same examination.

B. FOUR BASIC STEPS

1) Study the announcement

How, then, can you know what subjects to study? Our best answer is: "Learn as much as possible about the class of positions for which you've applied." The exam will test the knowledge, skills and abilities needed to do the work.

Your most valuable source of information about the position you want is the official exam announcement. This announcement lists the training and experience qualifications. Check these standards and apply only if you come reasonably close to meeting them.

The brief description of the position in the examination announcement offers some clues to the subjects which will be tested. Think about the job itself. Review the duties in your mind. Can you perform them, or are there some in which you are rusty? Fill in the blank spots in your preparation.

Many jurisdictions preview the written test in the exam announcement by including a section called "Knowledge and Abilities Required," "Scope of the Examination," or some similar heading. Here you will find out specifically what fields will be tested.

2) Review your own background

Once you learn in general what the position is all about, and what you need to know to do the work, ask yourself which subjects you already know fairly well and which need improvement. You may wonder whether to concentrate on improving your strong areas or on building some background in your fields of weakness. When the announcement has specified "some knowledge" or "considerable knowledge," or has used adjectives like "beginning principles of…" or "advanced … methods," you can get a clue as to the number and difficulty of questions to be asked in any given field. More questions, and hence broader coverage, would be included for those subjects which are more important in the work. Now weigh your strengths and weaknesses against the job requirements and prepare accordingly.

3) Determine the level of the position

Another way to tell how intensively you should prepare is to understand the level of the job for which you are applying. Is it the entering level? In other words, is this the position in which beginners in a field of work are hired? Or is it an intermediate or advanced level? Sometimes this is indicated by such words as "Junior" or "Senior" in the class title. Other jurisdictions use Roman numerals to designate the level – Clerk I, Clerk II, for example. The word "Supervisor" sometimes appears in the title. If the level is not indicated by the title, check the description of duties. Will you be working under very close supervision, or will you have responsibility for independent decisions in this work?

4) Choose appropriate study materials

Now that you know the subjects to be examined and the relative amount of each subject to be covered, you can choose suitable study materials. For beginning level jobs, or even advanced ones, if you have a pronounced weakness in some aspect of your training, read a modern, standard textbook in that field. Be sure it is up to date and has general coverage. Such books are normally available at your library, and the librarian will be glad to help you locate one. For entry-level positions, questions of appropriate difficulty are chosen – neither highly advanced questions, nor those too simple. Such questions require careful thought but not advanced training.

If the position for which you are applying is technical or advanced, you will read more advanced, specialized material. If you are already familiar with the basic principles of your field, elementary textbooks would waste your time. Concentrate on advanced textbooks and technical periodicals. Think through the concepts and review difficult problems in your field.

These are all general sources. You can get more ideas on your own initiative, following these leads. For example, training manuals and publications of the government agency which employs workers in your field can be useful, particularly for technical and professional positions. A letter or visit to the government department involved may result in more specific study suggestions, and certainly will provide you with a more definite idea of the exact nature of the position you are seeking.

III. KINDS OF TESTS

Tests are used for purposes other than measuring knowledge and ability to perform specified duties. For some positions, it is equally important to test ability to make adjustments to new situations or to profit from training. In others, basic mental abilities not dependent on information are essential. Questions which test these things may not appear as pertinent to the duties of the position as those which test for knowledge and information. Yet they are often highly important parts of a fair examination. For very general questions, it is almost impossible to help you direct your study efforts. What we can do is to point out some of the more common of these general abilities needed in public service positions and describe some typical questions.

1) General information

Broad, general information has been found useful for predicting job success in some kinds of work. This is tested in a variety of ways, from vocabulary lists to questions about current events. Basic background in some field of work, such as sociology or economics, may be sampled in a group of questions. Often these are principles which have become familiar to most persons through exposure rather than through formal training. It is difficult to advise you how to study for these questions; being alert to the world around you is our best suggestion.

2) Verbal ability

An example of an ability needed in many positions is verbal or language ability. Verbal ability is, in brief, the ability to use and understand words. Vocabulary and grammar tests are typical measures of this ability. Reading comprehension or paragraph interpretation questions are common in many kinds of civil service tests. You are given a paragraph of written material and asked to find its central meaning.

3) Numerical ability

Number skills can be tested by the familiar arithmetic problem, by checking paired lists of numbers to see which are alike and which are different, or by interpreting charts and graphs. In the latter test, a graph may be printed in the test booklet which you are asked to use as the basis for answering questions.

4) Observation

A popular test for law-enforcement positions is the observation test. A picture is shown to you for several minutes, then taken away. Questions about the picture test your ability to observe both details and larger elements.

5) Following directions

In many positions in the public service, the employee must be able to carry out written instructions dependably and accurately. You may be given a chart with several columns, each column listing a variety of information. The questions require you to carry out directions involving the information given in the chart.

6) Skills and aptitudes

Performance tests effectively measure some manual skills and aptitudes. When the skill is one in which you are trained, such as typing or shorthand, you can practice. These tests are often very much like those given in business school or high school courses. For many of the other skills and aptitudes, however, no short-time preparation can be made. Skills and abilities natural to you or that you have developed throughout your lifetime are being tested.

Many of the general questions just described provide all the data needed to answer the questions and ask you to use your reasoning ability to find the answers. Your best preparation for these tests, as well as for tests of facts and ideas, is to be at your physical and mental best. You, no doubt, have your own methods of getting into an exam-taking mood and keeping "in shape." The next section lists some ideas on this subject.

IV. KINDS OF QUESTIONS

Only rarely is the "essay" question, which you answer in narrative form, used in civil service tests. Civil service tests are usually of the short-answer type. Full instructions for answering these questions will be given to you at the examination. But in case this is your first experience with short-answer questions and separate answer sheets, here is what you need to know:

1) **Multiple-choice Questions**

Most popular of the short-answer questions is the "multiple choice" or "best answer" question. It can be used, for example, to test for factual knowledge, ability to solve problems or judgment in meeting situations found at work.

A multiple-choice question is normally one of three types—
- It can begin with an incomplete statement followed by several possible endings. You are to find the one ending which *best* completes the statement, although some of the others may not be entirely wrong.
- It can also be a complete statement in the form of a question which is answered by choosing one of the statements listed.

- It can be in the form of a problem – again you select the best answer.

Here is an example of a multiple-choice question with a discussion which should give you some clues as to the method for choosing the right answer:

When an employee has a complaint about his assignment, the action which will *best* help him overcome his difficulty is to
   A. discuss his difficulty with his coworkers
   B. take the problem to the head of the organization
   C. take the problem to the person who gave him the assignment
   D. say nothing to anyone about his complaint

In answering this question, you should study each of the choices to find which is best. Consider choice "A" – Certainly an employee may discuss his complaint with fellow employees, but no change or improvement can result, and the complaint remains unresolved. Choice "B" is a poor choice since the head of the organization probably does not know what assignment you have been given, and taking your problem to him is known as "going over the head" of the supervisor. The supervisor, or person who made the assignment, is the person who can clarify it or correct any injustice. Choice "C" is, therefore, correct. To say nothing, as in choice "D," is unwise. Supervisors have and interest in knowing the problems employees are facing, and the employee is seeking a solution to his problem.

2) True/False Questions

The "true/false" or "right/wrong" form of question is sometimes used. Here a complete statement is given. Your job is to decide whether the statement is right or wrong.

SAMPLE: A roaming cell-phone call to a nearby city costs less than a non-roaming call to a distant city.

This statement is wrong, or false, since roaming calls are more expensive.

This is not a complete list of all possible question forms, although most of the others are variations of these common types. You will always get complete directions for answering questions. Be sure you understand *how* to mark your answers – ask questions until you do.

V. RECORDING YOUR ANSWERS

Computer terminals are used more and more today for many different kinds of exams.
For an examination with very few applicants, you may be told to record your answers in the test booklet itself. Separate answer sheets are much more common. If this separate answer sheet is to be scored by machine – and this is often the case – it is highly important that you mark your answers correctly in order to get credit.
An electronic scoring machine is often used in civil service offices because of the speed with which papers can be scored. Machine-scored answer sheets must be marked with a pencil, which will be given to you. This pencil has a high graphite content which responds to the electronic scoring machine. As a matter of fact, stray dots may register as answers, so do not let your pencil rest on the answer sheet while you are pondering the correct answer. Also, if your pencil lead breaks or is otherwise defective, ask for another.

Since the answer sheet will be dropped in a slot in the scoring machine, be careful not to bend the corners or get the paper crumpled.

The answer sheet normally has five vertical columns of numbers, with 30 numbers to a column. These numbers correspond to the question numbers in your test booklet. After each number, going across the page are four or five pairs of dotted lines. These short dotted lines have small letters or numbers above them. The first two pairs may also have a "T" or "F" above the letters. This indicates that the first two pairs only are to be used if the questions are of the true-false type. If the questions are multiple choice, disregard the "T" and "F" and pay attention only to the small letters or numbers.

Answer your questions in the manner of the sample that follows:

32. The largest city in the United States is
    A. Washington, D.C.
    B. New York City
    C. Chicago
    D. Detroit
    E. San Francisco

1) Choose the answer you think is best. (New York City is the largest, so "B" is correct.)
2) Find the row of dotted lines numbered the same as the question you are answering. (Find row number 32)
3) Find the pair of dotted lines corresponding to the answer. (Find the pair of lines under the mark "B.")
4) Make a solid black mark between the dotted lines.

VI. BEFORE THE TEST

Common sense will help you find procedures to follow to get ready for an examination. Too many of us, however, overlook these sensible measures. Indeed, nervousness and fatigue have been found to be the most serious reasons why applicants fail to do their best on civil service tests. Here is a list of reminders:

- Begin your preparation early – Don't wait until the last minute to go scurrying around for books and materials or to find out what the position is all about.
- Prepare continuously – An hour a night for a week is better than an all-night cram session. This has been definitely established. What is more, a night a week for a month will return better dividends than crowding your study into a shorter period of time.
- Locate the place of the exam – You have been sent a notice telling you when and where to report for the examination. If the location is in a different town or otherwise unfamiliar to you, it would be well to inquire the best route and learn something about the building.
- Relax the night before the test – Allow your mind to rest. Do not study at all that night. Plan some mild recreation or diversion; then go to bed early and get a good night's sleep.
- Get up early enough to make a leisurely trip to the place for the test – This way unforeseen events, traffic snarls, unfamiliar buildings, etc. will not upset you.
- Dress comfortably – A written test is not a fashion show. You will be known by number and not by name, so wear something comfortable.

- Leave excess paraphernalia at home – Shopping bags and odd bundles will get in your way. You need bring only the items mentioned in the official notice you received; usually everything you need is provided. Do not bring reference books to the exam. They will only confuse those last minutes and be taken away from you when in the test room.
- Arrive somewhat ahead of time – If because of transportation schedules you must get there very early, bring a newspaper or magazine to take your mind off yourself while waiting.
- Locate the examination room – When you have found the proper room, you will be directed to the seat or part of the room where you will sit. Sometimes you are given a sheet of instructions to read while you are waiting. Do not fill out any forms until you are told to do so; just read them and be prepared.
- Relax and prepare to listen to the instructions
- If you have any physical problem that may keep you from doing your best, be sure to tell the test administrator. If you are sick or in poor health, you really cannot do your best on the exam. You can come back and take the test some other time.

VII. AT THE TEST

The day of the test is here and you have the test booklet in your hand. The temptation to get going is very strong. Caution! There is more to success than knowing the right answers. You must know how to identify your papers and understand variations in the type of short-answer question used in this particular examination. Follow these suggestions for maximum results from your efforts:

1) Cooperate with the monitor

The test administrator has a duty to create a situation in which you can be as much at ease as possible. He will give instructions, tell you when to begin, check to see that you are marking your answer sheet correctly, and so on. He is not there to guard you, although he will see that your competitors do not take unfair advantage. He wants to help you do your best.

2) Listen to all instructions

Don't jump the gun! Wait until you understand all directions. In most civil service tests you get more time than you need to answer the questions. So don't be in a hurry. Read each word of instructions until you clearly understand the meaning. Study the examples, listen to all announcements and follow directions. Ask questions if you do not understand what to do.

3) Identify your papers

Civil service exams are usually identified by number only. You will be assigned a number; you must not put your name on your test papers. Be sure to copy your number correctly. Since more than one exam may be given, copy your exact examination title.

4) Plan your time

Unless you are told that a test is a "speed" or "rate of work" test, speed itself is usually not important. Time enough to answer all the questions will be provided, but this does not mean that you have all day. An overall time limit has been set. Divide the total time (in minutes) by the number of questions to determine the approximate time you have for each question.

5) Do not linger over difficult questions

If you come across a difficult question, mark it with a paper clip (useful to have along) and come back to it when you have been through the booklet. One caution if you do this – be sure to skip a number on your answer sheet as well. Check often to be sure that you have not lost your place and that you are marking in the row numbered the same as the question you are answering.

6) Read the questions

Be sure you know what the question asks! Many capable people are unsuccessful because they failed to *read* the questions correctly.

7) Answer all questions

Unless you have been instructed that a penalty will be deducted for incorrect answers, it is better to guess than to omit a question.

8) Speed tests

It is often better NOT to guess on speed tests. It has been found that on timed tests people are tempted to spend the last few seconds before time is called in marking answers at random – without even reading them – in the hope of picking up a few extra points. To discourage this practice, the instructions may warn you that your score will be "corrected" for guessing. That is, a penalty will be applied. The incorrect answers will be deducted from the correct ones, or some other penalty formula will be used.

9) Review your answers

If you finish before time is called, go back to the questions you guessed or omitted to give them further thought. Review other answers if you have time.

10) Return your test materials

If you are ready to leave before others have finished or time is called, take ALL your materials to the monitor and leave quietly. Never take any test material with you. The monitor can discover whose papers are not complete, and taking a test booklet may be grounds for disqualification.

VIII. EXAMINATION TECHNIQUES

1) Read the general instructions carefully. These are usually printed on the first page of the exam booklet. As a rule, these instructions refer to the timing of the examination; the fact that you should not start work until the signal and must stop work at a signal, etc. If there are any *special* instructions, such as a choice of questions to be answered, make sure that you note this instruction carefully.

2) When you are ready to start work on the examination, that is as soon as the signal has been given, read the instructions to each question booklet, underline any key words or phrases, such as *least, best, outline, describe* and the like. In this way you will tend to answer as requested rather than discover on reviewing your paper that you *listed without describing*, that you selected the *worst* choice rather than the *best* choice, etc.

3) If the examination is of the objective or multiple-choice type – that is, each question will also give a series of possible answers: A, B, C or D, and you are called upon to select the best answer and write the letter next to that answer on your answer paper – it is advisable to start answering each question in turn. There may be anywhere from 50 to 100 such questions in the three or four hours allotted and you can see how much time would be taken if you read through all the questions before beginning to answer any. Furthermore, if you come across a question or group of questions which you know would be difficult to answer, it would undoubtedly affect your handling of all the other questions.

4) If the examination is of the essay type and contains but a few questions, it is a moot point as to whether you should read all the questions before starting to answer any one. Of course, if you are given a choice – say five out of seven and the like – then it is essential to read all the questions so you can eliminate the two that are most difficult. If, however, you are asked to answer all the questions, there may be danger in trying to answer the easiest one first because you may find that you will spend too much time on it. The best technique is to answer the first question, then proceed to the second, etc.

5) Time your answers. Before the exam begins, write down the time it started, then add the time allowed for the examination and write down the time it must be completed, then divide the time available somewhat as follows:
    - If 3-1/2 hours are allowed, that would be 210 minutes. If you have 80 objective-type questions, that would be an average of 2-1/2 minutes per question. Allow yourself no more than 2 minutes per question, or a total of 160 minutes, which will permit about 50 minutes to review.
    - If for the time allotment of 210 minutes there are 7 essay questions to answer, that would average about 30 minutes a question. Give yourself only 25 minutes per question so that you have about 35 minutes to review.

6) The most important instruction is to *read each question* and make sure you know what is wanted. The second most important instruction is to *time yourself properly* so that you answer every question. The third most important instruction is to *answer every question*. Guess if you have to but include something for each question. Remember that you will receive no credit for a blank and will probably receive some credit if you write something in answer to an essay question. If you guess a letter – say "B" for a multiple-choice question – you may have guessed right. If you leave a blank as an answer to a multiple-choice question, the examiners may respect your feelings but it will not add a point to your score. Some exams may penalize you for wrong answers, so in such cases *only*, you may not want to guess unless you have some basis for your answer.

7) Suggestions
    a. Objective-type questions
        1. Examine the question booklet for proper sequence of pages and questions
        2. Read all instructions carefully
        3. Skip any question which seems too difficult; return to it after all other questions have been answered
        4. Apportion your time properly; do not spend too much time on any single question or group of questions

5. Note and underline key words – *all, most, fewest, least, best, worst, same, opposite,* etc.
6. Pay particular attention to negatives
7. Note unusual option, e.g., unduly long, short, complex, different or similar in content to the body of the question
8. Observe the use of "hedging" words – *probably, may, most likely,* etc.
9. Make sure that your answer is put next to the same number as the question
10. Do not second-guess unless you have good reason to believe the second answer is definitely more correct
11. Cross out original answer if you decide another answer is more accurate; do not erase until you are ready to hand your paper in
12. Answer all questions; guess unless instructed otherwise
13. Leave time for review

  b. Essay questions
1. Read each question carefully
2. Determine exactly what is wanted. Underline key words or phrases.
3. Decide on outline or paragraph answer
4. Include many different points and elements unless asked to develop any one or two points or elements
5. Show impartiality by giving pros and cons unless directed to select one side only
6. Make and write down any assumptions you find necessary to answer the questions
7. Watch your English, grammar, punctuation and choice of words
8. Time your answers; don't crowd material

8) Answering the essay question

Most essay questions can be answered by framing the specific response around several key words or ideas. Here are a few such key words or ideas:

M's: manpower, materials, methods, money, management
P's: purpose, program, policy, plan, procedure, practice, problems, pitfalls, personnel, public relations

  a. Six basic steps in handling problems:
1. Preliminary plan and background development
2. Collect information, data and facts
3. Analyze and interpret information, data and facts
4. Analyze and develop solutions as well as make recommendations
5. Prepare report and sell recommendations
6. Install recommendations and follow up effectiveness

  b. Pitfalls to avoid
1. *Taking things for granted* – A statement of the situation does not necessarily imply that each of the elements is necessarily true; for example, a complaint may be invalid and biased so that all that can be taken for granted is that a complaint has been registered

2. *Considering only one side of a situation* – Wherever possible, indicate several alternatives and then point out the reasons you selected the best one
3. *Failing to indicate follow up* – Whenever your answer indicates action on your part, make certain that you will take proper follow-up action to see how successful your recommendations, procedures or actions turn out to be
4. *Taking too long in answering any single question* – Remember to time your answers properly

IX. AFTER THE TEST

Scoring procedures differ in detail among civil service jurisdictions although the general principles are the same. Whether the papers are hand-scored or graded by machine we have described, they are nearly always graded by number. That is, the person who marks the paper knows only the number – never the name – of the applicant. Not until all the papers have been graded will they be matched with names. If other tests, such as training and experience or oral interview ratings have been given, scores will be combined. Different parts of the examination usually have different weights. For example, the written test might count 60 percent of the final grade, and a rating of training and experience 40 percent. In many jurisdictions, veterans will have a certain number of points added to their grades.

After the final grade has been determined, the names are placed in grade order and an eligible list is established. There are various methods for resolving ties between those who get the same final grade – probably the most common is to place first the name of the person whose application was received first. Job offers are made from the eligible list in the order the names appear on it. You will be notified of your grade and your rank as soon as all these computations have been made. This will be done as rapidly as possible.

People who are found to meet the requirements in the announcement are called "eligibles." Their names are put on a list of eligible candidates. An eligible's chances of getting a job depend on how high he stands on this list and how fast agencies are filling jobs from the list.

When a job is to be filled from a list of eligibles, the agency asks for the names of people on the list of eligibles for that job. When the civil service commission receives this request, it sends to the agency the names of the three people highest on this list. Or, if the job to be filled has specialized requirements, the office sends the agency the names of the top three persons who meet these requirements from the general list.

The appointing officer makes a choice from among the three people whose names were sent to him. If the selected person accepts the appointment, the names of the others are put back on the list to be considered for future openings.

That is the rule in hiring from all kinds of eligible lists, whether they are for typist, carpenter, chemist, or something else. For every vacancy, the appointing officer has his choice of any one of the top three eligibles on the list. This explains why the person whose name is on top of the list sometimes does not get an appointment when some of the persons lower on the list do. If the appointing officer chooses the second or third eligible, the No. 1 eligible does not get a job at once, but stays on the list until he is appointed or the list is terminated.

X. HOW TO PASS THE INTERVIEW TEST

The examination for which you applied requires an oral interview test. You have already taken the written test and you are now being called for the interview test – the final part of the formal examination.

You may think that it is not possible to prepare for an interview test and that there are no procedures to follow during an interview. Our purpose is to point out some things you can do in advance that will help you and some good rules to follow and pitfalls to avoid while you are being interviewed.

What is an interview supposed to test?

The written examination is designed to test the technical knowledge and competence of the candidate; the oral is designed to evaluate intangible qualities, not readily measured otherwise, and to establish a list showing the relative fitness of each candidate – as measured against his competitors – for the position sought. Scoring is not on the basis of "right" and "wrong," but on a sliding scale of values ranging from "not passable" to "outstanding." As a matter of fact, it is possible to achieve a relatively low score without a single "incorrect" answer because of evident weakness in the qualities being measured.

Occasionally, an examination may consist entirely of an oral test – either an individual or a group oral. In such cases, information is sought concerning the technical knowledges and abilities of the candidate, since there has been no written examination for this purpose. More commonly, however, an oral test is used to supplement a written examination.

Who conducts interviews?

The composition of oral boards varies among different jurisdictions. In nearly all, a representative of the personnel department serves as chairman. One of the members of the board may be a representative of the department in which the candidate would work. In some cases, "outside experts" are used, and, frequently, a businessman or some other representative of the general public is asked to serve. Labor and management or other special groups may be represented. The aim is to secure the services of experts in the appropriate field.

However the board is composed, it is a good idea (and not at all improper or unethical) to ascertain in advance of the interview who the members are and what groups they represent. When you are introduced to them, you will have some idea of their backgrounds and interests, and at least you will not stutter and stammer over their names.

What should be done before the interview?

While knowledge about the board members is useful and takes some of the surprise element out of the interview, there is other preparation which is more substantive. It *is* possible to prepare for an oral interview – in several ways:

1) Keep a copy of your application and review it carefully before the interview

This may be the only document before the oral board, and the starting point of the interview. Know what education and experience you have listed there, and the sequence and dates of all of it. Sometimes the board will ask you to review the highlights of your experience for them; you should not have to hem and haw doing it.

2) Study the class specification and the examination announcement

Usually, the oral board has one or both of these to guide them. The qualities, characteristics or knowledges required by the position sought are stated in these documents. They offer valuable clues as to the nature of the oral interview. For example, if the job involves supervisory responsibilities, the announcement will usually indicate that knowledge of modern supervisory methods and the qualifications of the candidate as a supervisor will be tested. If so, you can expect such questions, frequently in the form of a hypothetical situation which you are expected to solve. NEVER go into an oral without knowledge of the duties and responsibilities of the job you seek.

3) Think through each qualification required

Try to visualize the kind of questions you would ask if you were a board member. How well could you answer them? Try especially to appraise your own knowledge and background in each area, *measured against the job sought*, and identify any areas in which you are weak. Be critical and realistic – do not flatter yourself.

4) Do some general reading in areas in which you feel you may be weak

For example, if the job involves supervision and your past experience has NOT, some general reading in supervisory methods and practices, particularly in the field of human relations, might be useful. Do NOT study agency procedures or detailed manuals. The oral board will be testing your understanding and capacity, not your memory.

5) Get a good night's sleep and watch your general health and mental attitude

You will want a clear head at the interview. Take care of a cold or any other minor ailment, and of course, no hangovers.

What should be done on the day of the interview?

Now comes the day of the interview itself. Give yourself plenty of time to get there. Plan to arrive somewhat ahead of the scheduled time, particularly if your appointment is in the fore part of the day. If a previous candidate fails to appear, the board might be ready for you a bit early. By early afternoon an oral board is almost invariably behind schedule if there are many candidates, and you may have to wait. Take along a book or magazine to read, or your application to review, but leave any extraneous material in the waiting room when you go in for your interview. In any event, relax and compose yourself.

The matter of dress is important. The board is forming impressions about you – from your experience, your manners, your attitude, and your appearance. Give your personal appearance careful attention. Dress your best, but not your flashiest. Choose conservative, appropriate clothing, and be sure it is immaculate. This is a business interview, and your appearance should indicate that you regard it as such. Besides, being well groomed and properly dressed will help boost your confidence.

Sooner or later, someone will call your name and escort you into the interview room. *This is it.* From here on you are on your own. It is too late for any more preparation. But remember, you asked for this opportunity to prove your fitness, and you are here because your request was granted.

What happens when you go in?

The usual sequence of events will be as follows: The clerk (who is often the board stenographer) will introduce you to the chairman of the oral board, who will introduce you to the other members of the board. Acknowledge the introductions before you sit down. Do not be surprised if you find a microphone facing you or a stenotypist sitting by. Oral interviews are usually recorded in the event of an appeal or other review.

Usually the chairman of the board will open the interview by reviewing the highlights of your education and work experience from your application – primarily for the benefit of the other members of the board, as well as to get the material into the record. Do not interrupt or comment unless there is an error or significant misinterpretation; if that is the case, do not hesitate. But do not quibble about insignificant matters. Also, he will usually ask you some question about your education, experience or your present job – partly to get you to start talking and to establish the interviewing "rapport." He may start the actual questioning, or turn it over to one of the other members. Frequently, each member undertakes the questioning on a particular area, one in which he is perhaps most competent, so you can expect each member to participate in the examination. Because time is limited, you may also expect some rather abrupt switches in the direction the questioning takes, so do not be upset by it. Normally, a board member will not pursue a single line of questioning unless he discovers a particular strength or weakness.

After each member has participated, the chairman will usually ask whether any member has any further questions, then will ask you if you have anything you wish to add. Unless you are expecting this question, it may floor you. Worse, it may start you off on an extended, extemporaneous speech. The board is not usually seeking more information. The question is principally to offer you a last opportunity to present further qualifications or to indicate that you have nothing to add. So, if you feel that a significant qualification or characteristic has been overlooked, it is proper to point it out in a sentence or so. Do not compliment the board on the thoroughness of their examination – they have been sketchy, and you know it. If you wish, merely say, "No thank you, I have nothing further to add." This is a point where you can "talk yourself out" of a good impression or fail to present an important bit of information. Remember, *you close the interview yourself*.

The chairman will then say, "That is all, Mr. _____, thank you." Do not be startled; the interview is over, and quicker than you think. Thank him, gather your belongings and take your leave. Save your sigh of relief for the other side of the door.

How to put your best foot forward

Throughout this entire process, you may feel that the board individually and collectively is trying to pierce your defenses, seek out your hidden weaknesses and embarrass and confuse you. Actually, this is not true. They are obliged to make an appraisal of your qualifications for the job you are seeking, and they want to see you in your best light. Remember, they must interview all candidates and a non-cooperative candidate may become a failure in spite of their best efforts to bring out his qualifications. Here are 15 suggestions that will help you:

1) Be natural – Keep your attitude confident, not cocky

If you are not confident that you can do the job, do not expect the board to be. Do not apologize for your weaknesses, try to bring out your strong points. The board is interested in a positive, not negative, presentation. Cockiness will antagonize any board member and make him wonder if you are covering up a weakness by a false show of strength.

2) Get comfortable, but don't lounge or sprawl

Sit erectly but not stiffly. A careless posture may lead the board to conclude that you are careless in other things, or at least that you are not impressed by the importance of the occasion. Either conclusion is natural, even if incorrect. Do not fuss with your clothing, a pencil or an ashtray. Your hands may occasionally be useful to emphasize a point; do not let them become a point of distraction.

3) Do not wisecrack or make small talk

This is a serious situation, and your attitude should show that you consider it as such. Further, the time of the board is limited – they do not want to waste it, and neither should you.

4) Do not exaggerate your experience or abilities

In the first place, from information in the application or other interviews and sources, the board may know more about you than you think. Secondly, you probably will not get away with it. An experienced board is rather adept at spotting such a situation, so do not take the chance.

5) If you know a board member, do not make a point of it, yet do not hide it

Certainly you are not fooling him, and probably not the other members of the board. Do not try to take advantage of your acquaintanceship – it will probably do you little good.

6) Do not dominate the interview

Let the board do that. They will give you the clues – do not assume that you have to do all the talking. Realize that the board has a number of questions to ask you, and do not try to take up all the interview time by showing off your extensive knowledge of the answer to the first one.

7) Be attentive

You only have 20 minutes or so, and you should keep your attention at its sharpest throughout. When a member is addressing a problem or question to you, give him your undivided attention. Address your reply principally to him, but do not exclude the other board members.

8) Do not interrupt

A board member may be stating a problem for you to analyze. He will ask you a question when the time comes. Let him state the problem, and wait for the question.

9) Make sure you understand the question

Do not try to answer until you are sure what the question is. If it is not clear, restate it in your own words or ask the board member to clarify it for you. However, do not haggle about minor elements.

10) Reply promptly but not hastily

A common entry on oral board rating sheets is "candidate responded readily," or "candidate hesitated in replies." Respond as promptly and quickly as you can, but do not jump to a hasty, ill-considered answer.

11) Do not be peremptory in your answers

A brief answer is proper – but do not fire your answer back. That is a losing game from your point of view. The board member can probably ask questions much faster than you can answer them.

12) Do not try to create the answer you think the board member wants

He is interested in what kind of mind you have and how it works – not in playing games. Furthermore, he can usually spot this practice and will actually grade you down on it.

13) Do not switch sides in your reply merely to agree with a board member

Frequently, a member will take a contrary position merely to draw you out and to see if you are willing and able to defend your point of view. Do not start a debate, yet do not surrender a good position. If a position is worth taking, it is worth defending.

14) Do not be afraid to admit an error in judgment if you are shown to be wrong

The board knows that you are forced to reply without any opportunity for careful consideration. Your answer may be demonstrably wrong. If so, admit it and get on with the interview.

15) Do not dwell at length on your present job

The opening question may relate to your present assignment. Answer the question but do not go into an extended discussion. You are being examined for a *new* job, not your present one. As a matter of fact, try to phrase ALL your answers in terms of the job for which you are being examined.

Basis of Rating

Probably you will forget most of these "do's" and "don'ts" when you walk into the oral interview room. Even remembering them all will not ensure you a passing grade. Perhaps you did not have the qualifications in the first place. But remembering them will help you to put your best foot forward, without treading on the toes of the board members.

Rumor and popular opinion to the contrary notwithstanding, an oral board wants you to make the best appearance possible. They know you are under pressure – but they also want to see how you respond to it as a guide to what your reaction would be under the pressures of the job you seek. They will be influenced by the degree of poise you display, the personal traits you show and the manner in which you respond.

ABOUT THIS BOOK

This book contains tests divided into Examination Sections. Go through each test, answering every question in the margin. We have also attached a sample answer sheet at the back of the book that can be removed and used. At the end of each test look at the answer key and check your answers. On the ones you got wrong, look at the right answer choice and learn. Do not fill in the answers first. Do not memorize the questions and answers, but understand the answer and principles involved. On your test, the questions will likely be different from the samples. Questions are changed and new ones added. If you understand these past questions you should have success with any changes that arise. Tests may consist of several types of questions. We have additional books on each subject should more study be advisable or necessary for you. Finally, the more you study, the better prepared you will be. This book is intended to be the last thing you study before you walk into the examination room. Prior study of relevant texts is also recommended. NLC publishes some of these in our Fundamental Series. Knowledge and good sense are important factors in passing your exam. Good luck also helps. So now study this Passbook, absorb the material contained within and take that knowledge into the examination. Then do your best to pass that exam.

EXAMINATION SECTION

EXAMINATION SECTION
TEST 1

DIRECTIONS: Each question or incomplete statement is followed by several suggested answers or completions. Select the one that BEST answers the question or completes the statement. *PRINT THE LETTER OF THE CORRECT ANSWER IN THE SPACE AT THE RIGHT.*

1. Of the following, the BEST reason for using vibrators in concrete construction is to

    A. remove excess water
    B. consolidate the concrete
    C. increase the slump of the concrete
    D. retard the setting of the concrete

    1.____

2. When a contractor fails to adhere to an approved progress schedule, he should

    A. revise the schedule without delay
    B. ask for an extension of time on account of delays
    C. adopt such additional means and methods of construction as will make up for the time lost
    D. take no immediate action with the hope that sufficient time will be available later on that will assure the completion in accordance with the schedule

    2.____

3. The usual contract for work includes a section entitled *Instructions to Bidders* which states that the

    A. contractor agrees that he has made his own examination and will make no claim for damages on account of errors or omissions
    B. contractor shall not make claims for damages of any discrepancy, error, or omission in any plans
    C. estimates of quantities and calculations are guaranteed by the board to be correct and are deemed to be a representation of the conditions affecting the work
    D. plans, measurements, dimensions, and conditions under which the work is to be performed are guaranteed by the board

    3.____

4. Specifications covering brickwork usually require special precautions and protection for work in cold weather.
   The HIGHEST temperature below which these measures are required is *most nearly*

    A. 50° F   B. 40° F   C. 30° F   D. 20° F

    4.____

5. Controlled concrete is required for the reinforced concrete frame of a large school building. The ultimate strength of this concrete will be *most nearly* _____ pounds per square inch.

    A. 1000   B. 3000   C. 5000   D. 7000

    5.____

6. A lump sum type of contract may require the contractor to submit a schedule of unit prices.
   The BEST reason for this is that it

    A. prevents the lump sum from being too high
    B. simplifies the selection of the lowest bidder

    6.____

C. enables the estimators to check the total cost
D. provides a means of making equitable partial payments

7. The concrete test that will BEST determine the consistency of a concrete mix is the

   A. slump test
   B. sieve analysis
   C. calorimetric test
   D. water-cement ratio test

8. The BEST way to evaluate the overall state of completion of a construction project is to check the progress estimate against the

   A. inspection work sheet
   B. construction schedule
   C. inspector's checklist
   D. equipment maintenance schedule

Questions 9-15.

DIRECTIONS: Questions 9 through 15 refer to the sketch below.

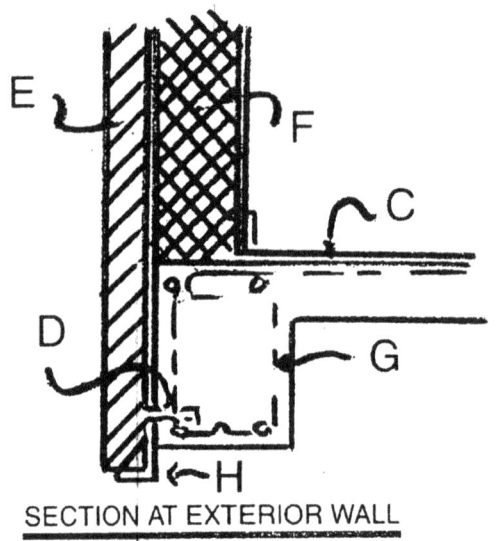
SECTION AT EXTERIOR WALL

9. The floor is made of

   A. air-entrained concrete
   B. reinforced concrete
   C. lightweight concrete
   D. concrete-encased structural steel

10. The exterior wall is a _____ wall.

    A. concrete block
    B. cavity construction
    C. veneer
    D. solid brick

11. Member C is a

    A. deformed bar
    B. hooked bar
    C. plain bar
    D. shear connector

12. Member E is made of

    A. steel   B. wood   C. brick   D. concrete

13. Member F is

    A. concrete block   B. facing brick
    C. glazed tile   D. sheetrock

14. Member G is a

    A. longitudinal bar   B. splice
    C. stirrup   D. tie wire

15. Member H is a

    A. purlin   B. brace   C. guy   D. lintel

16. A projected sash is a(n)

    A. architectural projection from a building exterior which breaks up a smooth pattern of the wall
    B. double-hung window
    C. window that opens inward or outward
    D. window that has a screen attachment

17. In the construction of cellar concrete floors resting on earth, the item that should be checked MOST carefully is that

    A. the earth is wet before pouring
    B. all backfill is granular soil
    C. the earth is dry before pouring
    D. all backfill is properly compacted

18. Specifications state that column dowels are embedded 24 diameters in the footing. The length of embedment for a number 6 bar is _____ inches.

    A. 6   B. 12   C. 18   D. 24

19. After excavating to the subgrade of a footing, an examination of the soil reveals that it is of a poorer quality than the soil in that area and at that elevation shown on the soil borings.
    Of the following types of footings, the one that would be LEAST affected by this condition is a

    A. footing on piles   B. plain concrete footing
    C. combined footing   D. spread footing

20. The MAIN reason for requiring written job reports is to

    A. avoid the necessity of oral orders
    B. develop better methods of doing the work
    C. provide a permanent record of what was done
    D. increase the amount of work that can be done

21. Of the following items, the one which should NOT be included in a proposed work schedule is

    A. a schedule of hourly wage rates and supplementary benefits
    B. an estimated time required for delivery of materials and equipment
    C. the anticipated commencement and completion of the various operations
    D. the sequence and inter-relationship of various operations with those of related contracts

22. A specification requires that brick be laid with *shoved* joints. The BEST reason for this requirement is that it helps the bricklayer to obtain _____ joint(s).

    A. full
    B. plumb vertical
    C. level horizontal
    D. the required thickness of

23. A specification states that access panels to suspended ceilings will be of metal. The MAIN reason for providing access panels is to

    A. improve the insulation of the ceiling
    B. improve the appearance of the ceiling
    C. make it easier to construct the building
    D. make it easier to maintain the building

24. A three-coat plaster job is to be 7/8 inches thick. Of the following, the thickness of the individual coats, in inches, would be *most nearly* scratch

    A. 1/8, brown 1/2, finish 1/4
    B. 3/8, brown 3/8, finish 1/8
    C. 11/16, brown 1/8, finish 1/16
    D. 5/16, brown 1/4, finish 5/16

25. You are assigned to keep a record of the number and volume of all boulders excavated that exceed one cubic yard in volume.
    The MOST probable reason for this order is:

    A. Any delays in excavating due to the boulders may result in a claim
    B. The contractor may receive additional payment for rock excavation
    C. There may be an extra charge for hauling boulders from the jobsite
    D. Excavation where there are large boulders involved is dangerous, and in the event of an accident, you will have appropriate records

KEY (CORRECT ANSWERS)

1. B
2. C
3. A
4. B
5. B

6. D
7. A
8. B
9. B
10. C

11. B
12. C
13. A
14. C
15. D

16. C
17. D
18. C
19. A
20. C

21. A
22. A
23. D
24. B
25. C

TEST 2

DIRECTIONS: Each question or incomplete statement is followed by several suggested answers or completions. Select the one that BEST answers the question or completes the statement. *PRINT THE LETTER OF THE CORRECT ANSWER IN THE SPACE AT THE RIGHT.*

1. Which one of the following is the PRIMARY object in drawing up a set of specifications for materials to be purchased?

    A. Control of quality
    B. Outline of intended use
    C. Establishment of standard sizes
    D. Location and method of inspection

2. In order to avoid disputes over payments for extra work in a contract for construction, the BEST procedure to follow would be to

    A. have contractor submit work progress reports daily
    B. insert a special clause in the contract specifications
    C. have a representative on the job at all times to verify conditions
    D. allocate a certain percentage of the cost of the job to cover such expenses

3. If there is a small amount of water on the surface of a newly-laid concrete sidewalk, the recommended procedure *before* finishing is to

    A. allow it to evaporate
    B. remove it with a broom
    C. sprinkle some dry cement on top
    D. remove it with a float

4. Prior to the installation of equipment called for in the specifications, the contractor is *usually* required to submit for approval

    A. sets of shop drawings
    B. a set of revised specifications
    C. a detailed description of the methods of work to be used
    D. a complete list of skilled and unskilled tradesmen he proposes to use

5. A specification on piles states that plumbness must be within 2% of the pile length. If the pile length is 30 feet, the MAXIMUM amount that the pile may be out of plumb is, in inches, *most nearly*

    A. 5   B. 6   C. 7   D. 8

6. The number of days that it will take high early strength concrete to equal the 28-day strength of normal portland cement concrete is *most nearly*

    A. 1   B. 3   C. 7   D. 12

7. Specifications may state that a standpipe system will be provided in each building. The MAIN purpose of a standpipe system is to

    A. supply the roof water tank
    B. provide water for firefighting

C. circulate water for the heating system
D. provide adequate pressure for the water supply

8. The drawing which should be used as a legal reference when checking completed construction work is the _____ drawing.

   A. contract
   B. assembly
   C. working or shop
   D. preliminary

9. Efflorescence may BEST be removed from brickwork by washing with a solution of _____ acid.

   A. muriatic   B. citric   C. carbonic   D. nitric

10. The MAIN difference between sheet glass and plate glass is

    A. the surface finish of the two types of glass
    B. the heat absorbing qualities of the two types of glass
    C. plate glass is thinner than sheet glass
    D. plate glass is tempered while sheet glass is not tempered

11. Construction joints in the concrete columns of a multistory building are *usually* located

    A. at floor level
    B. 1 foot above floor level
    C. at the underside of floor slab
    D. at the underside of deepest beam framing into the column

12. A contractor on a large construction project *usually* receives partial payments based on

    A. estimates of completed work
    B. actual cost of materials delivered and work completed
    C. estimates of material delivered and not paid for by the contractor
    D. the breakdown estimate submitted after the contract was signed and prorated over the estimated duration of the contract

13. According to the building code, masonry footings shall extend at least 4' below finished grade.
    The PRIMARY reason for this is to

    A. get below the frost line
    B. make the foundation stronger
    C. keep water out of the basement
    D. reach a lower soil strata where better bearing material can be found

14. Good inspection methods require that the inspector

    A. be observant and check all details
    B. constantly check with the engineer who designed the school
    C. apply specifications according to his interpretation
    D. permit slight job variation to establish good public relations

Questions 15-19.

DIRECTIONS: Questions 15 through 19 refer to the following specification for wood flooring. In answering these questions, refer to this specification.

2" x 4" wood sleepers laid flat @ 16" o.c.
1" x 6" sub flooring, laid diagonally; cut at butt joints with parallel cuts; joints at center of sleepers, well staggered, no two joints side by side. Not less than 1/8" space between boards.
One layer of 15# asphalt felt on top of sub-floor.
Finish floor - North Rock Maple, T & G, laid perpendicular to sleepers; 8d nails not more than 12" apart; end joints well scattered with at least 2 flooring strips between joints.
Flooring 25/32" x 2 1/4" face - 1st quality.

15. It is *most likely* that the floor referred to in the specification is to be laid

    A. directly on the ground
    B. on a concrete base
    C. on wood joists
    D. on steel beams

16. The BEST reason for specifying that the sub-flooring be parallel cut at butt joints is that this

    A. requires less material
    B. provides staggered joints
    C. provides more nailing surface
    D. allows the joint to fall between sleepers

17. The BEST reason for specifying a minimum space between the sub-floor boards is that it

    A. saves on material
    B. reduces creaking
    C. allows for expansion
    D. prevents dry rot

18. The BEST reason for specifying at least 2 flooring strips between joints in the finish flooring is that

    A. it looks better
    B. it is more economical
    C. each board is supported by two adjoining boards
    D. each finish board is supported by at least two sub-floor boards

19. The BEST reason for placing asphalt felt on top of the sub-floor is to

    A. deaden noise
    B. preserve the wood
    C. reduce dampness
    D. permit movement

20. Assume you are recommending in a report to your superior that a radical change in a standard maintenance procedure should be adopted.
    Of the following, the MOST important information to be included in this report is

    A. a list of the reasons for making this change
    B. the names of the other GSSM who favor the change
    C. a complete description of the present procedure
    D. amount of training time needed for the new procedure

21. Specifications require that the first floor beams of a building must be in place before backfill is placed against the foundation walls.
The BEST reason for this requirement is that

   A. without the first floor beams in place, the wall may become overstressed
   B. it is easier to inspect the first floor construction when the backfill is not in place
   C. the utilities up to the first floor level should be in place before backfill is placed
   D. the boiler setting hung from the first floor must be in place before backfill is placed

21.____

22. The frequency with which job reports are submitted should depend MAINLY on

   A. how comprehensive the report has to be
   B. the amount of information in the report
   C. the availability of an experienced man to write the report
   D. the importance of changes in the information included in the report

22.____

23. Assume that a contractor proposed to start the roofing three days after pouring the concrete roof slab.
This proposal is

   A. *good,* mainly since it will speed the construction
   B. *good,* mainly since it will assist in curing the concrete
   C. *poor* in cold weather but is all right in warm weather
   D. *poor,* mainly since excess water in the concrete may bulge the roofing

23.____

24. In performing field inspectional work, an inspector is the contact man between the public and the board, and it is his job to secure compliance through the maximum utilization of persuasion and education and the minimum application of coercion.
According to the above statement, an inspector performing inspectional duties should

   A. seek to obtain voluntary compliance and use coercion only as a last resort
   B. be conciliatory on all issues of non-compliance and not take an attitude of firmness and authority
   C. maintain a strictly impersonal attitude in the exercise of his duties at all times
   D. use the threat of legal action to secure conformance with specified requirements

24.____

25. A specification requires that brick should be thoroughly wet before using.
Of the following, the BEST reason for this requirement is that

   A. wetting the brick uncovers hidden flaws
   B. it is easier to shove wet brick into place
   C. wetting cleans the pores of the brick ensuring a stronger bond
   D. wetting decreases absorption of water from the mortar

25.____

KEY (CORRECT ANSWERS)

1.	A	11.	A
2.	C	12.	A
3.	A	13.	A
4.	A	14.	A
5.	C	15.	B
6.	C	16.	C
7.	B	17.	C
8.	A	18.	C
9.	A	19.	C
10.	A	20.	A

21. A
22. D
23. D
24. A
25. D

TEST 3

DIRECTIONS: Each question or incomplete statement is followed by several suggested answers or completions. Select the one that BEST answers the question or completes the statement. *PRINT THE LETTER OF THE CORRECT ANSWER IN THE SPACE AT THE RIGHT.*

Questions 1-4.

DIRECTIONS: Questions 1 to 4 refer to the sketch below.

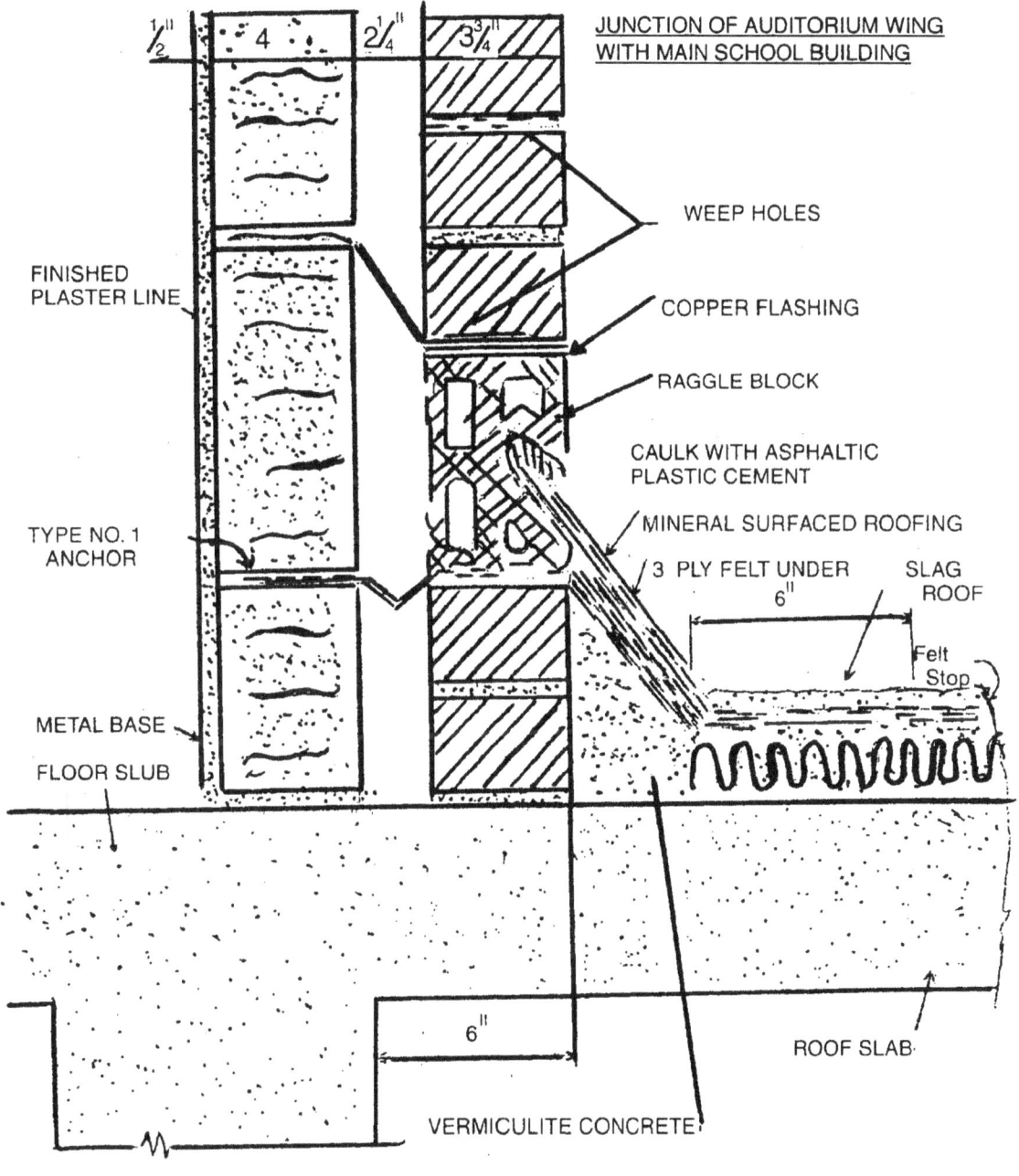

1. The 1/2" of plaster would *most likely* be applied in _____ coats. 1.____

   A. one B. two C. three D. four

2. Vermiculite concrete is PRIMARILY _____ concrete.

   A. low-slump
   B. water-resistant
   C. an air-entrained
   D. a lightweight

3. Which of the following statements relating to copper flashing is CORRECT? It

   A. is perforated in the air space
   B. consists of one solid continuous sheet
   C. consists of 2-inch strips spaced every foot
   D. is provided to prevent the fall of mortar into the air space

4. The 4-inch thick material is *most likely*

   A. cinder block
   B. gypsum block
   C. brick
   D. terra cotta

5. A rowlock course of brick is one in which the bricks are laid

   A. on their 2 1/4" x 8" surface
   B. in an interlocking fashion
   C. with dowels at set intervals
   D. in a one-header followed by a one-stretcher course

6. Specifications for excavation for spread footings require that machine excavation be to within a foot of the final subgrade and the remainder of the excavation shall be by hand. The BEST reason for this requirement is to

   A. prevent cave-ins near the excavation
   B. cut down on the amount of fill needed
   C. prevent excavation below the subgrade
   D. insure that the area in the vicinity of the footing not be excessively disturbed

7. The CHIEF purpose in preparing an outline for a report is *usually* to insure that

   A. the report will be grammatically correct
   B. every point will be given equal emphasis
   C. principal and secondary points will be properly integrated
   D. the language of the report will be of the same level and include the same technical terms

8. One of the properties of tempered plate glass which affects installation is that it

   A. has a blue tinge
   B. cannot be cut after the glass is tempered
   C. does not bond with putty or glazing compound
   D. cracks more easily than ordinary plate glass

9. In assigning the men to various jobs, the BEST principle for a supervisor to follow is to

   A. study the men's abilities and assign them accordingly
   B. rotate a man from job to job until you find one which he can do well
   C. assign each of them to a job and let them adjust to it in their own way
   D. assume that men appointed to the position can do all parts of the work equally well

10. With respect to waterproofing existing basements, the MOST effective and lasting repairs are those made

   A. on the earth side of a basement wall
   B. on the inside basement wall surface
   C. on the floor
   D. in the mortar joints

11. During the actual construction work, the CHIEF value of a construction schedule is to

   A. insure that the work will be done on time
   B. reveal when production is behind schedule
   C. show how much equipment and material is required for the project
   D. furnish data as to the methods and techniques of construction operations

12. When building the formwork for a 12" doubly reinforced concrete wall, the USUAL order of construction is place the

   A. formwork for both faces of the wall; then place the reinforcing steel
   B. reinforcing steel and then place the formwork for both faces of the wall
   C. formwork for one face of the wall, place the reinforcing steel, and then place the formwork for the other face of the wall
   D. formwork for one face of the wall, place the reinforcing steel for one face, place the formwork for the other face of the wall, and then place the reinforcement for the second face

13. The GREATEST period of time must elapse between

   A. pouring and stripping concrete formwork
   B. placing reinforcing steel and pouring concrete
   C. applying the finish plaster coat and painting a plastered wall
   D. applying the first and second coats of a 3-coat plaster job for a wall

14. A fixed amount of money is generally withheld from the contractor for a definite period after the completion of construction.
The BEST reason for this is

   A. that the money will be available for taxes due
   B. to penalize the contractor for poor work
   C. that it is a security for the repair of any defective work
   D. that the money will be available for modifications in the design of the structure

15. The practice of applying the brown coat to a wall on the day after the scratch coat of gypsum plaster was applied is GENERALLY considered

   A. satisfactory
   B. satisfactory only if the temperature is between 50° and 70° F
   C. unsatisfactory because 7 days must elapse between the application of the scratch and brown coats
   D. unsatisfactory because at least 3 days must elapse between the application of the scratch and brown coats

16. Fiberboard material 2 inches thick is placed on a flat reinforced concrete roof. The PRIMARY function of this 2 inch thick material is to

    A. act as a vapor barrier
    B. soundproof the rooms below
    C. prevent loss of heat from the building
    D. keep water from penetrating the ceiling below

17. The PRIMARY purpose of adding lime to a mortar mix is to

    A. improve the appearance of the mortar
    B. increase the workability of the mortar
    C. increase the strength of the mortar
    D. improve the bearing capacity of the wall

18. Assume that excavation is taking place adjacent to a building on a spread footing and a building on pile foundations.
    Extreme care must be exercised in excavating

    A. near the pile-supported building because the soil in the area is of poor quality
    B. near a building on spread footings because the concrete footings may crack
    C. for a pile-supported foundation because heavy loads are involved
    D. near a building on spread footings because of the danger of undermining the foundations

19. An inspector inspecting a large building under construction inspected brickwork at 9 M., formwork at 10 A.M., and concrete at 11 A.M. and did his office work in the afternoon. He followed the same pattern daily for months.
    This procedure is

    A. *bad* because not enough time is devoted to concrete work
    B. *bad* because the tradesmen know when the inspections will occur
    C. *good* because it is methodical and he does not miss any of the trades
    D. *good* because it gives equal amount of time to the important trades

20. If a supervisor finds a discrepancy between the plans and specifications, he should

    A. always follow the plans
    B. ask for an interpretation
    C. always follow the specifications
    D. follow the plans if the difference is in dimensions

KEY (CORRECT ANSWERS)

1. B
2. D
3. B
4. A
5. A

6. D
7. C
8. B
9. A
10. A

11. B
12. C
13. C
14. C
15. A

16. C
17. B
18. D
19. B
20. B

EXAMINATION SECTION
TEST 1

DIRECTIONS: Each question or incomplete statement is followed by several suggested answers or completions. Select the one that BEST answers the question or completes the statement. *PRINT THE LETTER OF THE CORRECT ANSWER IN THE SPACE AT THE RIGHT.*

1. Of the following aggregates, the one LEAST frequently used in the manufacture of lightweight concrete is

    A. cinders B. slag C. perlite D. mica

2. The purpose of a chase is to

    A. accommodate pipes in a wall
    B. act as a support for a stair stringer
    C. provide clearance between wood frame and a chimney
    D. flash block into a parapet

3. In masonry work, a bullnose brick would be used at

    A. an inside corner
    B. an outside corner
    C. the key of an arch
    D. the roof of a boiler setting

4. When asphalt shingles are applied to a sloping roof, a cant strip is frequently used. The purpose of this cant strip is to

    A. prevent leaking at the ridge
    B. hold together opposite sides of a valley
    C. eliminate the possibility of wind lifting the shingles
    D. raise the lower edge of the first course of shingles

5. Air entrained concrete is used rather than ordinary concrete MAINLY to provide additional resistance to

    A. fire
    B. impact
    C. freezing and thawing
    D. water penetration

6. The type of construction MOST commonly used in new wood frame dwellings is the _____ frame.

    A. platform B. braced C. balloon D. butt

7. Of the following, the one LEAST commonly used for flashing is

    A. copper
    B. monel
    C. polyethylene
    D. asphalt felt

8. The end of a wood joist resting directly on a concrete wall has to be brought up to level. The BEST material to use as a shim for this purpose is

    A. slate
    B. wood shingles
    C. dressed wood
    D. grout

9. In foundation work, an example of a rock that would be considered a SOFT rock is

   A. gneiss   B. granite   C. shale   D. limestone

10. Segregation in concrete will result from improper

    A. curing   B. placing   C. formwork   D. finishing

11. One method of dewatering an excavation for a foundation is the use of

    A. inverted siphons
    B. line holes
    C. well points
    D. suction heads

12. An excavation for a concrete footing to support a steel column was accidentally dug 4" too deep.
    Of the following, the BEST practice would be to

    A. make the footing 4" thicker
    B. backfill the 4" with stone
    C. backfill the 4" with clean sand and puddle the fill carefully
    D. lower the footing 4"

13. The MOST common finish for a concrete walk is a _____ finish.

    A. steel trowel
    B. screeded
    C. sealed
    D. wood float

14. In setting diagonal cross bridging on wood joists, the BEST method is to

    A. nail at top and bottom before subflooring is in place
    B. nail at bottom, place subflooring, then nail at top
    C. nail at top, place subflooring, then nail at bottom
    D. place subflooring, then nail at top and bottom

15. In a fireproof building, purlins used to support a suspended ceiling are USUALLY

    A. T   B. channel   C. I   D. lattice

16. *Standing seams* are MOST frequently found in _____ roofs.

    A. built up
    B. poured gypsum
    C. copper
    D. concrete plank

17. Long span steel floor joists differ from ordinary light steel beams used as joists in that the long span joists

    A. come with welded plank clips on the top flange
    B. do not require fireproofing
    C. have lower flanges with adaptors for suspended ceilings
    D. have open diagonal lacing rather than solid webs

18. In fireproofing steel girders (4 hour fire rating), the minimum thickness of concrete (ordinary concrete made with trap rock) required to protect the girder is

    A. 1"   B. 2"   C. 3"   D. 4"

19. The base composition of plaster boards is

    A. cement
    B. vermiculite
    C. gypsum
    D. perlite

20. In the ordinary cantilever type retaining wall, the main steel reinforcing in the upright part will be _____ and nearest the side of the wall _____ the earth.

    A. vertical; next to
    B. horizontal; next to
    C. vertical; away from
    D. horizontal; away from

21. A major disadvantage in the use of lime mortar for brickwork is that the lime

    A. sets too slowly
    B. is too difficult to apply
    C. discolors the brick too much
    D. reduces the fire resistance of the masonry

22. Mortar joints in old brick walls are BEST repaired by

    A. setting   B. framing   C. taping   D. pointing

23. Of the following, the MAIN advantage of a 10" brick cavity wall over an 8" solid brick wall is that the cavity wall

    A. is stronger
    B. resists rain penetration better
    C. is not affected by freezing and thawing
    D. can be used with more varieties of bond

24. In large metropolitan cities, masonry structural units are considered *solid* structural units when they are (select SMALLEST acceptable value) _____ *solid*.

    A. 70%   B. 75%   C. 80%   D. 85%

25. The PRIMARY function of a vapor barrier is to

    A. stop water from entering the space between a parapet wall and a roof surface
    B. prevent a driving rain from penetrating a roof surface
    C. seal openings around a hot water pipe in a wall
    D. block moisture in warm air from entering unheated ceiling and wall spaces

KEY (CORRECT ANSWERS)

1.	D	11.	C
2.	A	12.	A
3.	B	13.	D
4.	D	14.	C
5.	C	15.	B
6.	A	16.	C
7.	B	17.	D
8.	A	18.	B
9.	C	19.	C
10.	B	20.	A

21. A
22. D
23. B
24. B
25. D

TEST 2

DIRECTIONS: Each question or incomplete statement is followed by several suggested answers or completions. Select the one that BEST answers the question or completes the statement. *PRINT THE LETTER OF THE CORRECT ANSWER IN THE SPACE AT THE RIGHT.*

1. On a plan, the symbol ⌷⌷ represents

    A. brick
    B. cinder concrete block
    C. hollow clay tile
    D. gypsum block

2. Where a continuous concrete floor slab is supported on concrete beams and girders, poured integrally, the BEST place to make a construction joint is at a point

    A. midway between the beams
    B. directly over the center of a beam
    C. a distance from the face of the beam equal to the depth of the beam
    D. one-third of the distance from the face of the beam to the center of the beam

3. If legal curb grade is at elevation 134.27, and the first floor level is 4'2 1/4" above legal curb grade, then the elevation of the first floor is MOST NEARLY

    A. 138.40   B. 138.42   C. 138.44   D. 138.46

4. Of the following practices, the one that is MOST likely to result in segregation in concrete is

    A. inadequate floating
    B. vibrating mixes that can be readily consolidated by hand
    C. placing the chutes in such a way that the discharge end is always at the end of the fresh concrete surface
    D. placing the concrete in thin layers over the entire area to be concreted

5. Stone sills frequently have a groove cut into the underside.
   This is done MAINLY to

    A. assist in anchoring the sill with clips
    B. allow flashing to be inserted
    C. give the mortar a *key* or grip
    D. prevent rain dripping onto the wall

6. A permit to store paint in quantities greater than 20 gallons must be obtained from the

    A. Police Department
    B. Department of Air Resources
    C. Fire Department
    D. Building Department

7. The specifications state that glass shall have a thickness of 1/8" 1/32".
   Of the following thicknesses of glass, the one that does NOT meet the above specification is

    A. .090"   B. .110"   C. .130"   D. .150"

8. Of the following, the one that designates a quality of clear glass is

   A. Class II
   B. B
   C. select grade
   D. transparent

9. A section of the specifications calls for concrete fill. This concrete is MOST likely to be _____ concrete.

   A. reinforced
   B. high early strength
   C. cinder
   D. sulfate resisting

10. When concrete is to have a rubbed finish,

    A. the concrete must be thoroughly dry before the rubbing operation commences
    B. mortar is usually used in the rubbing operation
    C. grout is usually used in the rubbing operation
    D. the surfaces should be kept thoroughly wet during rubbing operations

11. The specification for Average A concrete is as follows:

    A. 1:1:3   B. 1:2:3 1/2   C. 1:2:4   D. 1:1 1/2:3

12. The specification states: *The value of each change order shall be computed separately by cost of labor and materials, plus equipment allowance, plus overhead and profit.*

    The MOST probable value of overhead and profit is _____ of the cost of labor and materials plus equipment allowance.

    A. 5%   B. 15%   C. 34%   D. 55%

13. In the specifications is an item, *Equipment Allowance: Shall include rental of necessary equipment plus 9% of this rental.*
    According to the above specification, if a piece of equipment rents for $35 per day, Equipment Allowance for this equipment rented for 11 days is MOST NEARLY

    A. $484.00   B. $378.42   C. $385.00   D. $419.65

14. Plank clips that are .062 inches thick are MOST NEARLY _____ thick.

    A. 1/32"   B. 2/32"   C. 3/32"   D. 4/32"

15. Of the following types of structured steel shapes, the one of the following that is UNLIKE the others in general is

    A. WF   B. H   C. I   D. T

16. Terra cotta is composed primarily of

    A. limestone
    B. portland cement
    C. gypsum
    D. clay

17. In the specification for brickwork is a paragraph entitled *bond.*
    With reference to brickwork, bond refers to

    A. the pattern of the brickwork
    B. the guarantee of the life of the brick

C. the mortar joining the brick
D. water tightness of the brick wall

18. The specifications for the laying of block state that the joint shall be slightly concave. This would appear MOST likely as in

A. B. C. D.

19. The maximum size of a sand particle beyond which it is NOT considered sand is _____ inch.

A. 1/16   B. 1/8   C. 3/16   D. 1/4

20. The specifications state that concrete shall have an ultimate compressive strength of 4000 psi. This means the compressive strength at the end of _____ days.

A. 7   B. 14   C. 21   D. 28

21. The primary purpose of curing a freshly poured concrete slab is to _____ the concrete.

A. prevent loss of water from
B. minimize segregation in
C. minimize honeycombing in
D. prevent efflorescense in

22. Silicone water repellent would MOST likely be used on

A. the inside of a foundation wall
B. the outside of a foundation wall
C. an exposed brick wall
D. the roof of a building

23. *Parging* of a brick wall is also known as

A. buttering   B. backplastering
C. slushing   D. scratching

24. The specifications require 2.2 lbs. metal lath. The 2.2 lbs. represents the weight per

A. foot   B. yard
C. square foot   D. square yard

25. Cleaning of glazed surfaces of a completed structural facing tile surface is BEST done by

A. sandblasting
B. washing with soap powder in boiling water
C. wire brushing
D. scrubbing with a medium solution of muriatic acid

4 (#2)

KEY (CORRECT ANSWERS)

1. B
2. A
3. D
4. B
5. D

6. C
7. A
8. B
9. C
10. D

11. C
12. B
13. D
14. B
15. D

16. D
17. A
18. A
19. D
20. D

21. A
22. C
23. B
24. D
25. B

TEST 3

DIRECTIONS: Each question or incomplete statement is followed by several suggested answers or completions. Select the one that BEST answers the question or completes the statement. *PRINT THE LETTER OF THE CORRECT ANSWER IN THE SPACE AT THE RIGHT.*

1. A metal support for plaster is 1 1/4" x 1/2" x 1/8". The 1/2" refers to

   A. A
   B. B
   C. C
   D. D

2. The specification requires stove bolts.
   The head of a stove bolt would MOST LIKELY appear as in

   A.   B.   C.   D.

3. In a hung plaster ceiling, the metal lath is tied to the

   A. runner   B. hanger
   C. tee insert   D. cross furring

4. Plastering has just been completed in a room.
   The proper way to ventilate the room to dry out the plaster when the outside weather conditions are moderate is to

   A. keep the window shut
   B. open the bottom window all the way
   C. open the top and bottom window 2 inches
   D. open the top window all the way

5. The specification for a wood door states: *Stiles and rails of doors M & T together and assembled with hardwood wedges.*
   M & T stands for

   A. mitred and tongued   B. matches and tacked
   C. milled and tacked   D. mortise and tenon

6. The weight of a gallon of ordinary paint, in pounds, is MOST NEARLY

   A. 5   B. 13   C. 21   D. 29

7. A section in the specification is entitled *Resilient Flooring*.
   Of the following types of flooring, the one that is NOT considered resilient flooring is

   A. linoleum   B. asphalt tile
   C. vinyl asbestos tile   D. quarry tile

8. The specifications state: *All exposed surfaces shall be free from knot spots, spalls, ohips, and mineral stains.* The material referred to is MOST likely

   A. brick   B. wood   C. marble   D. quarry tile

25

9. A protective transparent coating is to be placed on the aluminum surface of an aluminum window.
   The coating would MOST likely be a transparent coating of

   A. gum arable   B. shellac
   C. stain   D. lacquer

10. The vertical side of a window frame is known as the

    A. sill   B. muntin   C. rail   D. jamb

11. The specifications state: *Sill and head shall be No. 12 B & S gauge minimum.*
    B & S is an abbreviation of

    A. Black & Stone   B. Birmingham & Stone
    C. Black & Sloane   D. Brown & Sharpe

12. In three coat plaster, the finish coat follows the brown coat.
    The minimum number of days that must elapse after the brown coat is completed before the finish coat may be applied is MOST NEARLY

    A. 1   B. 3   C. 17   D. 32

13. Of the following, the method of construction that is encountering difficulty with governmental agencies because of environmental pollution is

    A. guniting
    B. spray painting
    C. sprayed on insulation
    D. air entraining of concrete

14. The specifications on piping require the use of graphite on cleanout plugs.
    Of the following, the BEST reason for the use of graphite is to

    A. facilitate installing the plug
    B. facilitate removing the plug
    C. make the plug watertight
    D. give the plug a dark color for identification purposes

15. The specifications state that the concrete shall have a certain minimum *cement factor.*
    Cement factor is the

    A. number of bags of cement per cubic yard of concrete
    B. gallons of water per bag of cement
    C. number of bags of cement per gallon of water
    D. slump of the concrete

16. The specifications state that the ends of a wood beam shall be firecut.
    The end of the beam would appear in place as shown in

17. One of the unit price items in the contract for extra or omitted work in a building is reinforcing steel in place.
This price is MOST likely _____ /pound.

   A. 12¢   B. 22¢   C. 32¢   D. 42¢

18. The specifications require that porous fill be placed under a concrete slab.
The material LEAST likely to be permitted as porous fill is

   A. crushed stone   B. sand
   C. gravel   D. loam

19. Of the following, the organization NOT concerned with standards for construction material is

   A. A.I.S.C.   B. A.C.I.   C. A.S.T.M.   D. A.I.E.M.

20. The specification on grouting states: *The contractor shall furnish all material and labor for properly bedding on Portland cement grout, the equipment or its supporting base.*
Grout of this type would usually consist of

   A. Portland cement only
   B. 1 part Portland cement and 1 part sand
   C. 1 part Portland cement and 4 parts sand
   D. 1 part Portland cement and 8 parts sand

21. Referring to the above question, the thickness of grout for the bases of machinery and equipment normally found in buildings would be, in inches, MOST NEARLY _____ inch(es).

   A. 1/4   B. 1/2   C. 1   D. 3

22. One of the duties of a superintendent is to keep a record of all delays caused by strikes, walkouts, rain, or other causes beyond the contractor's control.
Of the following, the BEST reason for keeping this record is to

   A. penalize the contractor for delays
   B. enable the city to plan future jobs more accurately
   C. allow the contractor additional time to complete the contract when necessary
   D. require the contractor to put on additional forces to meet the contract deadline

23. In setting, the reinforcing steel for a concrete slab 3/8" temperature reinforcing rod interfered with a one inch vertical sleeve for a cold water line. The contractor moved the temperature bar 1/2 inch at the sleeve to avoid the interference.
This action on the part of the contractor was

   A. *improper,* since the bar should have been cut at the point of interference
   B. *improper,* since the layout of all the 3/8 inch bars was incorrect according to the plans
   C. *proper,* because very minor changes in location of temperature reinforcing steel is permissible
   D. *proper,* because cutting steel and placing additional reinforcing steel around the opening would weaken the slab

24. Of the following permits for a new school building, the one NOT issued by the department of buildings is the pernit to

    A. build
    B. install elevators
    C. erect sidewalk shed when necessary
    D. store material on sidewalk

24.____

25. A reinforced concrete canopy is to be constructed. The reinforcing steel would MOST likely appear as in

25.____

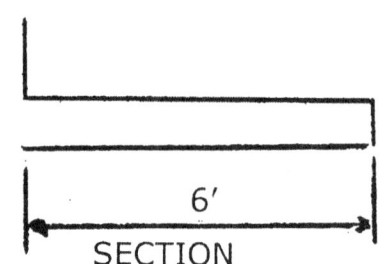
SECTION

A.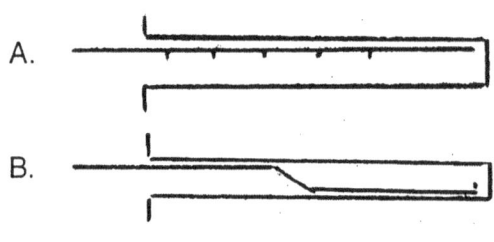

B.

C.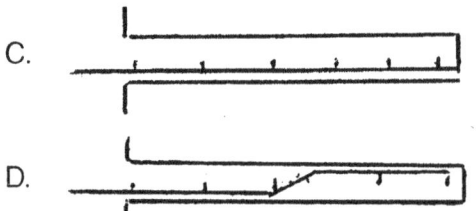

D.

KEY (CORRECT ANSWERS)

1. B
2. B
3. D
4. C
5. D

6. B
7. D
8. C
9. D
10. D

11. D
12. B
13. C
14. B
15. A

16. C
17. B
18. D
19. D
20. B

21. C
22. C
23. C
24. D
25. A

EXAMINATION SECTION
TEST 1

DIRECTIONS: Each question or incomplete statement is followed by several suggested answers or completions. Select the one that BEST answers the question or completes the statement. *PRINT THE LETTER OF THE CORRECT ANSWER IN THE SPACE AT THE RIGHT.*

1. The specifications for a construction job state that the bench top of a table shall be made of 1/2-inch transite. Transite is a(n)   1._____
   - A. thermo-setting plastic
   - B. titanium steel alloy
   - C. gypsum-cement product
   - D. asbestos-cement product

2. High early-strength cement is designated as Type   2._____
   - A. I
   - B. II
   - C. III
   - D. IV

3. The average weight of stone concrete is MOST NEARLY _____ lbs./cu.ft.   3._____
   - A. 100
   - B. 150
   - C. 200
   - D. 250

4. Concrete mixes made with lightweight aggregate USUALLY require the addition of an air-entraining agent in order to   4._____
   - A. reduce the weight of the concrete
   - B. make the concrete more workable
   - C. make the concrete more waterproof
   - D. reduce the setting time of the concrete

5. The addition of lime to cement mortar improves the workability of the mortar and   5._____
   - A. *decreases* the setting time
   - B. *increases* the water tightness
   - C. *increases* the strength
   - D. *decreases* the shrinkage

6. A mortar joint in a brick wall in which the joint is made flush with the brick is called a _____ joint.   6._____
   - A. cut
   - B. weather
   - C. painted
   - D. stripped

7. Quarry tile is made of   7._____
   - A. marble
   - B. cement and sand
   - C. clay
   - D. limestone

8. The base composition of *drywall* is   8._____
   - A. vermiculite
   - B. perlite
   - C. gypsum
   - D. Portland cement

9. The specifications for a construction job state: Furnish and erect chair rail of birch with continuous kerfing where required by room finish schedule.
Kerfing means MOST NEARLY   9._____
   - A. planing
   - B. rounding
   - C. jointing
   - D. grooving

10. Cement that has become lumpy after being stored on a job site may

    A. be used anywhere if screened
    B. be used only for foundations
    C. not be used at all
    D. be used anywhere if dried out thoroughly

11. The BEST of the following sources of information to use to obtain information concerning the product of a particular manufacturer of flooring is

    A. Sweet's Catalog
    B. Architectural Standards
    C. The Flooring Institute
    D. The ASTM

12. In masonry work, a bull nose brick would be located

    A. at the inside corner of a wall
    B. at an outside corner of a wall
    C. on the inside of a boiler flue
    D. in the key of an arch

13. The thickness of double-strength glass (D.S.) is MOST NEARLY

    A. 1/8"   B. 3/16"   C. 1/4"   D. 5/16"

14. Of the following types of paint, the one that can MOST readily be applied by spraying is

    A. lacquer
    B. shellac
    C. varnish
    D. bituminous-based paints

15. Of the following, the designation that would apply to brick is

    A. Grade A
    B. Grade SW
    C. Select Quality
    D. No. 1 Common

16. The size of the hole that is punched in structural steel to accommodate a 3/4-inch rivet should be _____ inch.

    A. 3/4   B. 13/16   C. 7/8   D. 15/16

17. In lightweight concrete, the lightweight material is substituted PRIMARILY for

    A. water   B. sand   C. cement   D. gravel

18. The thickness of a sheet of 16-ounce copper is MOST NEARLY _____ inch.

    A. 1/50   B. 1/30   C. 1/20   D. 1/8

19. One cubic foot of dry sand weighs MOST NEARLY _____ lbs.

    A. 70   B. 94   C. 110   D. 150

20. The main difference between plate glass and sheet glass is that plate glass

    A. has a better surface finish than sheet glass
    B. absorbs heat better than sheet glass
    C. is tempered, while sheet glass is not
    D. is thinner than sheet glass

21. Stainless steel (18-8) contains 18% _____ nickel and 8% _____.

    A. nickel; zinc
    B. nickel; chromium
    C. zinc; nickel
    D. zinc; chromium

22. The specifications for a construction job state: The subframe shall be formed 1/4" thick aluminum bar with corners mitered.
Which of the following is so formed?

    A.   B.   C.   D.

23. The coarse aggregate used in making terrazzo floors is MOST usually chips of

    A. limestone   B. granite   C. brick   D. marble

24. Projected sash are

    A. windows that open inward or outward
    B. double hung windows
    C. storm windows
    D. fixed picture windows

25. For a school building, the number of reinforcing bars in a slab would be indicated on the

    A. architectural plans
    B. structural engineer's plans
    C. reinforcing steel shop drawings
    D. standard detail drawings

KEY (CORRECT ANSWERS)

1. D
2. C
3. B
4. B
5. D

6. A
7. C
8. C
9. D
10. C

11. A
12. B
13. A
14. A
15. B

16. B
17. D
18. A
19. C
20. A

21. B
22. A
23. D
24. A
25. C

TEST 2

DIRECTIONS: Each question or incomplete statement is followed by several suggested answers or completions. Select the one that BEST answers the question or completes the statement. *PRINT THE LETTER OF THE CORRECT ANSWER IN THE SPACE AT THE RIGHT.*

1. The ADVANTAGES of gypsum mortar over lime mortar for use in plaster work are that gypsum mortar is stronger and _____ than lime mortar.

    A. is more compact
    B. sets more quickly
    C. works more easily
    D. contains more entrained air

    1._____

2. In concrete work, a dummy joint is MOST similar in purpose to a(n) _____ joint.

    A. construction
    B. expansion
    C. contraction
    D. shear

    2._____

3. In the welding symbol, ⟍ 3/8 ⟋ 2-5 ↗ , the 2 represents the

    A. length of the individual weld, in inches
    B. spacing between the welds, in inches
    C. number of sides to be welded
    D. thickness of the throat of the weld, in eighths of an inch

    3._____

4. Where vinyl tile is to be laid directly upon a concrete floor, the finish on the concrete surface should be

    A. wood floated
    B. broomed
    C. steel trowelled
    D. darbied

    4._____

5. Specifications for hollow metal doors to be used on a construction job state: Double door without mullions; spot weld astragal to inactive door.
Astragal, as used in the above statement, means MOST NEARLY

    A. louver   B. hinge   C. molding   D. veneer

    5._____

6. The concrete surface of a reinforced concrete building is 1/4 inch below the finished floor. Of the following, the floor finish MOST likely to be installed is

    A. wood flooring
    B. ceramic tile
    C. asphalt tile
    D. terrazzo

    6._____

7. Of the following, aluminum castings are USUALLY made from alloy

    A. 43   B. 3003   C. 1100   D. 6063

    7._____

8. Specifications for a building state that reinforcing bars must lap 40 diameters in the concrete.
The length of lap for a number 5 bar should be

    A. 15"   B. 25"   C. 30"   D. 35"

    8._____

9. The MAXIMUM size fillet weld that can usually be made in a single pass for other than vertical welds in ordinary structural steel work is _____ inch.

    A. 3/16   B. 5/16   C. 7/16   D. 9/16

10. The specifications for a construction job state: The contractor shall make additional borings at locations directed by the executive director, for which he will receive additional payment at the rate of $6.00 per lineal foot for earth borings, and $7.50 per lineal foot for rock borings. In addition to rate per lineal foot for borings, the contractor will be paid an additional sum of money in the amount of $150.00 to defray the cost of transporting drilling equipment to the site, setting up the equipment, dismantling same, and transporting equipment away from the site after completion of the work. If an additional boring is ordered that is through 40 feet of earth and 5 feet of rock, the contractor would be entitled to

    A. $187.50   B. $277.50   C. $390.00   D. $427.50

11. The specifications for a construction job state: Cement content shall not exceed 7 1/2 sacks nor be less than 6 sacks per cubic yard of concrete.
    The ratio of the number of sacks of cement per cubic yard of concrete is known as the

    A. water-cement ratio   B. yield
    C. ultimate strength   D. cement factor

12. The specifications for a construction job state that the deflection of the facing materials between the studs as well as the deflection of the studs shall be limited to .0025 times the span.
    If the span is 8 1/4", the MAXIMUM allowable deflection is _____ inch.

    A. 1/8   B. 1/4   C. 3/8   D. 1/2

13. The specifications for a construction job state that job chutes for placing concrete shall have a slope of not more than one vertical to two horizontal and not less than one vertical to three horizontal.
    If the horizontal distance of the run of chute is 20 feet, a difference in elevation between the start and the end of the chute that is acceptable is _____ feet.

    A. 6   B. 9   C. 12   D. 15

14. The specifications relating to cavity wall brick construction state: In laying up face brick, the mason shall leave temporary openings (one brick) approximately five feet on centers and at all internal and external corners in the first course of brick above the foundation wall and in brick courses resting on angle lintels.
    The purpose of these temporary openings is to allow for

    A. expansion or contraction
    B. the erection of scaffolds
    C. cleaning off the wall flashings
    D. draining off water that may get into the wall cavity

15. Of the following size electrodes for ordinary structural steel welding, the one that would MOST likely be used for vertical and overhead welding is _____ inch.

    A. 1/16   B. 3/16   C. 5/16   D. 7/16

16. The number of anchor bolts used to anchor a steel column to a footing is USUALLY   16.____

    A. 1   B. 2   C. 3   D. 4

17. Specifications for precasting for a construction job state: Dimensions shall be within a tolerance of plus 0 to minus 3/32.   17.____
    If the specified dimension is 24 inches, the one of the following actual dimensions which would be UNACCEPTABLE is _____ inches.

    A. 24-1/32   B. 24   C. 23-31/32   D. 23-15/16

18. Of the following, the one that would be the composition of grout under a billet plate is   18.____

    A. neat cement
    B. 1 part cement, 2 parts sand
    C. 1 part cement, 2 parts sand, 3 parts gravel
    D. 1 part cement, 1 part lime, 2 parts sand

19. Specifications for concrete for a construction job state that slab forms shall be set with a camber of 1/4 inch per 10 feet of slab.   19.____
    Of the following, the BEST reason for providing camber in the forms is to

    A. allow for adjustment during pouring
    B. prevent overloading of the wood forms during pouring
    C. allow for drainage before pouring
    D. eliminate sag in the finishing slab

20. Specifications for concrete construction state that the contractor must provide for rebates, reglets, keys, and chamfers.   20.____
    Rebates are

    A. grooves   B. grounds   C. chases   D. ties

21. Concrete driveways built across sidewalks must have a MINIMUM thickness of _____ inches.   21.____

    A. 4   B. 6   C. 7   D. 8

22. Wire mesh is designated 4 x 16 - 3/8.   22.____
    The *16* represents the _____ of the wires.

    A. spacing; longitudinal   B. spacing; transverse
    C. size; longitudinal   D. size; transverse

23. Specifications for a construction job state: Install 6 mil carbon vinyl membrane.   23.____
    The *6 mil* means 6

    A. millimeters   B. thousandths of an inch
    C. hundredths of an inch   D. tenths of an inch

24. It is poor practice to use a vibrator to move newly poured concrete into place.   24.____
    Of the following, the BEST reason for not using a vibrator for this purpose is to prevent

    A. air entrapment in the concrete
    B. segregation of the aggregates
    C. premature setting of the concrete
    D. premature drying out of the surface of the concrete

25. Expanded slag, shale, or clay would weigh MOST NEARLY _____ pounds per cubic foot. 25._____

    A. 30   B. 90   C. 150   D. 210

KEY (CORRECT ANSWERS)

1.	B		11.	D
2.	C		12.	B
3.	A		13.	B
4.	C		14.	C
5.	C		15.	B
6.	C		16.	B
7.	A		17.	A
8.	B		18.	B
9.	B		19.	D
10.	D		20.	A

21. C
22. B
23. B
24. B
25. B

EXAMINATION SECTION
TEST 1

DIRECTIONS: Each question or incomplete statement is followed by several suggested answers or completions. Select the one that BEST answers the question or completes the statement. *PRINT THE LETTER OF THE CORRECT ANSWER IN THE SPACE AT THE RIGHT.*

1. A percentage of the payment for a contract is held back until the job is completed for one year.
   The MAIN reason for this practice is to insure that the

   A. city doesn't overpay the contractor for the job
   B. contractor will return to correct defective work after the job is completed
   C. contractor will not make unwarranted claims against the city
   D. contractor will pay all his subcontractors

   1.____

2. There are four separate major contracts on a certain building construction project.
   The MAJOR disadvantage of this practice, as compared to the practice of having a single contract, is

   A. the difficulty in coordinating the work
   B. the low level of productivity of the tradesman
   C. cost of the material going into the building is greater
   D. the difficulty in finding competent bidders on the contracts

   2.____

3. Of the following, the PREFERRED way to authorize a contractor to perform work other than required by the contract is by a

   A. T & M order   B. unit price order
   C. lump sum modification D. change order

   3.____

4. A contract requires that the prime contractor do a certain minimum percentage of the work with his own forces.
   Of the following, the BEST reason for this requirement is to

   A. insure good work
   B. discourage bidders who may not have the ability to do the job
   C. encourage more people to bid the job, thus lowering the bid price
   D. freeze out incompetent subcontractors

   4.____

5. In computing an extra based on the actual cost of work done, the THREE MAJOR items that go into the cost are

   A. taxes, labor, and material
   B. time, taxes, and material
   C. labor, material, and equipment
   D. taxes, labor, and equipment

   5.____

6. A contractor is to be penalized if he exceeds a certain completion date. There is a major strike lasting a month that shuts down all construction.
   Under these conditions, the completion date should be

   6.____

A. held unchanged
B. made two weeks later than the original date
C. made one month later than the original date
D. made six weeks later than the original completion date

7. The one of the following that refers to a Federal safety program in construction is

A. OSHA   B. AISC   C. AIEE   D. UL

8. With regard to the placing of concrete, the contractor is GENERALLY

A. limited to a specific method by the contract
B. not permitted to rent equipment to place the concrete
C. not permitted to pump the concrete into place
D. permitted to choose his own method of placing the concrete

9. The MOST practical control the inspector or resident engineer has over the contractor when the inspector is not satisfied with the quality of the work is to

A. discuss withholding payment on that part of the work that is unsatisfactory
B. threaten to have the contractor thrown off the job
C. request that the contractor fire the men responsible for the unsatisfactory work
D. call the owner of the company and explain the situation to him

10. The MOST practical method of being sure that the architect will be satisfied with the appearance of the exterior brick work for a building is to

A. build a sample wall section, for the architect's approval, with the brick that is delivered to the job site
B. send the architect to the plant supplying the brick to insure that the color and tone of the brick is satisfactory
C. have the architect's representative on the job while the brick work is being erected to be sure the finished product is satisfactory
D. put a damage clause in the contract penalizing the contractor if the brick work is not satisfactory to the architect

11. Of the following, the MOST frequent problem that will arise during the construction of a building is

A. inability to fit all the reinforcing steel in the space allotted to it
B. interference in piping and ductwork
C. inability to keep walls level
D. settling of the foundation as the load comes on the building

12. To find the number of reinforcing bars that should be in a slab, the inspector SHOULD refer to the

A. architect's plan
B. reinforcing steel design drawings
C. standard detail drawings
D. reinforcing steel detail drawings

13. The specifications for a building state that a certain brick type shall be *Stark Brick type XX or equal.*
    The BEST reason for inserting the *or equal* clause is to

    A. permit other companies to compete in supplying the brick
    B. allow other companies to submit their product to determine which is best
    C. limit the suppliers only to those companies whose product is superior to that produced by Stark
    D. allow Stark Brick Company to set the standard for the industry

14. In the absence of a formal training program for inspectors, the BEST of the following ways to train a new man who is to do inspection work is to

    A. give him the literature on the subject so that he can learn what he has to know
    B. have him accompany an inspector as the inspector does his work so that he can learn by observing
    C. assign him the job and let him learn on his own
    D. tell him to go to a school at night that specializes in this field so that he will gain the necessary background

15. Of the following, the safety practice that is REQUIRED on the construction job site is

    A. safety shoes must be worn by all workers
    B. safety goggles must be worn by all workers
    C. safety helmets must be worn by all workers
    D. all workers must have a safety kit in their possession

16. Safety on the job is the concern of

    A. the individual workman only
    B. the contractor only
    C. all parties on the job
    D. the insuring company only

17. Frequently, payments due the contractor are delayed many months because of a backlog of work in the agency.
    This practice is considered

    A. *good* because the city saves money by delaying payment
    B. *poor* because the contractors will raise their bids in the future to compensate for the added cost
    C. *poor* because it becomes difficult to compute payments
    D. *good* because it forces the contractor to do good work in order to be sure that he will receive payment

18. Provisions are made in a contract for payment for certain items when delivered to the job before installation.
    The MAIN reason for this practice is to

    A. enable better inspection of the items
    B. prevent bottlenecks during construction
    C. give the contractor a quick profit on the items
    D. allow the contractor more time to shop for the items

19. The agency that approves payments to building contractors is the 19._____

    A. Corporation Counsel B. Comptroller's Office
    C. Board of Estimate D. City Planning Commission

20. The bond that the contractor puts up to insure that he will start work is the 20._____

    A. Bid Bond B. Payment Bond
    C. Performance Bond D. Liability Insurance

21. Of the following, the BEST practice to follow in order to minimize claims of damage to 21._____
    adjacent buildings during the construction of a building is to

    A. take out special insurance against such claims
    B. make a detailed survey of the condition of the nearby buildings before construction begins
    C. make a payment to adjacent property owners in advance so that they waive claims of damage to their property
    D. have the buildings underpinned

22. The four MAJOR contracts on a building project are: 22._____

    A. General Construction, Electrical, Plumbing and Drainage, Heating, Ventilating and Air Conditioning
    B. Plumbing, Heating and Ventilating, Air Conditioning, and General Construction
    C. Foundations, Superstructure, Mechanical, and Electrical
    D. Air Conditioning, Electrical, Mechanical, and Structural

23. Oil tanks, when set in place inside a building, are frequently filled with water. 23._____
    The BEST reason for this practice is

    A. to prevent them from floating off their foundation if water fills the room
    B. to enable them to be lifted up more easily
    C. to prevent them from becoming rusted
    D. for emergency use in case of fire

24. The filing system used in the field for correspondence is required to be uniform for all 24._____
    jobs.
    The BEST reason for this requirement is that

    A. there is only one good way of setting up the filing system
    B. the standardized system is compact, thereby saving space
    C. other interested parties such as engineers from the main office will be able to use the files
    D. the contractor's forces will understand the filing system and will be able to extract necessary correspondence

25. Upon excavation to the subgrade of a footing to be placed on piles, the inspector finds 25._____
    that the soil is very poor.
    Of the following, the PROPER action for the inspector to take is to

    A. do nothing
    B. add 20% to the number of piles
    C. notify the engineer's office of this condition
    D. order the contractor to keep excavating until he hits better soil

26. The general contractor is required to submit a progress schedule before starting work. Of the following, the BEST reason for this requirement is to

    A. determine if the contractor intends to complete the job
    B. enable the inspector to determine whether the contractor is on schedule
    C. enable the inspector to estimate monthly payments
    D. check minority hiring

27. If a contractor is falling behind schedule, the FIRST thing to check if the inspector is looking for the cause of this condition is the

    A. number of men he has on the job
    B. efficiency of his crew
    C. availability of equipment needed to do the job
    D. availability of the latest drawings needed by the contractor

28. The critical path method is a method for

    A. finding the best material needed for a specific use
    B. determining the best arrangement of equipment
    C. determining the best time to replace a piece of machinery
    D. scheduling work

29. The contractor states to the inspector that a given structural detail is undersized and unsafe.
    Of the following, the BEST action for the inspector to take in this situation is to

    A. ignore the complaint since the contractor is not an engineer
    B. change the detail by issuing a change order
    C. notify your superiors of the contractor's statements
    D. allow the contractor to modify the detail since it is his responsibility

30. The contractor proposes to use an additive to the concrete to accelerate its set. He asks you, the inspector, for permission to use it.
    Of the following, the FIRST action to take in response to his request is to

    A. check if the use of the additive is permitted by the specifications
    B. tell him to put the request in writing
    C. ask your superior if the use of the additive is acceptable
    D. deny him permission since additives to concrete are not permitted

KEY (CORRECT ANSWERS)

1.	B	16.	C
2.	A	17.	B
3.	D	18.	B
4.	B	19.	B
5.	C	20.	A
6.	C	21.	B
7.	A	22.	A
8.	D	23.	A
9.	A	24.	C
10.	A	25.	A
11.	B	26.	B
12.	D	27.	A
13.	A	28.	D
14.	B	29.	C
15.	C	30.	A

EXAMINATION SECTION
TEST 1

DIRECTIONS: Each question or incomplete statement is followed by several suggested answers or completions. Select the one that BEST answers the questions or completes the statement. *PRINT THE LETTER OF THE CORRECT ANSWER IN THE SPACE AT THE RIGHT.*

1. Of the following, the FIRST operation in the demolition of a 4-story building adjacent to the property line is the

    A. erection of railings around the stairwells
    B. shoring of adjoining buildings
    C. erection of a sidewalk shed
    D. removal of windows

    1.____

2. Projected sash is defined as a(n)

    A. double hung window
    B. window that opens inward or outward
    C. architectural projection from a building exterior
    D. storm window

    2.____

3. Specifications for a reinforced concrete structure call for a roof fill to be placed on the concrete roof slab. Of the following, the PURPOSE of the fill is to

    A. reduce sound transmission
    B. facilitate drainage
    C. provide a smooth base for insulation
    D. protect the concrete slab

    3.____

4. The Building Department requires a location survey by a licensed surveyor

    A. *only* if it is suspected that the building is not in the proper place and may impinge on adjacent property
    B. *only* of the completed foundation
    C. *only* of the completed superstructure
    D. *after* the foundation is completed and a second survey after the building is completed

    4.____

5. After excavating by a contractor for a footing, the sub-grade soil appears to be below the quality shown on the borings.
   Of the following types of footings, the one that would be LEAST affected by this condition is a

    A. spread footing   B. combined footing
    C. footing on piles   D. footing and pier

    5.____

6. Of the following, the information of GREATEST significance to be recorded for each pile during pile driving is the

    A. steam pressure and the temperature
    B. condition of the ground at the pile location

    6.____

C. number of hammer blows at the last inch
D. total number of hammer blows

7. One method of dewatering an excavation for a foundation is by the use of

    A. inverted siphons
    B. well points
    C. line holes
    D. suction heads

8. An excavation for a concrete footing to support a structural steel column was dug 4" too deep.
   Of the following, the BEST construction practice would be to

    A. backfill the 4" with stone
    B. backfill the 4" with sand
    C. lower the entire footing 4"
    D. make the footing 4" thicker

9. Spudding, in a pile driving operation, is used PRIMARILY to

    A. remove a broken pile
    B. pass an obstruction
    C. compact the soil in the area
    D. splice piles

10. Where walers and form ties are used in wood formwork for tall vertical concrete walls, the walers are

    A. more closely spaced at the top of the wall than at the bottom
    B. evenly spaced at the top to the bottom of the wall
    C. more closely spaced at the bottom of the wall than at the top
    D. more closely spaced at the middle of the wall than at either the top or the bottom

11. A non-bearing wall unit between columns enclosing a structure is known as a _____ wall.

    A. panel
    B. curtain
    C. apron
    D. spandrel

12. In a multi-story building, standpipes are installed FIRST by the plumber for

    A. water supply
    B. sanitary facilities
    C. fire protection
    D. steam supply

13. It is necessary to burn reinforcing steel while they are in the wood forms in order to change their lengths.
    The STANDARD safety precaution to observe during this process is to

    A. fireproof the wood forms
    B. use a low heat flame
    C. have a man stand by with a fire extinguisher
    D. soak a 20-foot radius around the area with water

14. Specifications for a building require that the first floor beams must be in place before backfilling against the foundation walls.
    Of the following, the BEST reason for this requirement is that

    A. the utilities up to the first floor level should be in place before backfilling
    B. without the first floor beams in place, the wall may become overstressed
    C. it facilitates the inspection of the first floor construction
    D. it facilitates the inspection of the backfilling operation

    14.____

15. The utility line that USUALLY enters the building at the *lowest* elevation is the

    A. electric cable   B. gas lines
    C. water lines   D. plumbing drain

    15.____

16. Specifications for a building require that machine excavation for foundation footings be within a foot of final subgrade and the remaining excavation be done by hand. Of the following, the BEST reasons for this requirement is to

    A. prevent cave-ins around the excavation
    B. save the amount of fill needed
    C. prevent disturbing the surrounding excavation
    D. prevent excavation below the subgrade

    16.____

17. Of the following outside lines entering a building, the one for which grades must be MOST carefully controlled is the

    A. sewer line   B. water line
    C. gas line   D. electric cable

    17.____

18. On a plan, the grades for a building are as follows:
    Datum ± 0 (Elev. 24.08')
    First floor El + 1' - 0" (Elev. 25.08').
    The elevation of a ledge 6'3" below the finished first floor level with respect to datum is

    A. El. - 6.25   B. El. - 5.25
    C. El. + 18.83   D. El. + 17.83

    18.____

19. Specifications for a building call for *defective material to be removed from the job site immediately*. The MAIN reason for this is to

    A. prevent accidents
    B. prevent accidental use of the defective material in the construction
    C. insure that the contractor does not make the same mistake again
    D. minimize claims against the department

    19.____

20. *Drywall* is installed by

    A. carpenters   B. lathers
    C. plasterers   D. masons

    20.____

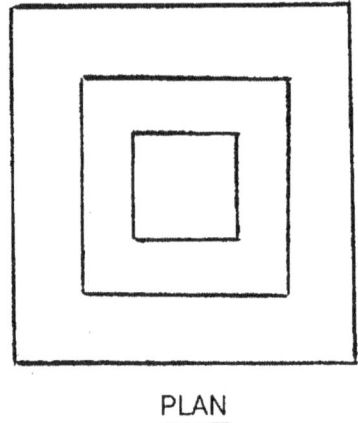

PLAN

21. The Plan of a footing and concrete column is shown above. An elevation of the footing would be shown as:

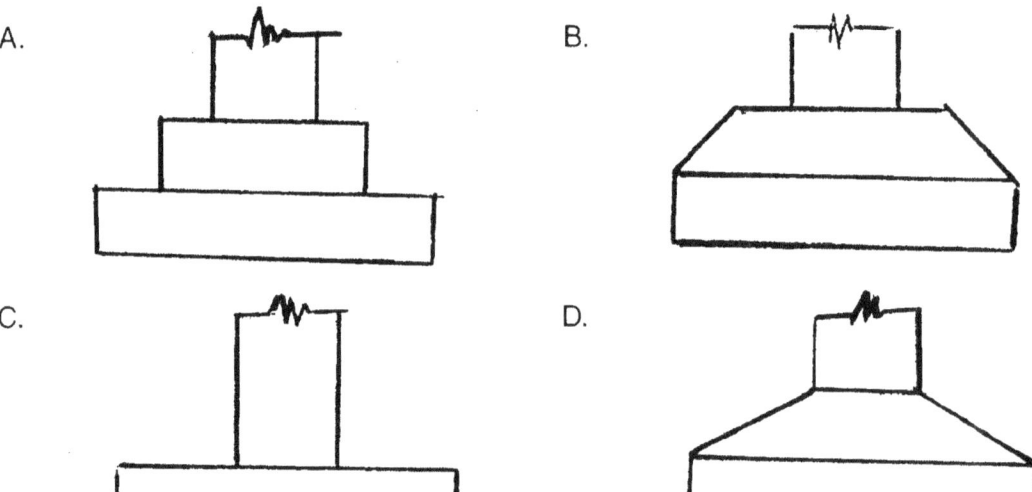

22. Of the following, the BEST sequence to follow in pouring the interior footing, concrete column and basement floor as shown below is pour the footing,

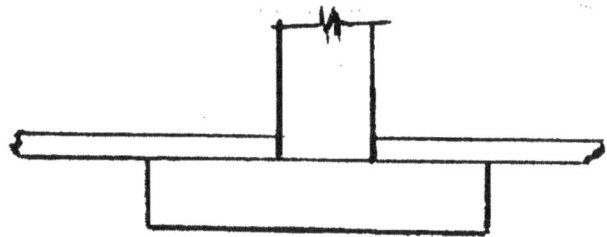

 A. and floor in one pour. Pour the column
 B. and column in one pour. Pour the floor
 C. pour the floor above the footing, pour the column above the floor
 D. box out for the floor, pour the column. Pour the floor

23. The PURPOSE of curing concrete is so that the 23._____

    A. forms for the concrete can be stripped quickly
    B. water content will not evaporate too quickly
    C. concrete will harden faster
    D. reinforcing rods will not rust

24. Air-entraining cement may be required so that the resulting concrete will resist 24._____

    A. freezing and thawing
    B. hot weather
    C. dampness
    D. heavy loads

25. Concrete test cylinders are required to 25._____

    A. provide an indication of the strength of the concrete poured in a specific location
    B. provide a basis of payment
    C. check on the inspector
    D. check the source of material

26. Concrete test cylinders are stored and cured on the job 26._____

    A. so that the contractor can then control the curing
    B. so that the inspector can then control the curing
    C. because the laboratory has no facilities for curing concrete cylinders
    D. because conditions of curing on the job are the same as at the location poured

27. The *water-cement ratio* refers to the quantity of water in a concrete mix as 27._____

    A. cubic feet of water per cubic foot of cement
    B. gallons of water per pound of cement
    C. gallons of water per sack of cement
    D. bags of cement per gallon of water

28. *Slump* of concrete refers to the 28._____

    A. shrinkage of concrete while setting
    B. drop in height relative to a standard testing cone
    C. amount of water introduced into the concrete
    D. cracking or crazing of the surface of concrete

29. Concrete mixes made with lightweight aggregate USUALLY require the addition of an air-entraining agent in order to 29._____

    A. increase the strength of the concrete
    B. reduce the weight of the concrete
    C. obtain the necessary plasticity without added water
    D. save aggregate material

30. Concrete in some instances requires integral waterproofing. 30._____
    This can BEST be achieved by

    A. addition of more cement in the mix
    B. longer vibration
    C. addition of a waterproofing agent to the mix
    D. longer curing period

6 (#1)

31. In placing concrete where the vertical drop is greater than 5 feet, the use of an elephant trunk is necessary.
　　The BEST reason for using an elephant trunk is to

　　　A. prevent segregation of the aggregate
　　　B. prevent waste of material
　　　C. safeguard health and property
　　　D. save time and labor

32. According to the Building Code, the maximum size of coarse aggregate for reinforced concrete shall be one-fifth of the narrowest dimension between forms or three-quarters of the clear spacing between reinforcing bars. Of the following, the MAXIMUM sized aggregate permitted for a 12" wall with #6 bars spaced at 3" center to center is

　　　A. 1 3/4"　　B. 1 1/2"　　C. 1 1/4"　　D. 1"

33. Of the following, the one that is NOT a name for a lightweight aggregate is

　　　A. Solite　　　　　B. Vitralite
　　　C. Lelite　　　　　D. Nitralite

34. High early strength cement is designated as

　　　A. Type I　　B. Type II　　C. Type III　　D. Type IV

35. The average weight of stone concrete is, MOST NEARLY, _____ lb./cu. ft.

　　　A. 125　　　　　B. 150
　　　C. 175　　　　　D. 200

KEY (CORRECT ANSWERS)

1.	C	16.	D
2.	B	17.	A
3.	B	18.	B
4.	D	19.	B
5.	C	20.	A
6.	C	21.	A
7.	B	22.	D
8.	D	23.	B
9.	B	24.	A
10.	C	25.	A
11.	B	26.	D
12.	C	27.	C
13.	C	28.	B
14.	B	29.	C
15.	D	30.	C

31. A
32. B
33. B
34. C
35. B

TEST 2

DIRECTIONS: Each question or incomplete statement is followed by several suggested answers or completions. Select the one that BEST answers the question or completes the statement. *PRINT THE LETTER OF THE CORRECT ANSWER IN THE SPACE AT THE RIGHT.*

1. The Building Code requires that concrete shall be kept in a moist condition, after placing, for at least the FIRST _____ days.

    A. 3   B. 7   C. 14   D. 28

2. In concrete work, a dummy joint is SIMILAR in purpose to a(n) _____ joint.

    A. expansion
    B. construction
    C. contraction
    D. shear

3. Specifications for concrete usually contain a statement disallowing the *retampering* of concrete. *Retampering* means

    A. adding more water to the drum after ingredients are mixed
    B. vibrating of concrete in the forms
    C. mixing of the remaining concrete after some concrete is taken from the truck
    D. mixing of concrete in the truck after it has partially set and adding water

4. Chamfers are placed on a concrete beam PRIMARILY to

    A. save weight
    B. eliminate honeycomb
    C. eliminate sharp corners
    D. save construction costs

5. Of the following, the BEST reason for using vibrators in concrete construction is to

    A. increase the workability of the concrete
    B. consolidate the concrete
    C. slow up the setting
    D. speed up the setting

6. The concrete test that will BEST determine the consistency of a concrete mix is the

    A. sieve analysis
    B. water-cement ratio test
    C. calorimetric test
    D. slump test

7. Specifications for the concrete floor treatment of a building require *dustproofing*. This process consists of

    A. scraping the floor surface to remove loose concrete material that will dust
    B. mopping the floor with a chemical solution that will harden the concrete surface
    C. adding a chemical compound to the concrete mix that will harden the surface of the concrete
    D. grinding the concrete floor with a terrazzo machine that will case harden the surface of the concrete

8. In checking the placement of reinforcing steel, it is discovered that reinforcing steel called for on the design drawings is not shown on the reinforcing steel shop drawings.
Of the following, the BEST procedure to follow is to

2 (#2)

    A. check the design drawings for the errors
    B. check the shop drawings for the errors
    C. subtract the missing steel in the field
    D. stop all work

9. While a large spread footing of about 50 cubic yards Is being poured, the supply plant breaks down. Concrete is available from another supplier.
The use of the other supplier should

    A. not be approved because the supplier may not be approved
    B. be approved since additional test cylinders can be taken
    C. not be approved since construction joints can be installed where the pour has ended
    D. be approved as the concrete in footings is relatively unimportant

10. Of the following species of lumber, the one MOST likely to be used for concrete formwork is

    A. oak   B. pine   C. maple   D. birch

11. A contractor proposes to install the roofing two days after the concrete roof slab is poured.
This proposal should

    A. *be recommended* as it will speed the construction
    B. *be recommended* as it will cure the concrete better
    C. *not be recommended* as excess water may bulge the roofing
    D. *not be recommended* in cold weather but would be recommended in warm weather

12. For the construction of concrete floors resting on earth, the item that should be MOST carefully checked is that

    A. the earth is dry before pouring
    B. the earth is wet before pouring
    C. all backfill is properly compacted
    D. all backfill is porous soil

13. Cracks in concrete are not necessarily caused by settlement of a structure.
Sometimes they are caused by

    A. shrinkage   B. plastic flow
    C. hydration   D. curing

14. Specifications for a building state that reinforcing bars must lap 40 diameters in the concrete.
The length of lap for a number 6 bar should be, MOST NEARLY, _____ inches.

    A. 12   B. 20   C. 30   D. 40

15. Cement stored on the job site that has become caked and lumpy may

    A. be used only for foundations
    B. be used only for slabs on ground
    C. be used anywhere if the lumps are broken up
    D. not be used

16. Of the following statements relating to the plies in plywood, the one that is CORRECT is: 16.____

   A. The primary difference between exterior and interior plywood is the quality of the exterior plies.
   B. Exterior plywood has more plies than interior plywood.
   C. Exterior plywood has no surface defects on the outer plies while interior plywood permits surface defects on the outer plies.
   D. Plywood has an odd number of plies.

17. Of the following, the one that is NOT a principal classification of lumber according to the American Lumber Standards is 17.____

   A. building B. structural
   C. yard   D. shop

18. Of the following types of lumber, the one that is classified as a hardwood is 18.____

   A. cedar   B. fir   C. pine   D. maple

19. When building the formwork for a 12" doubly reinforced concrete wall, the USUAL order of conctruction is to place the 19.____

   A. formwork for both faces of the wall; then place the steel
   B. formwork for one face of the wall, place all reinforcing steel, then place the formwork for the other face of the wall
   C. reinforcing steel, then place the formwork for both faces of the wall
   D. formwork for one face of the wall, place the reinforcing steel for one face, place the form-work for the other face of the wall, then place the reinforcing steel for the second face

20. To obtain information concerning the product of a particular major manufacturer of flooring, the BEST of the following sources of information is the 20.____

   A. Architectural Standards   B. ASTM
   C. Sweet's Catalogue   D. Flooring Institute

21. Of the following, loose lintels would MOST likely be found in the specifications under the item entitled 21.____

   A. Ornamental Iron   B. Miscellaneous Iron
   C. Structural Steel   D. Hollow Metal Work

22. Galvanized metal lath is metal lath coated with 22.____

   A. tin   B. copper   C. zinc   D. nickel

23. In the welding symbol the 2 represents the 23.____
   A. spacing between welds in inches
   B. length of the weld in inches
   C. number of sides to be welded
   D. thickness of the throat of the weld in inches

24. The specification for a building states that rib lath should be 3.4 pounds. This MEANS 3.4 pounds per

    A. square foot
    B. linear foot of a 3 foot roll
    C. square yard
    D. 10 square feet

25. Terrazzo floors are laid with brass dividing strips PRIMARILY for the purpose of

    A. preventing slipping
    B. appearance
    C. preventing irregular cracking
    D. easy screeding

26. The PURPOSE of a chase is to

    A. support stair stringers
    B. accomodate pipes in a wall
    C. accomodate flashing in a parapet
    D. provide venting

27. In masonry work, a bull nose brick would be located at

    A. an inside corner   B. an outside corner
    C. the key of an arch   D. the roof of a boiler setting

28. The addition of lime to cement mortar improves the workability of mortar and

    A. increases the strength
    B. decreases the shrinkage
    C. decreases the weight
    D. increases the watertightness

29. Brickwork must be cleaned after completion of setting by

    A. scrubbing with soap solution and water
    B. wire brushing
    C. washing with muriatic solution
    D. sand blasting

30. In a multi-story building, weep holes in cavity wall brick construction are USUALLY placed in the brickwork

    A. above all masonry openings
    B. at foundation level only
    C. at the parapet only
    D. at every floor

31. A brick wall which consists of all stretcher courses is said to be built with a _____ Bond.

    A. Flemish   B. Running
    C. English   D. Common

32. The whitish deposit frequently seen on brick walls can USUALLY be avoided by

    A. using brick that contains more soluable salts
    B. keeping the water-mortar ratio high
    C. adding muriatic acid to the mortar
    D. constructing properly filled weathertight joints

33. Specifications for a building require brick to be wet before using.
    Of the following, the BEST reason for this requirement is that wetting

    A. makes it easier to place brick
    B. cleans the brick
    C. prevents absorption of moisture from the mortar
    D. shows up flaws in the brick that would otherwise be hidden

34. In checking the ingredients that are to go into the concrete for a footing that is being poured, you notice that there is 5% too much cement.
    Of the following, the BEST action to take in this situation is to

    A. do nothing
    B. condemn the footing
    C. increase the amount of sand in the mix
    D. order core borings taken of the finished footing

35. The soil conditions for a new building are MOST frequently checked by

    A. augering   B. soundings
    C. rodding   D. borings

KEY (CORRECT ANSWERS)

1. B
2. C
3. D
4. C
5. B

6. D
7. B
8. B
9. B
10. B

11. C
12. C
13. A
14. C
15. D

16. D
17. A
18. D
19. B
20. C

21. B
22. C
23. B
24. C
25. C

26. B
27. B
28. B
29. C
30. D

31. B
32. D
33. C
34. A
35. D

EXAMINATION SECTION
TEST 1

DIRECTIONS: Each question or incomplete statement is followed by several suggested answers or completions. Select the one that BEST answers the question or completes the statement. *PRINT THE LETTER OF THE CORRECT ANSWER IN THE SPACE AT THE RIGHT.*

1. The material that is MOST often made from gypsum is

   A. lime
   C. grout
   B. mortar
   D. plaster of paris

   1._____

2. Of the following types of utility pipes, the one for which the slope of the line is USUALLY most important is a line.

   A. sewer   B. gas   C. water   D. steam

   2._____

3. Piles, as related to building construction, are located *most likely* in the

   A. foundation
   C. structural frame
   B. roof
   D. wall

   3._____

4. The scale of a drawing is 1/8" = 1'0". A rectangle on the drawing actually measures 7 1/8" x 6 1/4".
   This represents the true area, in square feet, of *most nearly*

   A. 72   B. 144   C. 1375   D. 2850

   4._____

5. The architectural symbol for brick as it would appear in section is USUALLY

   A. [symbol]   B. [symbol]   C. [symbol]   D. [symbol]

   5._____

6. [Diagram: triangle with A on left, B on upper right with height 60', left side 10', base 125']

   The length of AB is, in feet, *most nearly*

   A. 130   B. 135   C. 140   D. 145

   6._____

7. An inspector estimated that a paving job would require 30 cubic yards of concrete. The volume of the concrete actually used was 27.5 cubic yards.
   The percentage of error in the inspector's estimate is *most nearly*

   A. 4 1/2   B. 9   C. .08   D. .09

   7._____

8. The frame and cover of a sewer manhole is USUALLY made of

   A. stainless steel
   C. Monel metal
   B. cast iron
   D. structural steel

   8._____

9. Sleeves are used around anchor bolts that bolt steel columns to footings PRIMARILY to

   A. allow for minor lateral adjustments of anchor bolts
   B. provide better bearing of base plate on the footing
   C. provide greater bond between anchor bolt and footing
   D. allow the proper setting of the column as to elevation

10.

   The weld MOST commonly used to permanently connect the end of a structural steel angle to a plate as shown above is a _____ weld.

   A. tack   B. fillet   C. butt   D. plug

11. Cement is composed PRIMARILY of the following materials heated to fusion:

   A. Gypsum and sand
   B. Gypsum and limestone
   C. Clay and limestone
   D. Sand and clay

12. The capacity of storage batteries or its useful life is USUALLY expressed in

   A. amperes
   B. watts
   C. watt-hours
   D. ampere-hours

13. A transistor depends for its functioning on the flow of electrons through a

   A. gas   B. vapor   C. solid   D. vacuum

14. A bi-metallic element is made up by riveting a brass and iron strip together. When subjected to high temperature, the element will

   A. vibrate
   B. bend
   C. remain the same length
   D. shorten

15. Expansion bolts would *most likely* be used to attach electric equipment to walls made of

   A. concrete   B. hollow-tile   C. wood   D. steel

16. Of the following prefixes commonly used with electrical units, the one which would indicate one-millionth of a unit is

   A. mega   B. kilo   C. micro   D. milli

17.

   The voltage in volts, across the 2.4 ohms resistance in the circuit shown above is *most nearly* equal to

   A. 32   B. 48   C. 60   D. 72

18. The term *bell and spigot* in plumbing refers to

    A. soil pipes
    B. faucets
    C. hot water risers
    D. overflow alarm

19. The drafting symbol —⋈— on a line piping diagram USUALLY indicates a _____ valve.

    A. ball
    B. globe
    C. check
    D. gate

20. The babbit metals are used

    A. for dies and cutting tools
    B. for high speed shafts
    C. in the manufacture of gears
    D. as bearing metals

21. The safety device that can be used instead of a fuse to protect a piece of electrical equipment in case of overload is a

    A. toggle switch
    B. circuit shunt
    C. circuit rheostat
    D. circuit breaker

22. A device that is used to convert mechanical energy into electrical energy is USUALLY called a

    A. battery
    B. generator
    C. motor
    D. transformer

23. A pitot tube is used for measuring water

    A. density
    B. velocity
    C. temperature
    D. volatility

24. $\sqrt[x]{a^y}$ is equal to

    A. $a^{\frac{y}{x}}$
    B. a^{x+y}
    C. $a^{\frac{y}{x}}$
    D. a^{y-x}

25. Of the following, an approved means of obtaining the area of an irregular figure is by means of a

    A. slide caliper
    B. micrometer
    C. planimeter
    D. pantograph

KEY (CORRECT ANSWERS)

1.	D	11.	C
2.	A	12.	D
3.	A	13.	C
4.	D	14.	B
5.	B	15.	A
6.	B	16.	C
7.	B	17.	D
8.	B	18.	A
9.	A	19.	C
10.	B	20.	D

21. D
22. B
23. B
24. C
25. C

TEST 2

DIRECTIONS: Each question or incomplete statement is followed by several suggested answers or completions. Select the one that BEST answers the question or completes the statement. *PRINT THE LETTER OF THE CORRECT ANSWER IN THE SPACE AT THE RIGHT.*

1. Of the following, the BEST reason for using vibrators in concrete construction is to

    A. increase the slump of the concrete
    B. remove excess water
    C. retard the setting of the concrete
    D. consolidate the concrete

2. Specifications state that column dowels are embedded 24 diameters in the footing. The length of embedment for a number 8 bar in the footing is, in inches, *most nearly*

    A. 6 B. 12 C. 18 D. 24

3. A *tremie* is USUALLY used to

    A. weigh large quantities of sand
    B. support precast girders
    C. deposit concrete under water
    D. measure ground elevation very accurately

4. Of the following woods, the one that is the HARDEST is

    A. Hickory   B. Douglas Fir
    C. Southern Pine   D. Sitka Spruce

5. The total weight of a 10 WF 45 beam 8 feet long is, in pounds, *most nearly*

    A. 45 B. 80 C. 360 D. 450

6. The thickness 17 gage steel can be BEST checked with a

    A. finely divided steel scale
    B. depth gage
    C. hermaphrodite caliper
    D. micrometer

7. A specification for mixing concrete states *the minimum time of mixing concrete shall be one minute per cubic yard after all material, including the water, has been placed in the drum and the drum shall be reversed for an additional two minutes.*
   According to the above statement, the MINIMUM time for mixing a 3 cubic yard batch of concrete is *most nearly* _____ minutes.

    A. 3 B. 5 C. 8 D. 9

8. Of the following species of lumber, the one *most likely* used for wood formwork for concrete is

    A. birch B. pine C. oak D. maple

9. Of the following, the one that is NOT a lightweight aggregate is

   A. hematite
   B. perlite
   C. expanded shale
   D. pumice

10. Of the following, the MOST important factor that an individual must fulfill in order to insure his own safety on a construction job is to

    A. work slowly
    B. be familiar with the specifications
    C. wear clothing to suit climatic conditions
    D. be alert

11. A wall alongside of a ramp is 7'6" high at one end and 12'0" high at the other end. The length of the wall is 32'0".
    The area of one face of the wall, in square feet, is *most nearly*

    A. 310   B. 311   C. 312   D. 313

12. The equation $x^2 + y^2 = r^2$ is that of a

    A. parabola
    B. ellipse
    C. straight line
    D. circle

13. A round rod with a right-handed thread is to be coupled with another rod of the same diameter but with a left-handed thread.
    Of the following attachments, the one which is MOST appropriate to use is a(n)

    A. turnbuckle
    B. thimble
    C. clevis
    D. eye bolt

14. In the two simultaneous equations
    $(3x + y = 17)$
    $(2x - y = 8)$,
    the value of y is

    A. 1   B. 2   C. 3   D. 4

15. Leaks in gas piping may be BEST located by the use of

    A. cigarette lighter
    B. miner's lamp
    C. heated filament
    D. soapy water solution

16. The value of x that will satisfy the equation $x^3 - x^2 - 4 = 0$ is

    A. 3   B. 2   C. 1   D. -1

17. The number of board feet in a board 24 feet long, one foot wide, and 2 inches thick is _____ board feet.

    A. 4   B. 12   C. 24   D. 48

18. The distinguishing characteristic of safety shoes is

    A. their color
    B. their height
    C. the use of spikes on the sole
    D. the use of a steel toe box

19. For a 20 foot ladder, the base should extend back from the face of the wall *approximately*   19._____

   A. 3' B. 5' C. 7' D. 10'

20. π/2 radian is equivalent to, in degrees,   20._____

   A. 22 1/2 B. 45 C. 90 D. 180

21. Of the following conventional cross-hatching, the one that is for brass is   21._____

   A. [hatching] B. [hatching] C. [hatching] D. [hatching]

22. The $2\sqrt{690}$ is *most nearly*   22._____

   A. 26.25 B. 26.27 C. 26.29 D. 26.30

23. The line $y = 2x + 8$ intersects the *x* axis at   23._____

   A. -4 B. +4 C. -2 D. +8

24. If the radius of the circle shown is 5", the area of the shaded area, in square inches, is *most nearly*   24._____

   A. 6.1 B. 7.1 C. 7.6 D. 8.1

25. A cone has a base whose area is A and its altitude is h. The volume of this cone is   25._____

   A. Ah B. 1/2 Ah C. 1/3 Ah D. 1/4 Ah

KEY (CORRECT ANSWERS)

1. D
2. D
3. C
4. A
5. C

6. D
7. B
8. B
9. A
10. D

11. C
12. D
13. A
14. B
15. D

16. B
17. D
18. D
19. B
20. C

21. A
22. B
23. A
24. B
25. C

TEST 3

DIRECTIONS: Each question or incomplete statement is followed by several suggested answers or completions. Select the one that BEST answers the question or completes the statement. *PRINT THE LETTER OF THE CORRECT ANSWER IN THE SPACE AT THE RIGHT.*

1. A street has a grade of 1 1/2%.
   The distance the street rises in 1 1/2 miles is, in feet, *most nearly*

   A. 79.20   B. 98.75   C. 103.50   D. 118.80

2.

   The elevation of a steel member shown above represents a

   A. tee   B. channel   C. rail   D. zee

3. A circular tank is 12 feet in diameter and 9 feet high. The depth of water in the tank is 1/3 from the top. There are 7 1/2 gallons in a cubic foot.
   The number of gallons of water in the tank is *most nearly*

   A. 4820   B. 5070   C. 5320   D. 5570

4. If log of 2 = 0.3010 and log of 3 = 0.4772, then the log of 36 equals

   A. 0.7782   B. 1.0792   C. 1.2554   D. 1.5564

5. If there are 43,560 square feet in an acre, the number of acres in a tract 2 miles long by 3.2 miles wide is *most nearly*

   A. 3750   B. 4100   C. 4350   D. 4600

6. A foundation for a building consists of 9 concrete footings 8 ft. by 6 ft. by 18 inches deep.
   The total number of cubic yards of concrete in the footings is *most nearly*

   A. 12   B. 24   C. 36   D. 72

7. A drawing showing the longitudinal slope in elevation of a street is known as

   A. perspective   B. plan
   C. profile   D. route

8. On a drawing showing front, rear, and side elevations, and roof plan, the projected views are *most likely*

   A. isogonic   B. orthographic
   C. isographic   D. isometric

9. A note on a drawing reads *#6 bottom bars 6'0" long, 6" o.c.* "The #6 means *most nearly* _____ diameter.

   A. 6/8"   B. 0.6"   C. 6/16"   D. 6/32"

10. The signs of the sine, cosine, and tangent of an angle are all positive in Quadrant 10.____

    A. I   B. II   C. III   D. IV

11. The sum of three interior angles of a four-sided parcel of land add up to 115°, The fourth 11.____
    interior angle, in degrees, is *most nearly*

    A. 25   B. 75   C. 245   D. 295

12. Of the following print processes, the one that is LEAST like blue printing is 12.____

    A. Van Dyke   B. black and white
    C. Ozalid   D. multilith

13. Railroad curves would *most likely* be used to draw 13.____

    A. arcs of large radii
    B. ellipses
    C. circles of small radii
    D. circles of large radii

14. Concrete test cylinders are USUALLY tested in 14.____

    A. bending   B. buckling
    C. compression   D. shear

15. The invert of a sewer is the elevation of the _____ surface. 15.____

    A. bottom of the inside   B. top of the outside
    C. bottom of the outside   D. top of the inside

16. The symbol ++++++++++++++++ on a topographic map USUALLY represents a(n) 16.____

    A. abandoned highway   B. underground stream
    C. single track railroad   D. picket fence

17. Terrazzo would *most likely* be found on a(n) 17.____

    A. interior wall   B. exterior wall
    C. ceiling   D. floor

18. Well points are USUALLY used in construction to 18.____

    A. provide water for cleaning the area under construction
    B. dewater the area under construction
    C. provide water for the concrete used in construction
    D. provide adequate drinking water where other sources are not available

19. A flexible pavement is a 19.____

    A. shoulder of compacted clay
    B. pavement containing an air entraining ingredient
    C. pavement of concrete without reinforcing
    D. pavement of graded granular materials with bitumen

20. Closely spaced contour lines on a topographic map USUALLY indicate a 20.____

    A. small contour interval   B. large contour interval
    C. steep slope   D. mild slope

21. If concrete weighs 150#/cubic foot, then the weight of a 15'0" long, 36" I.D. and 3" wall thickness concrete pipe is *most nearly* (I.D. - inside diameter) _____ lbs. 21.____

    A. 5300   B. 5500   C. 5700   D. 6000

22. Of the following mixes, the one that is *most likely* to be used as mortar for brickwork is cement(,) 22.____

    A. and water   B. sand and water
    C. lime and water   D. gypsum and water

23. The pattern of brickwork is USUALLY called the 23.____

    A. bond   B. lay   C. coursing   D. register

24. The MOST important precaution to be observed in the storage of cement is to protect the cement against 24.____

    A. heat   B. dampness
    C. corrosion D. decomposition

25. Lead was poured into the joint between two pipes. The material composition of each pipe was *most likely* 25.____

    A. cast iron   B. vitrified clay
    C. asbestos cement   D. concrete

KEY (CORRECT ANSWERS)

1. D		11. C	
2. D		12. D	
3. B		13. A	
4. D		14. C	
5. B		15. A	
6. B		16. C	
7. C		17. D	
8. B		18. B	
9. A		19. D	
10. A		20. C	

21. C
22. B
23. A
24. B
25. A

TEST 4

DIRECTIONS: Each question or incomplete statement is followed by several suggested answers or completions. Select the one that BEST answers the question or completes the statement. *PRINT THE LETTER OF THE CORRECT ANSWER IN THE SPACE AT THE RIGHT.*

1. The main danger of having oil on the surface of steel reinforcing bars is PRIMARILY that the

    A. setting time of the concrete will be too great
    B. bond between steel and concrete will be weakened
    C. concrete will be weakened
    D. steel will corrode

2. The Brinell number of a metal is GENERALLY a measure of its

    A. hardness   B. ductility
    C. tensile strength   D. malleability

3. Masonite is a

    A. gypsum product   B. cement product
    C. wood product   D. coal tar derivative

4. A stairway has 9 treads. It NORMALLY would have _____ risers.

    A. 8   B. 9   C. 10   D. 11

5. A beam projecting from a wall is called a _____ beam.

    A. dolly   B. stringer
    C. cantilever   D. lally

6. In a paint mixture, the pigment is added PRIMARILY to supply

    A. hardness   B. color   C. body   D. toughness

7. The chemical formula for sand is

    A. $CaCO_3$ B. CaO C. Al_2O_3 D. SiO_2

8. If steel is galvanized, it is coated with

    A. copper   B. zinc   C. tin   D. lead

9. A hod is MOST often used by a

    A. rigger   B. plumber
    C. carpenter   D. plasterer

10. An engine is delivering 300 horsepower.
    The equivalent delivery, in kilowatts, is *most nearly* (1 HP = 746 watts)

    A. 175   B. 200   C. 225   D. 250

11. Of the following drafting pencils, the one that has the SOFTEST lead is

    A. 3B   B. HB   C. H   D. F

12. Two applications at 0.4 gallons per square yard of bituminous material on a 1/2 mile of road 18 feet wide would require *most nearly* _____ gallons. 12.____

    A. 425   B. 3,875   C. 4,225   D. 38,000

13. Rock excavation is to be paid for at a unit price of $25/cubic yard. 13.____
    Of the following, the cost of rock between Sta. 3+35 and Sta. 8+65 for a width of 45 feet and a depth of five feet is *most nearly*

    A. $75,000   B. $110,000   C. $220,000   D. $330,000

14. Three 40 foot long piles are driven so that their top elevations are 79.6', 81.7', and 80.2' before being cut off at elevation 75.5'. 14.____
    If the contract unit price is $4.50 per foot in place, then the payment to the contractor is *most nearly*

    A. $405.00   B. $472.50   C. $540.00   D. $600.00

15. To void a contract means *most nearly* to _____ it. 15.____

    A. reinstate   B. nullify   C. amend   D. redeem

16. Of the following, the MOST important characteristic of a good inspector on construction work is 16.____

    A. punctuality
    B. good penmanship
    C. superior physical strength
    D. keen observation

17. The BEST method of making assignments of technicians would be ordinarily to make them according to the technician's 17.____

    A. seniority
    B. desire to do the work
    C. ability to do the work
    D. attitude towards other employees

18. Of the following, the BEST way to correct a mistake made by your subordinate is to 18.____

    A. correct the mistake yourself and privately explain correction to subordinate
    B. correct the mistake yourself and say nothing to subordinate
    C. give it to another subordinate to correct
    D. belittle him and then have him correct the mistake

19. If a draftsman cannot possibly complete a drawing on time, then the BEST action for him to take is 19.____

    A. work during lunchtime
    B. work overtime
    C. ask an employee to assist you
    D. notify the supervisor

20. Of the following, the BEST thing for a supervisor to do when a subordinate has done a very good job is to

    A. tell him to take it easy
    B. praise his work
    C. reduce his work load
    D. say nothing because he may become conceited

21. Of the following, the method MOST often used to keep a record of progress of construction of a project is a _____ chart.

    A. bar   B. pie   C. polar   D. Venn

22. Of the following, the BEST method of getting an employee who is not working up to his capacity to produce more work is to

    A. have another employee criticize his production
    B. privately criticize his production but encourage him to produce more
    C. criticize his production before his associates
    D. criticize his production and threaten to fire him

23. The ability of an employee to take the first step and follow through on a job is known as

    A. demeanor   B. indolence
    C. initiative   D. individuality

24. Of the following behavior characteristics of a supervisor, the one that is *most likely* to lower the morale of the men he supervises is

    A. diligence   B. favoritism
    C. punctuality   D. thoroughness

25. Of the following, the MOST important item in a good engineering report is

    A. brevity   B. promptness
    C. accuracy   D. good grammar

KEY (CORRECT ANSWERS)

1.	B	11.	A
2.	A	12.	C
3.	C	13.	B
4.	C	14.	B
5.	C	15.	B
6.	B	16.	D
7.	D	17.	C
8.	B	18.	A
9.	D	19.	D
10.	C	20.	B

21. A
22. B
23. C
24. B
25. C

ENGINEERING PROBLEMS

EXAMINATION SECTION
TEST 1

DIRECTIONS: Each question or incomplete statement is followed by several suggested answers or completions. Select the one that BEST answers the question or completes the statement. *PRINT THE LETTER OF THE CORRECT ANSWER IN THE SPACE AT THE RIGHT.*

1. The distance in inches from the back of the short leg to the center of gravity of a 5" x 4" x 1/2" steel angle is, APPROXIMATELY,

    A. 0.80 B. 0.95 C. 1.50 D. 1.55 E. 1.75

2. A wide flange I-Beam has a depth of 12 inches and a flange width of 10 inches. The thickness of the material is one inch. The moment of inertia of the cross-section about an axis normal and through the centerline of the web is

    A. 540 in.^{4} B. 575 in.^{4} C. 595 in.^{4} D. 625 in.^{4} E. 690 in.^{4}

3. Two 2" x 4" steel plates are welded together in the shape of a "T". The distance from the centroid to the top of the "T" is 2.5 inches. The moment of inertia of the "T" about a gravity axis parallel to its top, in inches^4, is

    A. 32.6 B. 39.2 C. 45.6 D. 49.4 E. 55.6

4. The section modulus of a 3" x 12" deep wooden beam is

    A. 36 B. 72 C. 108 D. 121 E. 144

5. A steel I beam with a section mudulus of 120 inches cubed is to carry a uniformly distributed load including its own weight on a simple span of 12'. The maximum allowable fibre stress is 16,000 psi. Of the following loads in pounds per foot (including the weight of the beam), the LARGEST load the beam can carry is

    A. 1050 B. 4900 C. 8800 D. 12,600 E. 15,400

6. A round steel bar, one inch in diameter and three feet long, is elongated .022 inches by a load applied at one end of the bar. The magnitude of the load is, in lbs, MOST NEARLY, (E is 30×10^6 lb/sq. in.),

    A. 13,800 B. 14,400 C. 15,000 D. 16,600 E. 17,700

7. A steel bar, cross-sectional area 2 in.^{2} and 150 ft. long, is supported at one end and hangs vertically. The elongation of the bar due to its own weight, in inches, is

    A. 0.0039 B. 0.0121 C. 0.0154 D. 0.0167 E. 0.0200

8. A tie rod 25 feet long and one inch in diameter is fastened to rigid supports at its ends. If the temperature rises 40, the resulting stress in the rod will be, in psi,

    A. 5,220 B. 5,780 C. 6,436 D. 7,225 E. 7,740

9. A 6" x 8" timber (actual size) is being used as a gin pole. The radius of gyration of this column which would be used in a column formula to determine safe load for the gin pole is, in inches, MOST NEARLY,

   A. 1.73   B. 2.42   C. 2.77   D. 2.85   E. 3.01

10. Two plates, each 7 inches wide by 1/2 inch thick, under a tensile load of 45,000 pounds, are lap riveted. The single shear and single bearing stresses are 13,500 and 24,000 pounds per square inch, respectively. The number of 7/8 inch rivets required is

    A. 3   B. 6   C. 9   D. 12   E. 15

KEY (CORRECT ANSWERS)

1. D
2. E
3. D
4. B
5. C

6. B
7. C
8. E
9. A
10. B

TEST 2

DIRECTIONS: Each question or incomplete statement is followed by several suggested answers or completions. Select the one that BEST answers the question or completes the statement. *PRINT THE LETTER OF THE CORRECT ANSWER IN THE SPACE AT THE RIGHT.*

1. A riveted joint is made up of two 3/8" outside plates and a 3/4" thick inside plate. The allowable stresses for double shear, single bearing, and double bearing are 15,000, 32,000, and 40,000 pounds per square inch, respectively. The number of rivets, using 7/8" rivets, required for this joint if P is 40,000#, is

   A. 1   B. 2   C. 3   D. 4   E. 5

   1.____

2. A boiler is to be formed of steel plates 1/2" thick, riveted together by single lap joints with 7/8" rivets and 3 inches pitch. The efficiency for tension is, MOST NEARLY, (assume rivet diameter is 1 inch),

   A. 43%   B. 59%   C. 67%   D. 69%   E. 75%

   2.____

3. If the allowable shearing unit stresses of welds is 12,500 psi, to connect an angle having a total axial tensile stress of 60,000 pounds to a gusset plate at the end, by a 3/8" fillet weld, will require a total length of weld of (in inches)

   A. 12.3   B. 14.4   C. 16.2   D. 18.1   E. 19.5

   3.____

4. A cantilever beam, length 10 feet, carries a concentrated load of 8,000 pounds at its free end. If the moment of inertia of the beam is 2,000 in.^{4}, and E is 1,600,000 psi, the MAXIMUM deflection of the beam is (in inches)

   A. .98   B. 1.02   C. 1.44   D. 1.92   E. 2.04

   4.____

5. The distance from the centroid of the compression flange to the centroid of the tension flange on a steel plate girder is 42". The girder is subjected to a bending moment of 20,000,000 inch pounds. If the allowable tensile unit stress is 20,000 pounds per square inch, the area of the tension flange should be

   A. 17.3 in.^{2} B. 20.8 in.^{2} C. 21.6 in.^{2} D. 22.7 in.^{2} E. 23.8 in^2

   5.____

6. The reaction at joint C of the frame is, in kips, MOST NEARLY,
   A. 4.17
   B. 4.33
   C. 4.57
   D. 5.68
   E. 5.91

   6.____

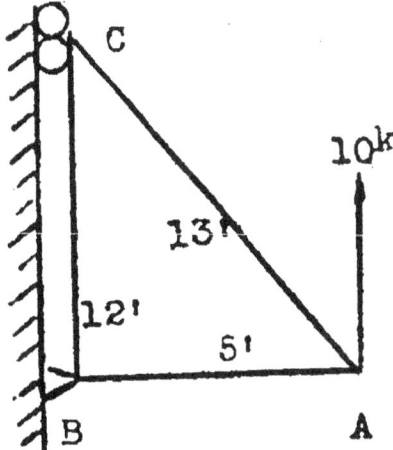

2 (#2)

7. Two wheels spaced 8 feet apart move over a simple span of 24 feet between end supports, from right to left. Wheel No. 1 (the wheel to the left) carries 12 kips and wheel No. 2 carries 4 kips. The absolute maximum bending moment due to these loads will occur under wheel No. 1 when it is at a distance, in feet, to the right of the left support, of

   A. 7   B. 9   C. 11   D. 13   E. 15

8. Three moving loads of 10^k, 15k, and 20k, from left to right, are spaced 8 feet apart on a simple span of 40 feet, the MAXIMUM moment the loads can cause on the beam, in kip feet, is

   A. 187   B. 209   C. 283   D. 311   E. 331

9. A symmetrical triangular roof truss of four panels at 10' having a span of 40' between end supports and a rise of 10' carries a vertical load at the top center of 20,000 pounds. The stress in the upper chord of the end panel, in pounds, is, APPROXIMATELY,

   A. 10,500   B. 19,500   C. 22,500   D. 24,500   E. 26,500

10. A reinforced concrete beam is 10" wide by 16" effective depth. If fs is 20,000 psi, fc is 1,350 psi, and n is 10, then the value of "k" is, MOST NEARLY,

   A. 0.367   B. 0.388   C. 0.403   D. 0.439   E. 0.477

KEY (CORRECT ANSWERS)

1. C
2. C
3. D
4. C
5. E

6. A
7. C
8. E
9. C
10. C

TEST 3

DIRECTIONS: Each question or incomplete statement is followed by several suggested answers or completions. Select the one that BEST answers the question or completes the statement. *PRINT THE LETTER OF THE CORRECT ANSWER IN THE SPACE AT THE RIGHT.*

1. A reinforced concrete beam 12" x 25" is subjected to a bending moment of 55,000 foot pounds. If f_s is 18,000 psi and "j" is 7/8, the area of reinforcing steel required, in square inches, is

    A. 1.09   B. 1.46   C. 1.59   D. 1.82   E. 1.94

    1.____

2. A rectangular reinforced concrete beam has b=8 inches, d = 12 inches, A_s = 0.8 square inches, n = 15; allowable fs = 18,000 psi and fc = 900 psi. Its safe resisting moment, in inch pounds, as determined by the steel, is about

    A. 114,000   B. 128,000   C. 134,000   D. 148,000   E. 156,000

    2.____

3. A 12 inch by 12 inch reinforced concrete column 8 feet long, reinforced with four 7/8 inch round steel rods, and having an allowable stress of 450 psi in the concrete, will, if n = 15, carry an axial load of

    A. 58,600#   B. 65,500#   C. 79,900#   D. 81,700#   E. 85,500#

    3.____

4. The allowable tensile and bond stresses in reinforcing bars for concrete are 16,000 and 100 psi, respectively. The depth of embedment in inches required to develop the allowable tensile strength of a 3/4 inch diameter bar is

    A. 40   B. 30   C. 20   D. 10   E. 5

    4.____

5. A round steel bar, one inch in diameter, is embedded 40 inches in concrete. The unit tensile stress in the bar which will develop a bond stress of 100 psi is, in psi, about

    A. 12,000   B. 14,000   C. 16,000   D. 18,000   E. 20,000

    5.____

6. A concrete rectangular footing whose depth is 25 inches carries a load resting on a 12 inch by 12 inch base plate. Using 120 psi as the allowable punching shear, the MAXIMUM load, in pounds, that this footing can safely carry is

    A. 115,000   B. 125,000   C. 135,000   D. 144,000   E. 154,000

    6.____

7. The length of a 6 curve whose central angle is .45 is

    A. 646'   B. 724'   C. 750'   D. 767'   E. 812'

    7.____

8. The middle ordinate of a 100 foot length of a 4 curve, in inches to the NEAREST eighth, is

    A. 7 3/8   B. 8 5/8   C. 9 7/8   D. 10 1/8   E. 812'

    8.____

9. The degree of a simple curve (circular) is 342' and the central angle is 3918'. The tangent length, in feet, is APPROXIMATELY,

    A. 422   B. 553   C. 578   D. 604   E. 632

    9.____

10. The point of intersection of two grade tangents occurs at Station 46+00 at an elevation of 42.40 feet. The back tangent has a grade of plus 5% and the forward tangent a grade of minus 1%. The elevation on a vertical parabolic curve 500 feet long at Station 46+00 is, in feet,

    A. 34.33   B. 35.35   C. 36.65   D. 37.33   E. 38.65

10.____

KEY (CORRECT ANSWERS)

1. D
2. D
3. C
4. B
5. C

6. D
7. C
8. E
9. B
10. E

TEST 4

DIRECTIONS: Each question or incomplete statement is followed by several suggested answers or completions. Select the one that BEST answers the question or completes the statement. *PRINT THE LETTER OF THE CORRECT ANSWER IN THE SPACE AT THE RIGHT.*

1. The width of a street pavement is 50 feet, the crown is at the center and is 6 inches, and the curve of the surface is parabolic. The drop in the surface from the center to a point 15 feet from the center is (to the nearest sixteenth of an inch)

    A. 3 5/16 B. 3 3/16 C. 2 9/16 D. 2 3/16 E. 1 7/16

2. A line 375.27 ft. long is to be laid out with a 100 ft. tape which is actually 99.92 ft. long. The taped length which should be laid out in the field is, in feet,

    A. 297.97 B. 313.13 C. 345.39 D. 375.57 E. 381.18

3. To lay out a line 170.00 feet long with a 100 foot tape which is actually 100.03 feet long, the taped distance should be, in feet,

    A. 144.44 B. 169.95 C. 171.01 D. 182.25 E. 194.27

4. A distance taped on a 3 percent slope is 231.24 feet. The length, in feet, of the horizontal projection is

    A. 231.14 B. 231.11 C. 231.02 D. 230.97 E. 230.91

5. In laying out an angle with a transit, an error of one minute will result in locating a point 1,000 ft. from the transit off the true line by, APPROXIMATELY,

    A. 0.05 ft. B. 0.25 ft. C. 0.3 ft. D. 0.35 ft. E. 0.4 ft.

6. In laying out a building, a right angle was turned off. The angle was then measured by repetition, the plates were set to zero, and three repetitions were taken with the telescope direct and three with the telescope reversed. The reading of the vernier after the sixth repetition was 180 0.01'30'. The TRUE value of the angle turned off is

    A. 85 35' 40"
    B. 87 45' 30"
    C. 88 05' 10"
    D. 89 15' 20"
    E. 90 00' 15"

7. In the closed traverse ABC, the bearings of lines AB and BC are N 45°E and N 60°E, respectively. The lengths of these lines are 200 ft. and 300 ft., respectively. The bearing of line CA is, MOST NEARLY,

    A. S 54° W B. S 58° W C. S 62° W D. S 66° W E. S 70° W

8. The notes for a level run are as follows:

STA.	B.S.	H.I.	F.S.	ELEV.
BM 1	3.26			100.23
A	2.13		1.19	
B	4.05		3.20	
C	2.26		4.03	
BM 2			4.22	

    The elevation of BM 2 is

    A. 99.08 B. 99.15 C. 99.22 D. 99.29 E. 99.36

9. The bearing of a line 550 feet long is S 30° W. The departure of the line is, in feet, 9.___

   A. 250　　　B. 275　　　C. 300　　　D. 325　　　E. 350

10. The sum of the positive departures of a closed traverse ex- ceeds that of the negative departures by 0.31 ft. The sum of the negative latitudes exceeds that of the positive latitudes by 0.67 ft. The linear error of closure is, in feet, MOST NEARLY, 10.___

    A. 0.38　　　B. 0.50　　　C. 0.62　　　D. 0.74　　　E. 0.86

KEY (CORRECT ANSWERS)

1. D
2. D
3. B
4. A
5. C

6. E
7. A
8. D
9. B
10. D

TEST 5

DIRECTIONS: Each question or incomplete statement is followed by several suggested answers or completions. Select the one that BEST answers the question or completes the statement. *PRINT THE LETTER OF THE CORRECT ANSWER IN THE SPACE AT THE RIGHT.*

1. The balanced latitudes and departures of the sides of a closed traverse are:

LINE	LAT.	DEP.
AB	152.27	212.06
BC	316.19	83.92
CD	-522.34	119.30
DA	53.88	-415.28

    The DMD of line CD referred to a meridian through A is
    A. 548.23   B. 660.77   C. 711.26   D. 834.34   E. 986.26

    1.___

2. A concrete road 20 feet wide is on a curve whose radius is 1500 feet. The surface has a uniform transverse slope such that the pressure on the wheels of an automobile moving at a speed of 40 miles per hour will be normal to the surface. The necessary elevation of the outer edge above the inner edge of the pavement should be, in feet,

    A. 1.17   B. 1.43   C. 1.63   D. 1.78   E. 1.86

    2.___

3. A map drawn to a scale of 1 inch equals 400 feet shows contours having an interval of 2 feet. If the scaled distance between contours is 0.5 inches, the percent of slope of the surface is

    A. 1%   B. 1.5%   C. 2.0%   D. 2.5%   E. 3.0%

    3.___

4. The hydraulic radius of a rectangular canal 4 feet wide is 1.20. The depth of flow, in feet, is

    A. 1.0   B. 1.5   C. 2.0   D. 3.0   E. 4.0

    4.___

5. A rectangular open channel 12 feet wide has a slope of 2 feet per 100 feet. Assuming that the coefficient C is 120 in the Chezy Formula, the discharge, in cubic feet per second, when water is flowing at a depth of 6 feet, is

    A. 717   B. 917   C. 1,117   D. 2,117   E. 3,117

    5.___

6. The discharge of a 12 in. diameter drain pipe running full and having a slope of 2 ft. in 100 ft. is 5.55 cubic ft. per second. Assuming that the Chezy Formula is applicable, the coefficient in this formula for this case is equal to

    A. 20   B. 40   C. 60   D. 80   E. 100

    6.___

7. A 3 in. diameter orifice on the side of a tank has water flowing through under a head of 55 feet of water. The coefficient of discharge is equal to 0.8. The discharge, in cubic ft. per second, is

    A. .34   B. 1.34   C. 2.34   D. 3.34   E. 4.34

    7.___

2 (#5)

8. Water flows from reservoir "A", elevation 200', to reservoir "B", elevation 100', through 6440 ft. of six-inch pipe. If the friction factor "f" is 0.02, the velocity of flow in feet per second is

   A. 3   B. 5   C. 7   D. 9   E. 11

9. The loss in head per 1,000 ft. in a 12 in. water pipe is 9 ft. and the friction factor, f, is 0.0161. The velocity of flow in the pipe is, in ft. per second,

   A. 6.0   B. 5.0   C. 4.0   D. 3.0   E. 2.0

10. A rectangular gate, 5 ft. wide by 8 ft. high, makes an angle of 30 with the horizontal. If the top of the gate is 8 ft. below the water surface, the total water pressure on one face of the gate, in pounds, is

    A. 25,000   B. 21,000   C. 17,000   D. 13,000   E. 9,000

KEY (CORRECT ANSWERS)

1. C
2. B
3. A
4. D
5. D

6. E
7. C
8. B
9. A
10. A

TEST 6

DIRECTIONS: Each question or incomplete statement is followed by several suggested answers or completions. Select the one that BEST answers the question or completes the statement. *PRINT THE LETTER OF THE CORRECT ANSWER IN THE SPACE AT THE RIGHT.*

1. Water exerts a force of 50 pounds on an area of 2 square inches at a depth of

    A. 34.6' B. 46.4' C. 57.7' D. 69.5' E. 77.7'

2. Water is 5 ft. high against a vertical 6 ft. sluice gate. The distance, in ft., from the top of the gate to the center of pressure, is

    A. 3.47 B. 4.33 C. 3.67 D. 4.63 E. 5.47

3. If one cubic foot of water per second under a head of 55 feet is delivered to a turbine, the theoretical horsepower that can be developed is

    A. 18 B. 12 C. 6 D. 24 E. 30

4. If the allowable stress in tension is 13,000 psi, the thickness of the wall of an 8 ft. diameter boiler required to sustain a pressure of 90 psi is, in inches,

    A. 0.13 B. 0.23 C. 0.33 D. 0.43 E. 0.53

5. A welded cylindrical horizontal steel tank, 36 inches in diameter, is subjected to an internal pressure caused by a 72-foot head of water. The ends of the tank are capped with hemispherical heads extending outward. If the allowable tensile strength of the steel is taken as 18,000 psi, the theoretical thickness of the heads should be, in inches,

    A. 0.0005 B. 0.015 C. 0.025 D. 0.035 E. 0.045

6. A 30' x 30' x 20' deep tank filled with water is to be emptied by having its water pumped to a standpipe. The stand-pipe, 25' in diameter, has its base level with the top of the tank. The energy required to transfer the water from the tank to the standpipe is, in foot pounds,

    A. 28,000,000   B. 30,000,000   C. 32,000,000
    D. 34,000,000   E. 36,000,000

7. A differential gage on a venturi meter shows the mercury column at the throat 10 inches higher than at the mouth. The specific gravity of the mercury is 13.57. The difference of pressure in the meter, in feet of water, is

    A. 10.48 B. 11.38 C. 12.48 D. 13.38 E. 15.48

8. The specific gravity of sand is 2.60. The weight of a cubic foot of sand in air is 162.5 pounds. The weight of the sand in water is

    A. 40# B. 60# C. 80# D. 100# E. 120#

9. A rectangular footing, 6 ft. long by 4 ft. wide, carries a vertical load of 20,000 pounds, located on the long axis 6 inches from the center of the footing. The maximum soil pressure under the footing due to this load is, in pounds per square foot, MOST NEARLY,

    A. 1150 B. 1200 C. 1250 D. 1300 E. 1350

10. The average penetration of the last 5 blows of a 6000 pound steam hammer is 2.5 inches. The hammer drops a distance of 12 feet. The bearing capacity of the pile is, in pounds,

   A. 15,400   B. 25,400   C. 35,400   D. 45,400   E. 55,400

KEY (CORRECT ANSWERS)

1. C
2. B
3. C
4. C
5. B

6. C
7. A
8. D
9. C
10. E

TEST 7

DIRECTIONS: Each question or incomplete statement is followed by several suggested answers or completions. Select the one that BEST answers the question or completes the statement. *PRINT THE LETTER OF THE CORRECT ANSWER IN THE SPACE AT THE RIGHT.*

1. Water rises to a point four feet below the top of a 60 foot high dam. The TOTAL water pressure per foot length of dam is

    A. 94,000#   B. 95,000#   C. 96,000#   D. 97,000#   E. 98,000#

    1.____

2. A rectangular concrete retaining wall (150 pounds per cubic foot), 15 feet high and 6 feet wide, resists a horizontal force, due to earth pressure, of 1280 pounds per lineal foot of wall, acting 10 feet below the top of the wall. If the coefficient of friction is 0.5, the factor of safety against sliding is

    A. 4.27   B. 5.27   C. 6.27   D. 7.27   E. 8.27

    2.____

3. The four sides of a rectangular pier have a uniform batter of 2 in. per ft. If the top of the pier is 4 ft. by 10 ft., and the pier is 12 ft. high, the volume, to the NEAREST cubic foot, is

    A. 568   B. 670   C. 748   D. 880   E. 936

    3.____

4. A 3" x 6" rectangular beam has a uniformly distributed load of 300 #/ft. on a 10' span. The MAXIMUM horizontal shearing stress is

    A. 77.7 psi   B. 90 psi   C. 125 psi   D. 140.5 psi   E. 150 psi

    4.____

5. The notes for a three level section for a 20' wide roadway are $\frac{C7.5}{15} \quad \frac{C9}{0} \quad \frac{C12}{18}$.

    The cross-sectional area of cut is, in square feet,

    A. 196   B. 246   C. 288   D. 314   E. 344

    5.____

6. The yield of a 1:2:4 concrete with a water content of 6 gallons, for one sack of cement, will be, if the voids in the cement are 48%, and 41% in the sand and gravel, in cubic feet,

    A. 1.43   B. 2.97   C. 3.54   D. 4.13   E. 4.86

    6.____

7. The amount of cement required for 8 cubic yards of 1:3:5 concrete is estimated to be, in cubic feet,

    A. 15.9   B. 27.8   C. 37.4   D. 49.9   E. 51.3

    7.____

8. A bill of timber calls for 2 pieces of 8" x 12" - 16'0", 5 pieces of 4" x 4" - 18'0", 6 pieces of 1" x 8" - 14' 0". The total F.B.M. is

    A. 6,912   B. 3,456   C. 1,728   D. 864   E. 432

    8.____

9. The distance, in inches, from the back of the long leg to the centroid of an 8" x 6" x 1" steel angle is, in inches,

    A. 1.31   B. 1.47   C. 1.53   D. 1.65   E. 1.71

    9.____

10. The elongation of a steel bar, 100 ft. long, cross-sectional area 1 in.^{2}, supported at one end and hanging vertically, due to its own weight, in inches, is 10.____

    A. .0029   B. .0037   C. .0045   D. .0059   E. .0068

KEY (CORRECT ANSWERS)

1. E
2. B
3. D
4. C
5. B

6. E
7. C
8. E
9. D
10. E

TEST 8

DIRECTIONS: Each question or incomplete statement is followed by several suggested answers or completions. Select the one that BEST answers the question or completes the statement. *PRINT THE LETTER OF THE CORRECT ANSWER IN THE SPACE AT THE RIGHT.*

1. The Moment of Inertia of the area of an H beam, 14" deep and 14" wide, both web and flanges 1" thick, about an axis through the center of gravity (centroid) and perpendicular to the web is, in inches^4,

    A. 1242   B. 1298   C. 1328   D. 1412   E. 1444

    1.____

2. The distance from the back of the short leg of a 6"x4"x1" angle to its centroid is 2.17". The Moment of Inertia of the angle about a gravity axis parallel to the short leg, in inches^4, is

    A. 21.4   B. 23.7   C. 25.5   D. 28.9   E. 30.7

    2.____

3. A 24" beam is made up of two 12" steel I beams, the flanges in contact being riveted. If the Moment of Inertia of a single 12" beam is 300 inches^4 and the cross-sectional area is 15 in.2, the Moment of Inertia of the 24" beam is, in inches4,

    A. 1327   B. 1481   C. 1524   D. 1680   E. 1722

    3.____

4. If the maximum allowable bending stress is 1400#/in.^{2}, a simple 15 ft. between end supports, with a cross-section 4" wide and 12" deep, will carry a uniformly distributed load, including its own weight, in #/ft. of length, of

    A. 100   B. 200   C. 300   D. 350   E. 400

    4.____

5. The elongation due to an external load of 1200#, of a steel bar 17 ft. long with a cross-sectional area of 2 in.^{2}, in inches, is

    A. .00408   B. .0408   C. .408   D. 4.08   E. 40.8

    5.____

6. The stress in a steel bar 8 ft. long, cross-sectional area 4 in.^{2}, rigidly set in a wall at both ends, due to a temperature rise of 30°F. is, in #/in.2,

    A. 4820   B. 5820   C. 6820   D. 7820   E. 8820

    6.____

7. A gin pole is made up of two 2" x 4" steel plates in the form of a "T". The radius of gyration of this column, which would be used in a column formula, is, in inches,

    A. .564   B. .632   C. .784   D. .882   E. .914

    7.____

8. Two 3/8" plates under a tension of 50,000# are lap riveted with 7/8" rivets. Allowable unit values of rivets are 15,000#/in.^{2} for shear and 32,000#/in.2 for bearing. The number of 7/8" rivets for this joint are

    A. 2   B. 4   C. 6   D. 8   E. 10

    8.____

2 (#8)

9. A double lap joint consists of two outside plates l/2"thick and an inside plate 3/4" thick. The allowable stresses are: double shear, 15,000 #/in.^{2}; single bearing, 32,000 #/in.2; double bearing, 40,000 #/in.2. The joint is under a tension of 50,000#. Rivets are 7/8" diameter. The number of rivets required for this j.oint, is   9.____

   A. 1   B. 3   C. 5   D. 7   E. 9

10. A steel water pipe constructed of 3/8" thick plates has a longitudinal single riveted lap joint with 7/8" diameter rivets spaced 3" on center. Assuming the allowable bearing stress on the rivets is 27,000#/in.^{2} and the allowable tensile stress on the plates is 18,000 #/in.^{2}, the efficiency of this joint in bearing is, in percentage,   10.____

   A. A.21   B. B.29   C. C. 33   D. D.44   E. E.48

KEY (CORRECT ANSWERS)

1. C
2. E
3. D
4. E
5. A

6. B
7. E
8. C
9. B
10. D

TEST 9

DIRECTIONS: Each question or incomplete statement is followed by several suggested answers or completions. Select the one that BEST answers the question or completes the statement. *PRINT THE LETTER OF THE CORRECT ANSWER IN THE SPACE AT THE RIGHT.*

1. A double riveted lap joint in a boiler having 3/4" rivets and a rivet pitch of 3" in each line, has a tensile efficiency of, in %,   1.____

    A. 25   B. 50   C. 75   D. 100   E. 125

2. If the allowable shearing stress on welds is 11,300#/in.^{2}, to connect a plate having a total tension of 50,000#, to another plate at one end, by a 5/16" fillet weld, will require a total length of weld, in inches, of   2.____

    A. 5   B. 10   C. 15   D. 20   E. 25

3. Fillet welds are required along the sides of the flat leg of a 6" x 6" x 1/2" angle. The centroid of the angle is 1.68" from the heel. The length of the weld along the heel is 8". The length of weld along the toe, in inches, is   3.____

    A. 1.9   B. 2.33   C. 2.91   D. 3.001   E. 3.11

4. A simple beam on a 16 ft. span carries a concentrated load of 5,000# at the midpoint. If E = 1,600,000#/in.^{2} and I = 1728 in.4, the center deflection, in inches, is   4.____

    A. .143   B. .197   C. .239   D. .257   E. .266

5. A steel plate girder having a depth of 48 1/2" back to back of flange angles is subjected to a maximum bending moment of 18,000,000"#. If the allowable tensile unit stress is 18,000#/in.^{2}, the net area of the tension flange should be, in square inches,   5.____

    A. 21.5   B. 31.7   C. 35.5   D. 41.3   E. 48.8

6. In a linkage ABC, AB = 15', AC = 25', and BC = 20'. The linkage is in a vertical plane with AC horizontal and B uppermost. The pin at A is fixed in position while that at C is supported by rollers resting on a horizontal surface. If a horizontal force of 250# is applied at B in the direction of AC, the reaction at C is, in pounds,   6.____

    A. 80   B. 90   C. 100   D. 110   E. 120

7. Given the sketch below, find the reaction at joint B. The reaction at point B is   7.____

    A. 28^k
    B. 32^k
    C. 36^k
    D. 40^k
    E. 44^k

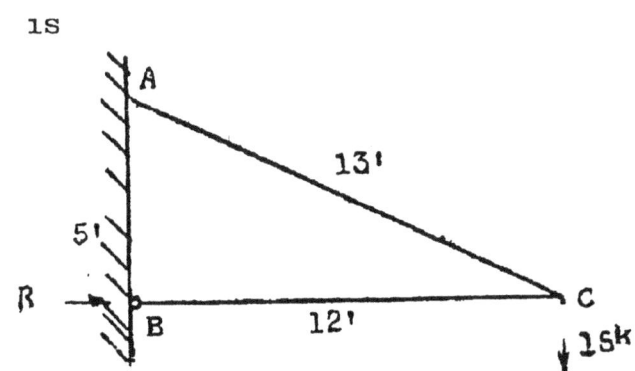

8. The absolute maximum bending moment on a simple beam 20' in length caused by two moving loads spaced 8' apart, 1000# and 2000#, is, in ft.#,

   A. 9.878   B. 10,657   C. 11,258   D. 12,339   E. 13,777

9. The maximum moment that three moving loads of 6^k, 8k and 10k, from left to right, respectively, spaced 6' apart, can cause on a span of 30' is, in ft.k,

   A. 100   B. 125   C. 132.2   D. 150   E. 175

10. In the truss below, find the stress in chord L_1L_2, in kips.

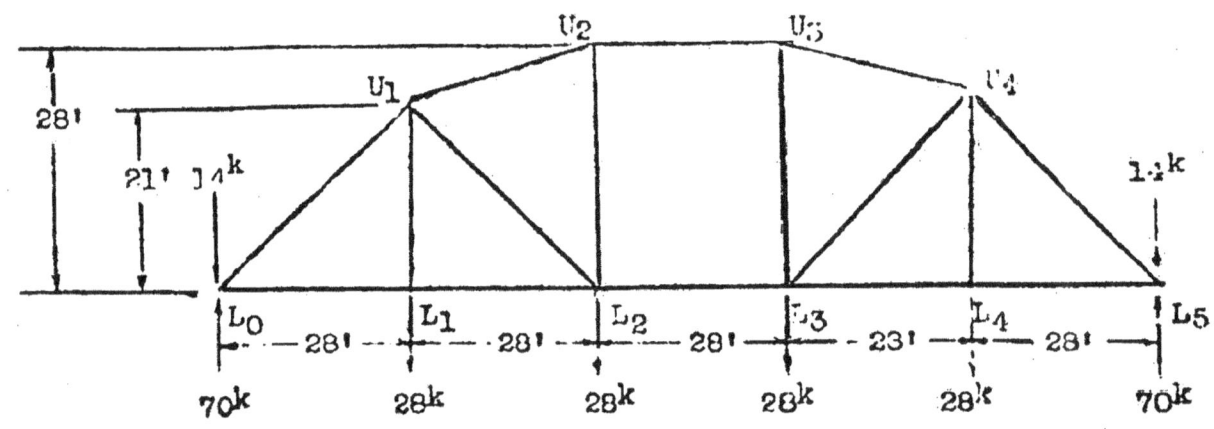

The CORRECT answer is:
A. 72.3   B. -72.3   C. 74.7   D. -74.7   E. 75

KEY (CORRECT ANSWERS)

1. C
2. D
3. E
4. E
5. A

6. E
7. C
8. C
9. B
10. C

TEST 10

DIRECTIONS: Each question or incomplete statement is followed by several suggested answers or completions. Select the one that BEST answers the question or completes the statement. *PRINT THE LETTER OF THE CORRECT ANSWER IN THE SPACE AT THE RIGHT.*

1. Refering to the truss in question 10 above, find the stress in chord U_2U_3, in kips.

    A. 51   B. 62   C. 73   D. 84   E. 95

    1.____

2. A symmetrical triangular roof truss having a span of 30' between end supports and a rise of 6', carries a vertical load at the top center of 10,000#. The stress in the upper chord, in #, is

    A. 12,000   B. 12,500   C. 13,000   D. 13,500   E. 14,000

    2.____

3. A rectangular reinforced concrete beam has b = 8", d = 12", As= .96 in.^{2}, n = 12, fs = 16,000#/in.^{2} and fc = 1000#in.^{2}. Its safe resisting moment, in in.#, is

    A. 128,000   B. 138,000   C. 148,000   D. 158,000   E. 168,000

    3.____

4. A reinforced concrete beam 10" wide by 12" effective depth on a simple span of 12' is reinforced in tension only with three 1/2" square rods. If the allowable steel and concrete stresses are 18,000#/in.^{2} and 600#/in.2, respectively, and k = .33, the MAXIMUM uniform load that the beam can carry (including its own weight) is, in #/ft.,

    A. 354   B. 488   C. 592   D. 618   E. 722

    4.____

5. Given a reinforced concrete beam with b = 12", d = 9", Es = 30,000,000, EC = 2,000,000, f_s = 18,000#/in.^{2}, fc = 650#/in.^{2}. To withstand a total bending moment of 8,000 ft.#, the area of steel reinforcement, in in.^{2}, should be

    A. .38   B. .43   C. .595   D. .67   E. .83

    5.____

6. A concrete column with an effective cross-section of 20" square has 1% vertical steel reinforcing with proper ties. Assuming f_c = 500#/in.^{2} and n = 15, the capacity of the column for taking axial load, in #, is

    A. 212,375   B. 228,000   C. 240,500   D. 244,444   E. 252,000

    6.____

7. A short column consists of a steel shell, 16 1/2" outside diameter and 16" inside diameter, filled with concrete. The Modulii of the steel and concrete are 30,000,000#/in.^{2} and 2,500,000 #/in.^{2}, respectively. When the column is subjected to an axial load of 200,000#, the unit stress in the concrete, in #/in.^{2}, is

    A. 460   B. 560   C. 640   D. 740   E. 840

    7.____

8. If the allowable bond stress is 100#/in.^{2} and the allowable tensile stress on reinforcing steel is 20,000 #/in.^{2}, it is necessary to embed reinforcing in the concrete, in order to develop in bond the tensile strength of the 1" square reinforcing bars, a distance, in inches, of

    A. 10   B. 20   C. 30   D. 40   E. 50

    8.____

9. A column carrying a load of 180,000# and resting on a base plate 15" x 15", is supported by a concrete rectangular footing. Using 120 #/in.² as the allowable punching shear, the MINIMUM depth of footing should be, in inches,

   A. 5   B. 10   C. 15   D. 20   E. 25

10. The PC of a 6 curve is at Station 18 + 25. The deflection angle to station 21 + 00 from the PC is

    A. 7°20'   B. 7°40'   C. 8°15'   D. 8°30'   E. 9°20'

KEY (CORRECT ANSWERS)

1. D
2. D
3. D
4. C
5. D

6. B
7. B
8. E
9. E
10. C

EXAMINATION SECTION
TEST 1

DIRECTIONS: Each question or incomplete statement is followed by several suggested answers or completions. Select the one that BEST answers the question or completes the statement. *PRINT THE LETTER OF THE CORRECT ANSWER IN THE SPACE AT THE RIGHT.*

1. The most common approach used by a prime contractor to hold its subcontractors to their initial bids is the doctrine of promissory estoppel. In order to bind a subcontractor to its bid price, the prime contractor must prove each of the following EXCEPT that the

    A. prime contractor relied on the subcontractor's offer when making its own bid
    B. subcontractor submitted a clear and definite offer
    C. subcontractor's bid was formally accepted by the prime contractor
    D. subcontractor could have expected the prime contractor to rely on the subcontractor's offer when making its own bid

1.____

2. Which type of specification in a construction contract is intended to invite the greatest amount of competition?

    A. Base bid
    B. Closed
    C. Open
    D. Bidder's choice

2.____

3. Written or graphic instruments issued prior to the execution of a contract, which modify or interpret the bidding documents by additions, deletions, clarifications, or corrections, are generally referred to as

    A. contract modifications
    B. addenda
    C. reference documents
    D. supplementary conditions

3.____

4. What type of warranty is used to limit the manufacturer's responsibility in a construction contract?

    A. Service agreement
    B. Correction of work
    C. Limited term
    D. Material-only

4.____

5. Which of the following statements represents the most important difference between drawings and specifications?

    A. Specifications constitute one of the contract documents.
    B. Specifications segregate information in order to aid in forming subcontracts.
    C. Drawings are used to show which materials are to be used.
    D. Drawings name the quantity of materials to be used.

5.____

6. The usual fidelity bond arrangement used in construction contracts is used to protect the contractor against

    A. loss, damage or excessive wear of rented equipment
    B. catastrophic damage to completed elements of the construction project
    C. dishonest acts of an employee such as theft, forgery or embezzlement
    D. bid stability of subcontractors

6.____

7. Each of the following is a common purpose of an agreement in construction contract documents EXCEPT to

   A. state the work to be done and the price to be paid for it
   B. specifically formalize the construction contract
   C. act as a single instrument that brings together all of the contract segments by reference
   D. list the technical specifications that must be adhered to in the construction project

8. Which of the following is an attribute that might be considered for the ceiling subsystem in a performance specification?

   A. Maximum claim spread 25
   B. Fire safety
   C. Smoke development shall not exceed 75
   D. ASTM E84

9. Of the following types of hold-harmless clauses, _____ indemnification used in construction contracts indemnifies the owner and/or architect engineer even when the party indemnified is solely responsible for the loss.

   A. limited-form   B. intermediate-form
   C. broad-form   D. omnibus

10. Unit kitchens are an item that would be described under the _____ Division heading in the CSI Masterformat of specifications.

    A. Equipment   B. Special Construction
    C. Furnishings   D. Specialties

11. Which of the following information is usually described in contract specifications?

    A. Test and code requirements
    B. Size of component parts
    C. Overall dimensions
    D. Schedules of finishes, windows, and doors

12. The PRIMARY advantage associated with unit-price construction contracts is

    A. open competition on projects involving quantities of work that cannot be accurately forecast at the time of bidding or negotiation
    B. fully completed drawings and specifications at the time of bidding or negotiation
    C. greater-than-usual flexibility with regard to special reimbursable costs
    D. flexibility in negotiating a unit price for agreed-upon work items

13. Which of the following information is typically shown by drawings?

    A. Methods of fabrication, installation, and erection
    B. Alternates and unit prices
    C. Interrelation of materials, equipment, and space
    D. Gages of manufacturer's equipment

14. Which of the following is/are typical purposes of a changed-condition clause in a construction contract?
    I. To protect the owner from unforeseen increases in project costs
    II. To reduce the contractor's liability for the unexpected
    III. To alleviate the need for including large contingency sums in the bid
    The CORRECT answer is:

    A. I only   B. II only   C. I, II   D. II, III

15. In construction contracts, a special warranty most frequently applies to the work of a(n)

    A. architect   B. subcontractor
    C. engineer   D. contractor

16. The MAIN advantage associated with the use of bid bonds as security for submitted proposals is that they

    A. will hold subcontractors accountable for their subbids
    B. don't require an annual service charge
    C. are estimated according to the minimum bid price
    D. don't immobilize appreciable sums of a contractor's money

17. Under most statutes governing construction contract law, a prime contractor may be relieved from its bid at any time after the opening of bids by the *doctrine of mistake.* Which of the following are conditions that would support an argument for applying the doctrine of mistake?
    The
    I. mistake relates to a material feature of the contract
    II. mistake is one of judgment, rather than fact
    III. owner is put in a status quo position, to the extent that he suffers no serious prejudice except the loss of his bargain
    IV. mistake is of a mechanical or clerical nature
    The CORRECT answer is:

    A. I only   B. III only   C. II, IV   D. I, III, IV

18. Which of the following is NOT typically a disadvantage associated with the use of retainage arrangements in construction contracts?

    A. Reduced bidding competition
    B. Higher construction costs for owners
    C. Tends to sacrifice workmanship for speed of completion
    D. Cash-flow problems for contractors

19. What is the term for a detailed compilation of the quantity of each elementary work item that is called for on the project?

    A. Specification   B. Takeoff
    C. Bid invitation   D. Summary sheet

20. Which of the following is NOT one of the general types of specifications used in construction contracts?

    A. Proprietary   B. Surety
    C. Descriptive   D. Performance

21. When negotiating a cost-plus contract, the owner and contractor must pay particular attention to each of the following considerations EXCEPT

    A. a list of job costs to be reimbursable to the contractor
    B. a common understanding regarding the accounting methods to be used
    C. the number of work units to be performed in executing the project
    D. a definite and mutually agreeable subcontract-letting procedure

22. According to construction contract law, what is the term for a promise by a party called the guarantor to make good the mistake, debt, or default of another party?

    A. Guaranty   B. Warranty   C. Guarantee   D. Surety

23. In a technical section that has been written according to the CSI standard format, which of the following descriptions would be sequenced FIRST?

    A. Warranty
    B. Summary
    C. Project/site conditions
    D. Maintenance

24. In a construction contract, addendum changes to _____ are typically sequenced first.

    A. drawings
    B. bid form
    C. prior addenda
    D. general conditions

25. Which of the following is typically added to a construction contract as a means of providing financial protection to a contractor?
    I. Value engineering clause
    II. Escalation clause
    III. Escape clause
    The CORRECT answer is:

    A. I only   B. I, II   C. I, III   D. II, III

KEY (CORRECT ANSWERS)

1. C		11. A
2. C		12. A
3. B		13. C
4. D		14. D
5. B		15. B
6. C		16. D
7. D		17. D
8. B		18. C
9. C		19. B
10. A		20. B

21. C
22. A
23. B
24. C
25. D

TEST 2

DIRECTIONS: Each question or incomplete statement is followed by several suggested answers or completions. Select the one that BEST answers the question or completes the statement. *PRINT THE LETTER OF THE CORRECT ANSWER IN THE SPACE AT THE RIGHT.*

1. Which type of specification is most commonly used for public work? 1._____

   A. Open
   B. Closed
   C. Restricted
   D. Bidder's choice

2. Changes in the general conditions of a contract are expressed in the form of 2._____

   A. contract modifications
   B. change orders
   C. supplementary conditions
   D. addenda

3. The listing of subcontractors is often troublesome for contractors when it comes to bidding on projects with 3._____

   A. unbalanced bids
   B. alternates
   C. contract bonds
   D. unit pricing

4. Of the following, it is NOT a typical right assigned to an owner under the terms of a construction contract to 4._____

   A. inspect the work as it proceeds
   B. terminate the contract for cause
   C. intervene in the direction and control of the work
   D. retain a specified portion of the contractor's periodic payments

5. In most states, oral purchase agreements are NOT enforceable when 5._____

   A. they are carried out without the knowledge or consent of the prime contractor
   B. the price of goods is $500 or more
   C. the seller has not been approved by the owner
   D. the seller is not required under the agreement to deliver the goods to the site

6. Which of the following elements of a project manual is NOT usually included under the Sample Forms heading? 6._____

   A. Bid bond
   B. Supplementary conditions
   C. Performance and payment bonds
   D. Agreement

7. As part of a construction contract, a retainage arrangement can substantially serve an owner in each of the following ways EXCEPT 7._____

   A. protection against a contractor's failure to remedy defective work
   B. collection of damages from the contractor for late completion
   C. protection against breach of contract
   D. protection against damages to others caused by the contractor's performance

8. In general, the submission of *qualified* bids by a contractor is not permissible in public bidding because it

   A. is considered to be an arbitrary and unfair practice.
   B. will make the bid subject to rejection
   C. avoids fixing a total cost for the project
   D. is an illegal practice

9. Which of the following bonds is given by a self-insured contractor to the state to guarantee payment of statutory benefits to injured employees?

   A. Union wage bond
   B. License bond
   C. Workman's compensation bond
   D. Fidelity bond

10. The Divisions of the CSI Masterformat of specifications are based on four major categories. Which of the following is NOT one of these categories?

    A. Trades
    B. Levels of specialization
    C. Place relationships
    D. Materials

11. In construction contract law, what is the term for the promise that certain facts are true as represented and that they will remain so?

    A. Guaranty   B. Guarantee   C. Surety   D. Warranty

12. An owner may occasionally want a contractor to start construction operations before the formalities associated with the signing of the contract can be completed. In this case, a(n) _____ should be conveyed to authorize the start of work.

    A. letter of intent
    B. escape clause
    C. proviso of estoppel
    D. writ of mediation

13. In performance specifying, the term *criterion* refers to a(n)

    A. set of physical measurements of the materials specified
    B. qualitative statement of the desired performance
    C. evaluative procedure to assure compliance with the standard
    D. quantitative statement of the desired performance

14. A construction contract may be terminated on the grounds of the doctrine of impossibility of performance. Which of the following would be most likely to be interpreted as constituting impossibility of performance?

    A. Prolonged infirmity of prime contractor
    B. Withdrawal of subbids that make the execution of construction too costly to be profitable
    C. Unexpected site conditions found that make the construction impracticable
    D. One party finds it an economic burden to continue

15. Which of the following contracts is NOT typically defined in a contractual liability insurance policy that is included in a construction contract?

    A. Hold-harmless agreements
    B. Lease of premises
    C. Easement agreements
    D. Sidetrack agreements

16. For a contractor, the main disadvantage associated with lump-sum contracts is that

- A. they increase the likelihood of impossibility of performance
- B. the total amount of payment will be unknown until project completion
- C. they make it more difficult to hold subcontractors to their subbids
- D. adverse changes in the contractor's project costs will not be compensated

17. When a bidder's list of substitutions is used in the specifications of a construction contract, each of the following is generally true EXCEPT

- A. the bid must include the net difference in cost if the substitutions are accepted
- B. each bidder is free to submit any substitution
- C. it is the best method for achieving pure competition
- D. each of the bidders is unaware of the substitution his competitor may offer

18. In a(n) _____ contract, it is especially important that the work must be of such a nature that it can be fairly well-defined and a reasonably good estimate of cost can be approximated at the time of negotiations.

- A. incentive
- B. cost-plus-fixed-fee
- C. progress payment
- D. cost-plus-percentage

19. In a typical surety bond arrangement written into a construction contract, the principal is the

- A. owner
- B. surety company
- C. contractor
- D. architect/engineer

20. When several prime contracts are desired in a construction project, the limits of each prime contract will usually be established in the

- A. specifications
- B. general conditions
- C. agreement
- D. bidding requirements

21. Under the terms of a *liquidated damages* bid bond, the surety agrees to pay the _____ as damages for a contractor's default on a bid.

- A. entire bond amount
- B. difference between the contractor's defaulted low bid and the price the owner must pay to the next lowest responsible bidder
- C. agreed-upon percentage, usually 5 to 10 percent, of the minimum bid price
- D. amount of the initial progress payment plus a penalty

22. Which of the following descriptions in a technical section would appear in Part 3, according to the CSI standard fornat?

- A. Manufacturers
- B. Installation
- C. Definitions
- D. Accessories

23. Before a contract award is made, the bids must be carefully studied and evaluated by the owner and architect-engineer, a process which is typically referred to as

- A. prepping
- B. polling
- C. canvassing
- D. bonding

24. On small projects, office functions are usually carried out in a contractor's main office and particular items of office overhead are difficult to establish. If the contractor is working such a project on a cost-plus basis, it is common practice to

   A. agree with the owner upon a disinterested third party who will estimate the total office overhead costs of the project, and incorporate this figure into the contract
   B. eliminate office overhead altogether as a reimbursed cost and increase the contractor's fee by a reasonable amount
   C. agree in advance with the owner upon an estimated percentage of total job costs that will be named as office overhead in the accounting of the contract
   D. agree in advance with the owner upon a fixed amount that will be named as office overhead in the accounting of the contract

25. In the absence of any clause in a construction contract that addresses the point of excusable delay by a contractor, the contractor may only expect relief from delays with specified causes. Which of the following is NOT one of these causes?

   A. The architect-engineer
   B. The law
   C. Subcontractors
   D. The owner

KEY (CORRECT ANSWERS)

1. A
2. C
3. B
4. C
5. B

6. B
7. C
8. B
9. C
10. B

11. D
12. A
13. D
14. C
15. A

16. D
17. C
18. B
19. C
20. A

21. A
22. B
23. C
24. B
25. C

READING COMPREHENSION
UNDERSTANDING AND INTERPRETING WRITTEN MATERIAL
EXAMINATION SECTION
TEST 1

DIRECTIONS: Each question or incomplete statement is followed by several suggested answers or completions. Select the one that BEST answers the question or completes the statement. *PRINT THE LETTER OF THE CORRECT ANSWER IN THE SPACE AT THE RIGHT.*

Questions 1-3.

DIRECTIONS: Questions 1 through 3, inclusive, are to be answered in accordance with the following paragraph.

All cement work contracts, more or less, in setting. The contraction in concrete walls and other structures causes fine cracks to develop at regular intervals. The tendency to contract increases in direct proportion to the quantity of cement in the concrete. A rich mixture will contract more than a lean mixture. A concrete wall which has been made of a very lean mixture and which has been built by filling only about one foot in depth of concrete in the form each day will frequently require close inspection to reveal the cracks.

1. According to the above paragraph,

    A. shrinkage seldom occurs in concrete
    B. shrinkage occurs only in certain types of concrete
    C. by placing concrete at regular intervals, shrinkage may be avoided
    D. it is impossible to prevent shrinkage

2. According to the above paragraph, the one of the factors which reduces shrinkage in concrete is the

    A. volume of concrete in wall
    B. height of each day's pour
    C. length of wall
    D. length and height of wall

3. According to the above paragraph, a rich mixture

    A. pours the easiest
    B. shows the largest amount of cracks
    C. is low in cement content
    D. need not be inspected since cracks are few

Questions 4-6.

DIRECTIONS: Questions 4 through 6, inclusive, are to be answered SOLELY on the basis of the following paragraph.

It is best to avoid surface water on freshly poured concrete in the first place. However, when there is a very small amount present, the recommended procedure is to allow it to evaporate before finishing. If there is considerable water, it is removed with a broom, belt, float, or by other convenient means. It is never good practice to sprinkle dry cement, or a mixture of cement and fine aggregate, on concrete to take up surface water. Such fine materials form a layer on the surface that is likely to dust or hair check when the concrete hardens.

4. The MAIN subject of the above passage is

   A. surface cracking of concrete
   B. evaporation of water from freshly poured concrete
   C. removing surface water from concrete
   D. final adjustments of ingredients in the concrete mix

5. According to the above passage, the sprinkling of dry cement on the surface of a concrete mix would MOST LIKELY

   A. prevent the mix from setting
   B. cause discoloration on the surface of the concrete
   C. cause the coarse aggregate to settle out too quickly
   D. cause powdering and small cracks on the surface of the concrete

6. According to the above passage, the thing to do when considerable surface water is present on the freshly poured concrete is to

   A. dump the concrete back into the mixer and drain the water
   B. allow the water to evaporate before finishing
   C. remove the water with a broom, belt, or float
   D. add more fine aggregate but not cement

Questions 7-9.

DIRECTIONS: Questions 7 through 9, inclusive, are to be answered ONLY in accordance with the information given in the paragraph below.

Before placing the concrete, check that the forms are rigid and well braced and place the concrete within 45 minutes after mixing it. Fill the forms to the top with the wearing-course concrete. Level off the surfaces with a strieboard. When the concrete becomes stiff but still workable (in a few hours), finish the surface with a wood float. This fills the hollows and compacts the concrete and produces a smooth but gritty finish. For a non-gritty and smoother surface (but one that is more slippery when wet), follow up with a steel trowel after the water sheen from the wood-troweling starts to disappear. If you wish, slant the tread forward a fraction of an inch so that it will shed rain water.

7. Slanting the tread a fraction of an inch gives a surface that will

   A. have added strength
   B. not be slippery when wet
   C. shed rain water
   D. not have hollows

8. In addition to giving a smooth but gritty finish, the use of a wood float will tend to

    A. give a finish that is slippery when wet
    B. compact the concrete
    C. give a better wearing course
    D. provide hollows to retain rain water

9. Which one of the following statements is most nearly correct?

    A. Having checked the forms, one may place the concrete immediately after mixing same.
    B. One must wait at least 15 minutes after mixing the concrete before it may be placed in the forms.
    C. A gritty compact finish and one which is more slippery when wet will result with the use of a wood float.
    D. A steel trowel used promptly after a wood float will tend to give a non-gritty smooth finish.

Questions 10-11.

DIRECTIONS: Questions 10 and 11 are to be answered SOLELY on the basis of information contained in the following paragraph.

Tools and plastering methods have changed very little over the years. Most of the changes are mere improvements of the basic tools. The tools formerly made by hand are now machine-made and are *rigidly* constructed of light, but strong, materials in contrast to the clumsy constructions of the early types. The power-driven mixers and hoisting equipment used on large plastering jobs today produce better mortars and lighten the tasks involved.

10. According to the above paragraph, present day tools used for plastering

    A. have made plastering much more complicated than it used to be
    B. are heavier than the old-fashioned tools they replaced
    C. produce poorer results but speed up the job
    D. are lighter and stronger than the hand-made tools of the past

11. As used in the above paragraph, the word *rigidly* means MOST NEARLY

    A. feeble   B. weakly   C. firmly   D. flexibly

Questions 12-18.

DIRECTIONS: Questions 12 through 18 are to be answered in accordance with the following paragraphs.

SURFACE RENEWING OVERLAYS

A surface renewing overlay should consist of material which can be constructed in very thin layers. The material must fill surface voids and provide an impervious skid-resistant surface. It must also be sufficiently resistant to traffic abrasion to provide an economical service life.

Materials meeting these requirements are:
    a. Asphalt concrete having small particle size
    b. Hot sand asphalts
    c. Surface seal coats

Fine-graded asphalt concrete or hot sand asphalt can be constructed in layers as thin as one-half inch and fulfill all requirements for surface renewing overlays. They are recommended for thin resurfacing of pavements having high traffic volumes, as their service lives are relatively long when constructed properly. They can be used for minor leveling, they are quiet riding, and their appearance is exceptionally pleasing. Seal coats or slurry seals may fulfill surface requirements for low traffic pavements.

12. A surface renewing overlay must fill surface voids, provide an impervious skid-resistant surface, and

    A. be resistant to traffic abrasion
    B. have small particle size
    C. be exceptionally pleasing in appearance
    D. be constructed in half-inch layers

13. An *impervious skid-resistant surface* means a surface that is

    A. rough to the touch and fixed firmly in place
    B. waterproof and provides good gripping for tires
    C. not damaged by skidding vehicles
    D. smooth to the touch and quiet riding

14. The number of types of materials that can be constructed in very thin layers and are also suitable for surface renewing overlays is

    A. 1   B. 2   C. 3   D. 4

15. The SMALLEST thickness of asphalt concrete or hot sand asphalt that can fulfill all requirements for surface renewing overlays is _____ inch(es).

    A. ¼   B. ½   C. 1   D. 2

16. The materials that are recommended for thin resurfacing of pavements having high traffic volumes are

    A. those that have relatively long service lives
    B. asphalt concretes with maximum particle size
    C. surface seal coats
    D. slurry seals with voids

17. Fine-graded asphalt concrete and hot sand asphalt are quiet riding and are also

    A. recommended for low traffic pavements
    B. used as slurry seal coats
    C. suitable for major leveling
    D. exceptionally pleasing in appearance

18. The materials that may fulfill surface requirements for low traffic pavements are

    A. fine-graded asphalt concretes
    B. hot sand asphalts
    C. seal coats or slurry seals
    D. those that can be used for minor leveling

Questions 19-25.

DIRECTIONS: Questions 19 through 25 are to be answered SOLELY on the basis of the paragraphs below.

OPEN-END WRENCHES

Solid, non-adjustable wrenches with openings in one or both ends are called open-end wrenches. Wrenches with small openings are usually shorter than wrenches with large openings. This proportions the lever advantage of the wrench to the bolt or stud and helps prevent wrench breakage or damage to the bolt or stud.

Open-end wrenches may have their jaws parallel to the handle or at angles anywhere up to 90 degrees. The average angle is 15 degrees. This angular displacement variation permits selection of a wrench suited for places where there is room to make only a part of a complete turn of a nut or bolt. Handles are usually straight, but may be curved. Those with curved handles are called S-wrenches. Other open-end wrenches may have offset handles. This allows the head to reach nut or bolt heads that are sunk below the surface.

There are a few basic rules that you should keep in mind when using wrenches. They are:
   I. ALWAYS use a wrench that fits the nut properly. Otherwise, the wrench may slip, or the nut may be damaged.
   II. Keep wrenches clean and free from oil. Otherwise, they may slip, resulting in possible serious injury to you or damage to the work.
   III. Do NOT increase the leverage of a wrench by placing a pipe over the handle. Increased leverage may damage the wrench or the work.

19. Open-end wrenches

    A. are adjustable
    B. are solid
    C. always have openings at both ends
    D. are always S-shaped

20. Wrench proportions are such that wrenches with _____ openings have _____ handles.

    A. larger; shorter   B. smaller; longer
    C. larger; longer   D. smaller; thicker

21. The average angle between the jaws and the handle of a wrench is _____ degrees.

    A. 0   B. 15   C. 22   D. 90

22. Offset handles are intended for use MAINLY with 22.____

    A. offset nuts
    B. bolts having fine threads
    C. nuts sunk below the surface
    D. bolts that permit limited swing

23. The wrench which is selected should fit the nut properly because this 23.____

    A. prevents distorting the wrench
    B. insures use of all wrench sizes
    C. avoids damaging the nut
    D. overstresses the bolt

24. Oil on wrenches is 24.____

    A. *good* because it prevents rust
    B. *good* because it permits easier turning
    C. *bad* because the wrench may slip off the nut
    D. *bad* because the oil may spoil the work

25. Extending the handle of a wrench by slipping a piece of pipe over it is considered 25.____

    A. *good* because it insures a tight nut
    B. *good* because less effort is needed to loosen a nut
    C. *bad* because the wrench may be damaged
    D. *bad* because the amount of tightening can not be controlled

KEY (CORRECT ANSWERS)

1. D		11. C	
2. B		12. A	
3. B		13. B	
4. C		14. C	
5. D		15. B	
6. C		16. A	
7. C		17. D	
8. B		18. C	
9. A		19. B	
10. D		20. C	

21. B
22. C
23. C
24. C
25. C

TEST 2

DIRECTIONS: Each question or incomplete statement is followed by several suggested answers or completions. Select the one that BEST answers the question or completes the statement. *PRINT THE LETTER OF THE CORRECT ANSWER IN THE SPACE AT THE RIGHT.*

Questions 1-3.

DIRECTIONS: Questions 1 through 3 are to be answered SOLELY on the basis of the following passage.

    A utility plan is a floor plan which shows the layout of a heating, electrical, plumbing, or other utility system. Utility plans are used primarily by the persons reponsible for the utilities, but they are important to the craftsman as well. Most utility installations require the leaving of openings in walls, floors, and roofs for the admission or installation of utility features. The craftsman who is, for example, pouring a concrete foundation wall must study the utility plans to determine the number, sizes, and locations of the openings he must leave for piping, electric lines, and the like.

1. The one of the following items of information which is LEAST likely to be provided by a utility plan is the

    A. location of the joists and frame members around stairwells
    B. location of the hot water supply and return piping
    C. location of light fixtures
    D. number of openings in the floor for radiators

1.____

2. According to the passage, the persons who will *most likely* have the GREATEST need for the information included in a utility plan of a building are those who

    A. maintain and repair the heating system
    B. clean the premises
    C. paint housing exteriors
    D. advertise property for sale

2.____

3. According to the passage, a repair crew member should find it MOST helpful to consult a utility plan when information is needed about the

    A. thickness of all doors in the structure
    B. number of electrical outlets located throughout the structure
    C. dimensions of each window in the structure
    D. length of a roof rafter

3.____

Questions 4-9.

DIRECTIONS: Questions 4 through 9 are to be answered SOLELY on the basis of the following passage.

    The basic hand-operated hoisting device is the tackle or purchase, consisting of a line called a fall, reeved through one or more blocks. To hoist a load of given size, you must set up a rig with a safe working load equal to or in excess of the load to be hoisted. In order to do this, you must be able to calculate the safe working load of a single part of line of given size, the safe working load of a given purchase which contains a line of given size, and the minimum size of hooks or shackles which you must use in a given type of purchase to hoist a given load. You must also be able to calculate the thrust which a given load will exert on a gin pole or a set of shears inclined at a given angle, the safe working load which a spar of a given size used as a gin pole or as one of a set of shears will sustain, and the stress which a given load will set up in the back guy of a gin pole or in the back guy of a set of shears inclined at a given angle.

4. The above passage refers to the lifting of loads by means of

   A. erected scaffolds
   B. manual rigging devices
   C. power-driven equipment
   D. conveyor belts

5. It can be concluded from the above passage that a set of shears serves to

   A. absorb the force and stress of the working load
   B. operate the tackle
   C. contain the working load
   D. compute the safe working load

6. According to the above passage, a spar can be used for a

   A. back guy   B. block   C. fall   D. gin pole

7. According to the above passage, the rule that a user of hand-operated tackle MUST follow is to make sure that the safe working load is AT LEAST

   A. equal to the weight of the given load
   B. twice the combined weight of the block and falls
   C. one-half the weight of the given load
   D. twice the weight of the given load

8. According to the above passage, the two parts that make up a tackle are

   A. back guys and gin poles
   B. blocks and falls
   C. rigs and shears
   D. spars and shackles

9. According to the above passage, in order to determine whether it is safe to hoist a particular load, you MUST

   A. use the maximum size hooks
   B. time the speed to bring a given load to a desired place
   C. calculate the forces exerted on various types of rigs
   D. repeatedly lift and lower various loads

Questions 10-15.

DIRECTIONS: Questions 10 through 15 are to be answered SOLELY on the basis of the following set of instructions.

PATCHING SIMPLE CRACKS IN A BUILT-UP ROOF

If there is a visible crack in built-up roofing, the repair is simple and straightforward:

1. With a brush, clean all loose gravel and dust out of the crack, and clean three or four inches around all sides of it.
2. With a trowel or putty knife, fill the crack with asphalt cement and then spread a layer of asphalt cement about 1/8 inch thick over the cleaned area.
3. Place a strip of roofing felt big enough to cover the crack into the wet cement and press it down firmly.
4. Spread a second layer of cement over the strip of felt and well past its edges.
5. Brush gravel back over the patch.

10. According to the above passage, in order to patch simple cracks in a built-up roof, it is necessary to use a

    A. putty knife and a drill
    B. knife and pliers
    C. tack hammer and a punch
    D. brush and a trowel

11. According to the above passage, the size of the area that should be clear of loose gravel and dust before the asphalt cement is first applied should

    A. be the exact size of the crack itself
    B. extend three or four inches on all sides of the crack
    C. be 1/8 inch greater than the size of the crack itself
    D. extend the length of the roofing strip

12. According to the above passage, loose gravel and dust in the crack should be removed with a

    A. brush   B. felt pad   C. trowel   D. dust mop

13. Assume that both layers of asphalt cement needed to patch the crack are of the same thickness.
    The total thickness of asphalt cement used in the patch should be MOST NEARLY _____ inch.

    A. 1/2   B. 1/3   C. 1/4   D. 1/8

14. According to the instructions in the above passage, how large should the strip of roofing felt be cut?

    A. Three of four inches square
    B. Smaller than the crack and small enough to be surrounded by cement on all sides of the strip
    C. Exactly the same size and shape of the area covered by the wet cement
    D. Large enough to completely cover the crack

15. The final or finishing action to be taken in patching a simple crack in a built-up roof is to

    A. clean out the inside of the crack
    B. spread a layer of asphalt a second time
    C. cover the crack with roofing felt
    D. cover the patch of roofing felt and cement with gravel

Questions 16-17.

DIRECTIONS: Questions 16 and 17 are to be answered SOLELY on the basis of the information given in the following paragraph.

Supplies are to be ordered from the stockroom once a week. The standard requisition form, Form SP21, is to be used for ordering all supplies. The form is prepared in triplicate, one white original and two green copies. The white and one green copy are sent to the stockroom, and the remaining green copy is to be kept by the orderer until the supplies are received.

16. According to the above paragraph, there is a limit on the

    A. amount of supplies that may be ordered
    B. day on which supplies may be ordered
    C. different kinds of supplies that may be ordered
    D. number of times supplies may be ordered in one year

17. According to the above paragraph, when the standard requisition form for supplies is prepared,

    A. a total of four requisition blanks is used
    B. a white form is the original
    C. each copy is printed in two colors
    D. one copy is kept by the stock clerk

Questions 18-21.

DIRECTION: Questions 18 through 21 are to be answered SOLELY on the basis of the following passage.

The Oil Pollution Act for U. S. waters defines an *oily mixture* as 100 parts or more of oil in one million parts of mixture. This mixture is not allowed to be discharged into the prohibited zone. The prohibited zone may, in special cases, be extended 100 miles out to sea but, in general, remains at 50 miles offshore. The United States Coast Guard must be contacted to report all *oily mixture* spills. The Federal Water Pollution Control Act provides for a fine of $10,000 for failure to notify the United States Coast Guard. An employer may take action against an employee if the employee causes an *oily mixture* spill. The law holds your employer responsible for either cleaning up or paying for the removal of the oil spillage.

18. According to the Oil Pollution Act, an *oily mixture* is defined as one in which there are _____ parts or more of oil in _____ parts of mixture.

    A. 50; 10,000
    B. 100; 10,000
    C. 100; 1,000,000
    D. 10,000; 1,000,000

19. Failure to notify the proper authorities of an *oily mixture* spill is punishable by a fine. Such fine is provided for by the

    A. United States Coast Guard
    B. Federal Water Pollution Control Act
    C. Oil Pollution Act
    D. United States Department of Environmental Protection

20. According to the law, the one responsible for the removal of an *oily mixture* spilled into U.S. waters is the

    A. employer
    B. employee
    C. U.S. Coast Guard
    D. U.S. Pollution Control Board

21. The *prohibited zone,* in general, is the body of water

    A. within 50 miles offshore
    B. beyond 100 miles offshore
    C. within 10,000 yards of the coastline
    D. beyond 10,000 yards from the coastline

Questions 22-25.

DIRECTIONS: Questions 22 through 25 are to be answered SOLELY on the basis of the following paragraph.

Synthetic detergents are materials produced from petroleum products or from animal or vegetable oils and fats. One of their advantages is the fact that they can be made to meet a particular cleaning problem by altering the foaming, wetting, and emulsifying properties of a cleaner. They are added to commonly used cleaning materials such as solvents, water, and alkalies to improve their cleaning performance. The adequate wetting of the surface to be cleaned is paramount in good cleaning performance. Because of the relatively high surface tension of water, it has poor wetting ability, unless its surface tension is decreased by addition of a detergent or soap. This allows water to flow into crevices and around small particles of soil, thus loosening them.

22. According to the above paragraph, synthetic detergents are made from all of the following EXCEPT

    A. petroleum products   B. vegetable oils
    C. surface tension oils   D. animal fats

23. According to the above paragraph, water's poor wetting ability is related to

    A. its low surface tension
    B. its high surface tension
    C. its vegetable oil content
    D. the amount of dirt on the surface to be cleaned

24. According to the above paragraph, synthetic detergents are added to all of the following EXCEPT

    A. alkalines   B. water   C. acids   D. solvents

25. According to the above paragraph, altering a property of a cleaner can give an advantage in meeting a certain cleaning problem.
The one of the following that is NOT a property altered by synthetic detergents is the cleaner's

   A. flow ability
   B. foaming property
   C. emulsifying property
   D. wetting ability

KEY (CORRECT ANSWERS)

1. A		11. B	
2. A		12. A	
3. B		13. C	
4. B		14. D	
5. A		15. D	
6. D		16. D	
7. A		17. B	
8. B		18. C	
9. C		19. B	
10. D		20. A	

21. A
22. C
23. B
24. C
25. A

PREPARING WRITTEN MATERIAL

PARAGRAPH REARRANGEMENT
COMMENTARY

The sentences that follow are in scrambled order. You are to rearrange them in proper order and indicate the letter choice containing the correct answer at the space at the right.

Each group of sentences in this section is actually a paragraph presented in scrambled order. Each sentence in the group has a place in that paragraph; no sentence is to be left out. You are to read each group of sentences and decide upon the best order in which to put the sentences so as to form a well-organized paragraph.

The questions in this section measure the ability to solve a problem when all the facts relevant to its solution are not given.

More specifically, certain positions of responsibility and authority require the employee to discover connection between events sometimes, apparently, unrelated. In order to do this, the employee will find it necessary to correctly infer that unspecified events have probably occurred or are likely to occur. This ability becomes especially important when action must be taken on incomplete information.

Accordingly, these questions require competitors to choose among several suggested alternatives, each of which presents a different sequential arrangement of the events. Competitors must choose the MOST logical of the suggested sequences.

In order to do so, they may be required to draw on general knowledge to infer missing concepts or events that are essential to sequencing the given events. Competitors should be careful to infer only what is essential to the sequence. The plausibility of the wrong alternatives will always require the inclusion of unlikely events or of additional chains of events which are NOT essential to sequencing the given events.

It's very important to remember that you are looking for the best of the four possible choices, and that the best choice of all may not even be one of the answers you're given to choose from.

There is no one right way to solve these problems. Many people have found it helpful to first write out the order of the sentences, as they would have arranged them, on their scrap paper before looking at the possible answers. If their optimum answer is there, this can save them some time. If it isn't, this method can still give insight into solving the problem. Others find it most helpful to just go through each of the possible choices, contrasting each as they go along. You should use whatever method feels comfortable and works for you.

While most of these types of questions are not that difficult, we've added a higher percentage of the difficult type, just to give you more practice. Usually there are only one or two questions on this section that contain such subtle distinctions that you're unable to answer confidently. And you then may find yourself stuck deciding between two possible choices, neither of which you're sure about.

EXAMINATION SECTION
TEST 1

DIRECTIONS: The sentences that follow are in scrambled order You are to rearrange them in proper order and indicate the letter choice containing the correct answer. *PRINT THE LETTER OF THE CORRECT ANSWER IN THE SPACE AT THE RIGHT.*

PARAGRAPH REARRANGEMENT

The following questions deal with paragraph rearrangement. Read the listed sentences and then select the suggested answer which MOST CORRECTLY indicates the proper continuity of sentences.

1. 1. One of the main benefits of the conference procedure is that those who are performing the actual operation can be given an opportunity to participate in making the decisions which affect them.
    2. They will usually respond more favorably when given this opportunity.
    3. Consultation between management and the members of an organization wherein employees share in the decision-making process will enhance morale and give employees a special feeling of status.
    4. The conference is particularly valuable when used by supervisors as a means of sharing information and experiences with subordinates and learning of their needs and desires.

    A. 2-1-4-3 B. 1-2-3-4
    C. 2-4-1-3 D. 4-3-2-1

    1.____

2. 1. It is highly desirable that he be occupationally competent to perform the task he expects his subordinates to learn about; but having technical proficiency does not insure that he can impart it to others.
    2. Rather, the technically competent supervisor who is also a good teacher will achieve a high degree of success in the training function because one ability will complement the other.
    3. Often a <u>lack of competency</u> or a failure on the part of the supervisor to prepare himself for his training role is the cause of his teaching ineffectiveness.
    4. It would be erroneous to assume that just because an individual is an excellent burglary investigator, he can effectively teach others how to catch burglars.

    A. 4-1-3-2 B. 2-3-1-4
    C. 3-1-4-2 D. 2-3-4-1

    2.____

3. 1. The true importance usually lies somewhere between these two diverse evaluations.
    2. Its determination is an important step in providing well-rounded police service.
    3. Policy decisions must be made about the extent of patrol participation in the performance of all tasks in the fields covered by special units.
    4. When the importance of a special task is evaluated differently by the patrol division and the specialized division, the effort spent by patrol in its performance is likely to be less than the specialists think it should be.
    5. As the range between the evaluations is diminished, the advantages of having the tasks performed by the members of the special divisions are lessened.

    A. 3-4-1-2-5 B. 1-4-3-5-2
    C. 2-5-4-3-1 D. 4-2-3-1-5

    3.____

117

4.
1. In some instances such action may be desirable, but the indiscriminate transfer of the most capable personnel from patrol to special units jeopardizes effective patrol service.
2. Not only are men drawn from patrol, but generally the most competent are taken in the creation of specialized units.
3. Police manpower is limited, and increased specialization usually results in a diminished patrol.
4. Although patrol is essential to effective police service, some specialization also is essential, and present evidence indicates a continuance of the marked trend of the past two decades toward specialization.

   A. 1-2-3-4 B. 2-1-4-3
   C. 3-4-1-2 D. 4-3-2-1

5.
1. He is a roving city-hall information and complaint counter for the distressed citizen, disgruntled by the inconvenience of trips to the city hall, unsatisfactory telephone calls, and sometimes apparent lack of attention to his complaints.
2. The consonant availability and mobility of the patrolman make his services useful to other city departments, and he improves both public and inter-department relationships by attending more immediately to citizen needs.
3. The patrolman is the ultimate in the decentralization of municipal service.
4. The extent to which patrol officers will provide extra police services is determined by the chief executive of the city and his department heads.

   A. 1-3-2-4 B. 4-1-3-2
   C. 2-4-1-3 D. 3-1-2-4

6.
1. For one thing, despite the objections of the administration and most business leaders, we must move to a shorter work week or work year, combined, if desired, with multiple shift operations.
2. If the national goal is to minimize technological displacement and unemployment without going back to horse-and-buggy production methods, then a variety of possible policies would achieve optimum employment.
3. For another, young people should be required to stay in school longer.
4. This would keep more people employed and would prevent expensive equipment from standing idle.
5. This requirement, combined with an earlier retirement age, would cut persons off from both ends of the labor force, thereby reducing the number of job seekers.

   A. 2-1-4-3-5 B. 2-1-4-5-3
   C. 3-1-5-2-4 D. 2-1-5-4-3

7.
1. Overly severe or excessively lenient penalties may cause a reaction from employees just opposite to that intended by the supervisor.
2. In neither case will the punishment accomplish what it should.
3. Such penalties may make the recipient a martyr or indicate that management considers the dereliction inconsequential.
4. Rather, it may set a dangerous precedent which may tend to "bindn management to an indesirable course of action in the future.

   A. 1-3-2-4 B. 1-2-3-4
   C. 1-4-2-3 D. 2-1-3-4

8.
1. Many of the personal traits supervisors are called upon to evaluate cannot be measured by precise tests.
2. Extreme difficulties are encountered in trying to compare the performance of the detective with that of the jailor, or the performance of the patrol officer with that of the staff officer.
3. Rating systems are inherently subjective since they involve a personal audit by one person of another's conduct or performance.
4. One of the inherently difficult problems in the police service is that of fairly comparing persons assigned to widely different tasks.

A. 4-2-1-3 B. 4-1-2-3
C. 3-1-4-2 D. 3-4-2-1

8._____

9.
1. Procedures should be standardized so that all raters may perform their tasks uniformly.
2. Employees may be ranked, they may be rated on the basis of a comparison with selected employees, or in comparison with the ideal employee, or they may be rated on a numerical basis.
3. He should be made conscious of the difference between ability and performance.
4. One of the biggest problems in performance evaluations is the selection of a rating method which will yield reliable results.
5. Whatever standards the supervisor is expected to use as guides in interpreting the performance norms of his subordinates should be clearly defined.

A. 4-3-2-1-5 B. 1-2-4-3-5
C. 4-2-5-3-1 D. 5-3-1-2-4

9._____

10.
1. It is the type of police behavior that is most objectionable to citizens.
2. Police decision making is complex enough in cases where discretion is authorized, let alone in situations where discretion is not authorized.
3. This leads to judgments that are of questionable validity and provides a controversial basis for subsequent actions.
4. In reacting to perceived dangers and to threats to their authority, policemen often rely on stereotypic symbolic assailants and other perceptual traits of suspiciousness.

A. 1-3-4-2 B. 2-4-3-1
C. 3-1-4-2 D. 2-4-3-1

10._____

11.
1. All of the councils have been active on an informal basis in promoting interjurisdictional agreements.
2. A council of governments, with a committee on law enforcement, can be an effective vehicle in metropolitan areas for promoting consolidation or cooperation in law enforcement activities.
3. It is a simple step to include law enforcement as part of a council's total program.
4. Four of the councils are now engaged in negotiating cooperative agreements among member units, and three also mediate disputes.

A. 3-2-1-4 B. 2-4-1-3
C. 1-2-4-3 D. 4-3-1-2

11._____

12. 1. However, in their attempts to uncover basic feelings regarding these factors, the researcher found that direct questions designed to find out how the subjects felt about specific aspects of their jobs resulted in superficial, "lifeless" answers.
    2. These studies were primarily concerned with the determinants of morale and productivity.
    3. Management first became aware of the value of interviewing in industrial relations during the 1930's as a consequence of studies conducted at the Hawthorne plant of the Western Electric Company.
    4. Even worse - or so it seemed at the time - instead of giving "straightforward" responses, some of the people interviewed tended to talk about what interested them most at the moment.

    A. 2-1-4-3   B. 3-2-1-4
    C. 1-2-3-4   D. 3-2-4-1

13. 1. Provision should be made for use of the system by Federal and regional law enforcement agencies, but parallel or duplicatory systems should be avoided unless for specific backup purposes.
    2. It is intended to complement, not to replace, local and State systems.
    3. The National system should be a coordinating mechanism that will further the exchange of information of mutual concern among smaller, independent but coordinated systems.
    4. The concept of the National Crime Information Center (NCIC) is clear.

    A. 4-2-3-1   B. 2-4-1-3
    C. 2-3-1-4   D. 3-2-4-1

14. 1. Traditionally, purchasing was primarily conducted on a departmental basis with little or no centralized purchasing for the jurisdiction.
    2. Purchasing is an activity undertaken by every public jurisdiction, large or small.
    3. The cities of Chicago, Cincinnati, and Milwaukee are in the forefront of this type of buying.
    4. More recently, however, governments, and especially the larger jurisdictions, are abandoning departmental in favor of centralized purchasing.

    A. 2-1-4-3   B. 1-2-3-4
    C. 3-2-1-4   D. 1-4-3-2

15. 1. These "qualities" are really a state of mind.
    2. They exist or are possessed by people who have their heads turned a special way.
    3. We all understand that "ethics and professionalism" do not come in a can or jar.
    4. You cannot order a supply for your department.

    A. 1-3-4-2   B. 3-1-2-4
    C. 3-4-1-2   D. 2-3-1-4

16.
1. This suggests to us that the greater stress lies upon the anvil and not the hammer.
2. It has been written that "Every man who strikes blows for power, for influence, for right, must be just as good an anvil as he is a hammer."
3. Here lies the greater stress.
4. But one does not stand reasonless before an anvil and strike it with a hammer.
5. Between the hammer and the anvil we always find an object which is being beaten, pulled, pursuaded, and shaped — at the mercy of both.

   A. 1-3-5-2-4   B. 2-1-4-5-3
   C. 2-4-5-3-1   D. 2-5-4-1-3

16.____

17.
1. The complaint is not centered in the community, but in the emotional context of the family, thus making an objective analysis of the situation very difficult.
2. Not only are the youth and his parents at the peak of escalated emotions, but the issue of ungovernability, by its very nature, is difficult to define and treat.
3. No more challenging situation exists then investigating a complaint of ungovernability.
4. While truly delinquent acts committed in the community can frequently be determined through the accounts of victims and witnesses, such is not the case with ungovernability.

   A. 3-2-4-1   B. 3-4-1-2
   C. 4-3-2-1   D. 2-1-4-3

17.____

18.
1. The private security sector must be sure thai its personnel are of the highest caliber and that their training is the very best that can be produced with available resources.
2. Certain responsibilities face both law enforcement and the private security sector in providing public safety.
3. Complacency can be more devastating than overzealousness.
4. In addition, the private security sector must be constantly aware that it cannot become lethargic to the point of letting its guard drop.

   A. 1-2-3-4   B. 2-1-4-3
   C. 2-3-4-1   D. 2-4-1-3

18.____

19.
1. This important service makes private security a natural ally of the police and a formidable foe of the criminal.
2. Together they can fashion a program which will foster public understanding and enlist public assistance in combating crime.
3. Both police and private security stand to gain, but more importantly, the public stands to gain the most.
4. The business of the private security sector is not only to sell safety and security but to educate people in the many ways they can protect themselves.

   A. 2-1-3-4   B. 4-2-1-3
   C. 4-1-2-3   D. 4-3-2-1

19.____

20.
1. But these mistakes do not change the economic nature of business.
2. Many private, public or institutional organizations to not plan, design, and manage positions on an economical or efficient basis.
3. However, the fact that some organizations manage more efficiently than others does not conflict with the thesis that positions are creatures of economic need.
4. Poorly made decisions on the number and kinds of positions will surely result in losses and inefficient use of funds that might better be used elsewhere.
5. A business management may make poor investments, it may create too many positions, it may not sell its product, it may tolerate high production costs.

A. 1-4-3-5-2
B. 2-3-5-1-4
C. 3-2-5-1-4
D. 1-2-3-4-5

21.
1. The search for release from stress may result in alcohol or chemical abuse, domestic or financial problems, illness, and sometimes suicide.
2. Long exposure to police work creates physical and mental stress on its practitioners.
3. For others, proper supervision and evaluations will identify potential problem areas in handling stress before adverse conditions take their toll.
4. In a small minority, the inability to cope manifests itself in poor job performance, disability or even death.
5. In the ideal, the strain is routinely handled by the officer who meets the demands of law enforcement and achieves the personal satisfaction associated with public service.

A. 1-5-2-3-4
B. 2-5-3-4-1
C. 1-2-5-3-4
D. 2-5-4-3-1

22.
1. Obviously, it benefits the user to have instructions on how to use an item correctly and how to avoid improper use.
2. Proper labeling serves many purposes, including product identification.
3. Similarly, labels often contain detailed information on how to maintain or care for a product.
4. Another purpose of labeling is to lessen the likelihood of product liability on the part of the manufacturer, and, in the case of police use, on the part of the department that issues an item of equipment to its officers for field use.
5. In some cases, the lable may contain shelf-life data that states a date beyond which the product should not be used, or can be expected to degrade as a consequence of aging.

A. 2-1-3-4-5
B. 2-4-5-1-3
C. 2-1-5-3-4
D. 2-1-3-5-4

23.
1. The same is true for those officers who routinely operate speed-measuring radar devices.
2. Each year, law enforcement equipment becomes more complex as the result of technological developments.
3. Consider the widespread use of mobile communication systems.
4. The very nature of this technology causes potential liability problems.
5. Several police departments have had questions raised by their officers as to whether the transmitted signal is a potentional health hazard.

A. 2-4-3-5-1
B. 5-4-3-2-1
C. 2-3-4-5-1
D. 2-4-5-3-1

24.
1. Terrorists generally do not have criminal records, and their motivation is typically political.
2. Combating terrorism is perhaps the most difficult task facing law enforcement.
3. They are organized in small cells and therefore are not as vulnerable to the use of informants and undercover agents.
4. Generally speaking, there has been a downtrend since the late 1970's.
5. Notwithstanding these problems, we have made progress against terrorists and the number of incidents last year was down from 1982's total.

A. 2-3-1-5-4 B. 1-2-3-5-4
C. 2-1-3-5-4 D. 1-3-2-5-4

25.
1. It is not uncommon for officers to gather at the corner bar when their shift is over to unwind, drink a few beers, and review the events of the day.
2. In many departments, these activities are the basis for the strong personal bonds that build trust and reliance among colleagues.
3. Unfortunately, they may also be the basis for the beginning stages of alcoholism for that percentage of officers who are either physiologically or psychologically prone to the disease.
4. Both public and law enforcement professionals tend to share a belief that police officers abuse alcohol to a greater extent than the population as a whole.
5. While surveys indicate that this is not true, it has been suggested that police social customs foster regular alcohol consumption.

A. 1-4-5-2-3 B. 4-5-1-2-3
C. 1-3-5-4-2 D. 4-5-2-1-3

26.
1. This approach to mental measurement fell out of favor when it became apparent that there was no correlation between performance on the tests and actual scholastic achievement.
2. The work of Alfred Binet in France suggested that questions tapping reasoning skills and general knowledge provided a more direct means of measuring intelligence.
3. With the development of mental tests, the variability hypothesis began to serve not as an explanation for women's inferior social position but as a justification for it.
4. The strength of a student's grip could not predict the student's grades in mathematics.
5. Tests conducted by Francis Galton had been based on the assumption that measurement of sensory and motor capacities could provide an estimate of intellectual functioning, and supported this assumption of women's inferiority.

A. 2-3-1-4-5 B. 5-3-1-4-2
C. 5-1-3-4-2 D. 3-5-1-4-2

27.
1. Only because of the rapidity of the enzyme's action can the carbon dioxide be freed fast enough from its compounds to leave the blood during that moment in the alveolus when it is separated from the air by the thinnest of membranes.
2. The result is that each is broken into one water and one carbon dioxide molecule.
3. Our ability to rid ourselves of CO_2 through the exhaled air is then utterly dependent on the presence of these critically located atoms of zinc.
4. During the one second that the blood is racing through the tiny capillaries of the lung, the single atom of zinc that is set in the center of the enzyme carbonic anhydrase is brought into contact with 600,000 of its target molecule, carbonic acid.
5. Yet the total amount of this mineral in the body is so little that it was, up until a few years ago, considered to be of no significance.

A. 3-4-5-1-2 B. 1-2-3-4-5
C. 4-2-1-3-5 D. 3-4-5-2-1

28.
1. The wise person realizes that everything everyone wants is already contained within himself or herself, and he or she begins to embody these qualities rather than search for them from others.
2. What we usually don't realize is that everyone has this tendency, and unless one knows himself or herself well, he or she is probably wondering the same things.
3. Everyone is wanting it, but few people have the courage to be the one to give it.
4. Usually when we relate to others, our normal tendency is to think, "I wonder if he or she likes me? I wonder if he or she thinks well of me?"
5. So normally we are hoping for approval from those who are hoping for our approval.

A. 1-2-3-4-5 B. 1-4-5-2-3
C. 4-2-5-3-1 D. 4-5-2-1-3

29.
1. At an earlier point in the process, some pure energy slowed down to a speed below that of light, at which point it congealed into mass; and at some point in the future, should the equilibrium of this stable form of energy be disturbed in any way, it can shed its temporary property called mass and become pure energy once more.
2. The moment its mass disappears, an energy pattern no longer projects a material appearance.
3. The manifestation we know as "matter" is simply one of the attendant effects of this energy's transformation into mass; thus, an object is really more of an event than it is a thing of substance.
4. Every material object, be it our own body, a tree, or a mountain, is essentially just a temporary phase in a dynamic process involving a certain amount of energy.
5. The fact that the mass of any material entity is nothing but a specific quantity of energy indicates that we can no longer look at the world around us as a collection of static objects, for matter is not composed of solid substance, it is in fact made up of dancing patterns of energy.

A. 5-1-3-4-2 B. 5-4-1-3-2
C. 4-2-1-5-3 D. 3-4-5-1-2

30.
1. As people get jobs, or move up from poverty-level to better paying employment, they stop receiving benefits and start paying taxes, decreasing the federal deficit.
2. The strategy of putting people to work in civilian rein-dustrialization - in clean energy development, public transportation and urban reconstruction - would not only provide socially useful products, but would lower social service costs and reduce the deficit as well.
3. Thus job creation programs are often a bargain for taxpayers, if the reductions in the costs of other programs and the increase in tax payments are counted.
4. Only poor or unemployed people are eligible for food stamps, welfare, unemployment compensation, housing subsidies and so on.
5. The best way to cut costs of many social programs is to create jobs.

A. 5-3-4-1-2
B. 2-3-4-1-5
C. 4-5-2-3-1
D. 2-1-3-4-5

30.____

KEY (CORRECT ANSWERS)

1.	B	16.	B
2.	C	17.	A
3.	D	18.	B
4.	D	19.	C
5.	D	20.	B
6.	A	21.	B
7.	A	22.	D
8.	C	23.	A
9.	C	24.	C
10.	B	25.	B
11.	B	26.	D
12.	B	27.	C
13.	A	28.	C
14.	A	29.	B
15.	C	30.	C

PREPARING WRITTEN MATERIAL
EXAMINATION SECTION
TEST 1

DIRECTIONS: Each of the sentences in this test may be classified under one of the following four categories:
    A. *Incorrect* because of faulty grammar or sentence structure
    B. *Incorrect* because of faulty punctuation
    C. *Incorrect* because of faulty capitalization
    D. *Correct*

Examine each sentence carefully to determine under which of the above four options it is best classified. Then, in the space at the right, print the capital letter preceding the option which is the BEST of the four suggested above.

(Each incorrect sentence contains but one type of error. Consider a sentence to be correct if it contains none of the types of errors mentioned, even though there may be other correct ways of expressing the same thought.)

1. This fact, together with those brought out at the previous meeting, prove that the schedule is satisfactory to the employees.   1.____

2. Like many employees in scientific fields, the work of bookkeepers and accountants requires accuracy and neatness.   2.____

3. "What can I do for you," the secretary asked as she motioned to the visitor to take a seat.   3.____

4. Our representative, Mr. Charles will call on you next week to determine whether or not your claim has merit.   4.____

5. We expect you to return in the spring; please do not disappoint us.   5.____

6. Any supervisor, who disregards the just complaints of his subordinates, is remiss in the performance of his duty.   6.____

7. Because she took less than an hour for lunch is no reason for permitting her to leave before five o'clock.   7.____

8. "Miss Smith," said the supervisor, "Please arrange a meeting of the staff for two o'clock on Monday."   8.____

9. A private company's vacation and sick leave allowance usually differs considerably from a public agency.   9.____

10. Therefore, in order to increase the efficiency of operations in the department, a report on the recommended changes in procedures was presented to the departmental committee in charge of the program.   10.____

11. We told him to assign the work to whoever was available. 11.____

12. Since John was the most efficient of any other employee in the bureau, he received the highest service rating. 12.____

13. Only those members of the national organization who resided in the middle West attended the conference in Chicago. 13.____

14. The question of whether the office manager has as yet attained, or indeed can ever hope to secure professional status is one which has been discussed for years. 14.____

15. No one knew who to blame for the error which, we later discovered, resulted in a considerable loss of time. 15.____

KEY (CORRECT ANSWERS)

1.	A	6.	B	11.	D
2.	A	7.	A	12.	A
3.	B	8.	C	13.	C
4.	B	9.	A	14.	B
5.	D	10.	D	15.	A

TEST 2

DIRECTIONS: Each of the sentences in this test may be classified under one of the following four categories:
   A. *Incorrect* because of faulty grammar or sentence structure
   B. *Incorrect* because of faulty punctuation
   C. *Incorrect* because of faulty capitalization
   D. *Correct*

1. The National alliance of Businessmen is trying to persuade private businesses to hire youth in the summertime.   1.____

2. The supervisor who is on vacation, is in charge of processing vouchers.   2.____

3. The activity of the committee at its conferences is always stimulating.   3.____

4. After checking the addresses again, the letters went to the mailroom.   4.____

5. The director, as well as the employees, are interested in sharing the dividends.   5.____

KEY (CORRECT ANSWERS)

1. C
2. B
3. D
4. A
5. A

TEST 3

DIRECTIONS: In each of the following groups of sentences, one of the four sentences is faulty in grammar, punctuation, or capitalization. Select the INCORRECT sentence in each case.

1. A. Sailing down the bay was a thrilling experience for me.
    B. He was not consulted about your joining the club.
    C. This story is different than the one I told you yesterday.
    D. There is no doubt about his being the best player.

    1.____

2. A. He maintains there is but one road to world peace.
    B. It is common knowledge that a child sees much he is not supposed to see.
    C. Much of the bitterness might have been avoided if arbitration had been resorted to earlier in the meeting.
    D. The man decided it would be advisable to marry a girl somewhat younger than him.

    2.____

3. A. In this book, the incident I liked least is where the hero tries to put out the forest fire.
    B. Learning a foreign language will undoubtedly give a person a better understanding of his mother tongue.
    C. His actions made us wonder what he planned to do next.
    D. Because of the war, we were unable to travel during the summer vacation.

    3.____

4. A. The class had no sooner become interested in the lesson than the dismissal bell rang.
    B. There is little agreement about the kind of world to be planned at the peace conference.
    C. "Today," said the teacher, "we shall read 'The Wind in the Willows,' I am sure you'll like it.
    D. The terms of the legal settlement of the family quarrel handicapped both sides for many years.

    4.____

5. A. I was so surprised that I was not able to say a word.
    B. She is taller than any other member of the class.
    C. It would be much more preferable if you were never seen in his company.
    D. We had no choice but to excuse her for being late.

    5.____

KEY (CORRECT ANSWERS)

1. C
2. D
3. A
4. C
5. C

TEST 4

DIRECTIONS: In each of the following groups of sentences, one of the four sentences is faulty in grammar, punctuation, or capitalization. Select the INCORRECT sentence in each case.

1. A. Please send me these data at the earliest opportunity.
   B. The loss of their material proved to be a severe handicap.
   C. My principal objection to this plan is that it is impracticable.
   D. The doll had laid in the rain for an hour and was ruined.

   1._____

2. A. The garden scissors, left out all night in the rain, were in a badly rusted condition.
   B. The girls felt bad about the misunderstanding which had arisen
   C. Sitting near the campfire, the old man told John and I about many exciting adventures he had had.
   D. Neither of us is in a position to undertake a task of that magnitude.

   2._____

3. A. The general concluded that one of the three roads would lead to the besieged city.
   B. The children didn't, as a rule, do hardly anything beyond what they were told to do.
   C. The reason the girl gave for her negligence was that she had acted on the spur of the moment.
   D. The daffodils and tulips look beautiful in that blue vase.

   3._____

4. A. If I was ten years older, I should be interested in this work.
   B. Give the prize to whoever has drawn the best picture.
   C. When you have finished reading the book, take it back to the library.
   D. My drawing is as good as or better than yours.

   4._____

5. A. He asked me whether the substance was animal or vegetable.
   B. An apple which is unripe should not be eaten by a child.
   C. That was an insult to me who am your friend.
   D. Some spy must of reported the matter to the enemy.

   5._____

6. A. Limited time makes quoting the entire message impossible.
   B. Who did she say was going?
   C. The girls in your class have dressed more dolls this year than we.
   D. There was such a large amount of books on the floor that I couldn't find a place for my rocking chair.

   6._____

7. A. What with his sleeplessness and his ill health, he was unable to assume any responsibility for the success of the meeting.
   B. If I had been born in February, I should be celebrating my birthday soon.
   C. In order to prevent breakage, she placed a sheet of paper between each of the plates when she packed them.
   D. After the spring shower, the violets smelled very sweet.

   7._____

8. A. He had laid the book down very reluctantly before the end of the lesson.
   B. The dog, I am sorry to say, had lain on the bed all night.
   C. The cloth was first lain on a flat surface; then it was pressed with a hot iron.
   D. While we were in Florida, we lay in the sun until we were noticeably tanned.

   8.____

9. A. If John was in New York during the recent holiday season, I have no doubt he spent most of the time with his parents.
   B. How could he enjoy the television program; the dog was barking and the baby was crying.
   C. When the problem was explained to the class, he must have been asleep.
   D. She wished that her new dress were finished so that she could go to the party.

   9.____

10. A. The engine not only furnishes power but light and heat as well.
    B. You're aware that we've forgotten whose guilt was established, aren't you?
    C. Everybody knows that the woman made many sacrifices for her children.
    D. A man with his dog and gun is a familiar sight in this neighborhood.

    10.____

KEY (CORRECT ANSWERS)

1.	D	6.	D
2.	C	7.	B
3.	B	8.	C
4.	A	9.	B
5.	D	10.	A

TEST 5

DIRECTIONS: Each of Questions 1 through 5 consists of a sentence which may be classified appropriately under one of the following four categories:
- A. *Incorrect* because of faulty grammar
- B. *Incorrect* because of faulty punctuation
- C. *Incorrect* because of faulty spelling
- D. *Correct*

Examine each sentence carefully. Then, print in the space at the right the letter preceding the category which is the BEST of the four suggested above
(Note: Each incorrect sentence contains only one type of error. Consider a sentence correct if it contains no errors, although there may be other correct ways of writing the sentence.)

1. Of the two employees, the one in our office is the most efficient. 1.____

2. No one can apply or even understand, the new rules and regulations. 2.____

3. A large amount of supplies were stored in the empty office. 3.____

4. If an employee is occassionally asked to work overtime, he should do so willingly. 4.____

5. It is true that the new procedures are difficult to use but, we are certain that you will learn them quickly. 5.____

6. The office manager said that he did not know who would be given a large allotment under the new plan. 6.____

7. It was at the supervisor's request that the clerk agreed to postpone his vacation. 7.____

8. We do not believe that it is necessary for both he and the clerk to attend the conference. 8.____

9. All employees, who display perseverance, will be given adequate recognition. 9.____

10. He regrets that some of us employees are dissatisfied with our new assignments. 10.____

11. "Do you think that the raise was merited," asked the supervisor? 11.____

12. The new manual of procedure is a valuable supplament to our rules and regulations. 12.____

13. The typist admitted that she had attempted to pursuade the other employees to assist her in her work. 13.____

14. The supervisor asked that all amendments to the regulations be handled by you and I.   14.____

15. The custodian seen the boy who broke the window.   15.____

KEY (CORRECT ANSWERS)

1.	A	6.	D	11.	B
2.	B	7.	D	12.	C
3.	A	8.	A	13.	C
4.	C	9.	B	14.	A
5.	B	10.	D	15.	A

REPORT WRITING

EXAMINATION SECTION

TEST 1

DIRECTIONS: Each question or incomplete statement is followed by several suggested answers or completions. Select the one that BEST answers the question or completes the statement. *PRINT THE LETTER OF THE CORRECT ANSWER IN THE SPACE AT THE RIGHT.*

1. Following are six steps that should be taken in the course of report preparation:
   - I. Outlining the material for presentation in the report
   - II. Analyzing and interpreting the facts
   - III. Analyzing the problem
   - IV. Reaching conclusions
   - V. Writing, revising, and rewriting the final copy
   - VI. Collecting data

   According to the principles of good report writing, the CORRECT order in which these steps should be taken is:
   - A. VI, III, II, I, IV, V
   - B. III, VI, II, IV, I, V
   - C. III, VI, II, I, IV, V
   - D. VI, II, III, IV, I, V

   1.____

2. Following are three statements concerning written reports:
   - I. Clarity is generally more essential in oral reports than in written reports.
   - II. Short sentences composed of simple words are generally preferred to complex sentences and difficult words.
   - III. Abbreviations may be used whenever they are customary and will not distract the attention of the reader.

   Which of the following choices correctly classifies the above statements in to those which are valid and those which are not valid?
   - A. I and II are valid, but III is not valid
   - B. I is valid, but II and III are not valid.
   - C. II and III are valid, but I is not valid.
   - D. III is valid, but I and II are not valid.

   2.____

3. In order to produce a report written in a style that is both understandable and effective, an investigator should apply the principles of unit, coherence, and emphasis.
   The one of the following which is the BEST example of the principle of coherence is
   - A. interlinking sentences so that thoughts flow smoothly
   - B. having each sentence express a single idea to facilitate comprehension
   - C. arranging important points in prominent positions so they are not overlooked
   - D. developing the main idea fully to insure complete consideration

   3.____

137

4. Assume that a supervisor is preparing a report recommending that a standard work procedure be changed.
Of the following, the MOST important information that he should include in this report is
   A. a complete description of the present procedure
   B. the details and advantages of the recommended procedure
   C. the type and amount of retraining needed
   D. the percentage of men who favor the change

5. When you include in your report on an inspection some information which you have obtained from other individuals, it is MOST important that
   A. this information have no bearing on the work these other people are performing
   B. you do not report as fact the opinions of other individuals
   C. you keep the source of the information confidential
   D. you do not tell the other individuals that their statements will be included in your report

6. Before turning in a report of an investigator of an accident, you discover some additional information you did not know about when you wrote the report. Whether or not you re-write your report to include this additional information should depend MAINLY on the
   A. source of this additional information
   B. established policy covering the subject matter of the report
   C. length of the report and the time it would take you to re-write it
   D. bearing this additional information will have on the conclusions in the report

7. The MOST desirable *first* step in the planning of a written report is to
   A. ascertain what necessary information is readily available in the files
   B. outline the methods you will employ to get the necessary information
   C. determine the objectives and uses of the report
   D. estimate the time and cost required to complete the report

8. In writing a report, the practice of taking up the least important points and the most important points last is a
   A. *good* technique since the final points made in a report will make the greatest impression on the reader
   B. *good* technique since the material is presented in a more logical manner and will lead directly to the conclusions
   C. *poor* technique since the reader's time is wasted by having to review irrelevant information before finishing the report
   D. *poor* technique since it may cause the reader to lose interest in the report and arrive at incorrect conclusions about the report

3 (#1)

9. Which one of the following serves as the BEST guideline for you to follow for effective written reports?
   Keep sentences
   A. short and limit sentences to one thought
   B. short and use as many thoughts as possible
   C. long and limit sentences to one thought
   D. long and use as many thoughts as possible

10. One method by which a supervisor might prepare written reports to management is to begin with the conclusions, results, or summary, and to follow this with the supporting data.
    The BEST reason why management may *prefer* this form of report is that
    A. management lacks the specific training to understand the data
    B. the data completely supports the conclusions
    C. time is saved by getting to the conclusions of the report first
    D. the data contains all the information that is required for making the conclusions

11. When making written reports, it is MOST important that they be
    A. well-worded
    B. accurate as to the facts
    C. brief
    D. submitted immediately

12. Of the following, the MOST important reason for a supervisor to prepare good written reports is that
    A. a supervisor is rated on the quality of his reports
    B. decisions are often made on the basis of the reports
    C. such reports take less time for superiors to review
    D. such reports demonstrate efficiency of department operations

13. Of the following, the BEST test of a good report is whether it
    A. provides the information needed
    B. shows the good sense of the writer
    C. is prepared according to a proper format
    D. is grammatical and neat

14. When a supervisor writes a report, he can BEST show that he has a understanding of the subject of the report by
    A. including necessary facts and omitting nonessential details
    B. using statistical data
    C. giving his conclusions but not the data on which they are based
    D. using a technical vocabulary

15. Suppose you and another supervisor on the same level are assigned to work together on a report. You disagree strongly with one of the recommendations the other supervisor wants to include in the report but you cannot change his views.

Of the following, it would be BEST that
- A. you refuse to accept responsibility for the report
- B. you ask that someone else be assigned to this project to replace you
- C. each of you state his own ideas about this recommendation in the report
- D. you give in to the other supervisor's opinion for the sake of harmony

16. Standardized forms are often provided for submitting reports. 16.____
 Of the following, the MOST important advantage of using standardized forms for reports is that
 - A. they take less time to prepare than individually written reports
 - B. the person making the report can omit information he considers unimportant
 - C. the responsibility for preparing these reports can be turned over to subordinates
 - D. necessary information is less likely to be omitted

17. A report which may BEST be classed as a *periodic* report is one which 17.____
 - A. requires the same type of information at regular intervals
 - B. contains detailed information which is to be retained in permanent records
 - C. is prepared whenever a special situation occurs
 - D. lists information in graphic form

18. In the writing of reports or letters, the ideas presented in a paragraph are usually of unequal importance and require varying degrees of emphasis. 18.____
 All of the following are methods of placing extra stress on an idea EXCEPT
 - A. repeating it in a number of forms
 - B. placing it in the middle of the paragraph
 - C. placing it either at the beginning or at the end of a paragraph
 - D. underlining it

Questions 19-25.

DIRECTIONS: Questions 19 through 25 concern the subject of report writing and are based on the information and incidents described in the following paragraph. (In answering these questions, assume that the facts and incidents in the paragraph are true.)

On December 15, at 8 A.M., seven Laborers reported to Foreman Joseph Meehan in the Greenbranch Yard in Queens. Meehan instructed the men to load some 50-pound boxes of books on a truck for delivery to an agency building in Brooklyn. Meehan told the men that, because the boxes were rather heavy, two men should work together, helping each other lift and load each box. Since Michael Harper, one of the Laborers, was without a partner, Meehan helped him with the boxes for a while. When Meehan was called to the telephone in a nearby building, however, Harper decided to lift a box himself. He appeared able to lift the box, but, as he got the box halfway up, he cried out that he had a sharp pain in his back. Another Laborer, Jorge Ortiz, who was passing by, ran over to help Harper put the box down. Harper suddenly dropped the box, which fell on Ortiz' right foot. By this time, Meehan had come out of the building. He immediately helped get the box off Ortiz' foot and had both men lie down. Meehan covered the men with blankets and called an ambulance, which arrived a half hour later. At the hospital, the doctor said that the X-ray results showed that Ortiz' right foot was broken in three places.

19. What would be the BEST term to use in a report describing the injury of Jorge Ortiz?
    A. Strain   B. Fracture   C. Hernia   D. Hemorrhage

    19.____

20. Which of the following would be the MOST accurate summary for the Foreman to put in his report of the incident?
    A. Ortiz attempted to help Harper carry a box which was too heavy for one person, but Harper dropped it before Ortiz got there.
    B. Ortiz tried to help Harper carry a box but Harper got a pain in his back and accidentally dropped the box on Ortiz' foot.
    C. Harper refused to follow Meehan's orders and lifted a box too heavy for him; he deliberately dropped it when Ortiz tried to help him carry it.
    D. Harper lifted a box and felt a pain in his back; Ortiz tried to help Harper put the box down but Harper accidentally dropped it on Ortiz' foot.

    20.____

21. One of the Laborers at the scene of the accident was asked his version of the incident.
    Which information obtained from this witness would be LEAST important for including in the accident report?
    A. His opinion as to the cause of the accident
    B. How much of the accident he saw
    C. His personal opinion of the victims
    D. His name and address

    21.____

22. What should be the MAIN objective of writing a report about the incident described in the above paragraph? To
    A. describe the important elements in the accident situation
    B. recommend that such Laborers as Ortiz be advised not to interfere in another's work unless given specific instructions
    C. analyze the problems occurring when there are not enough workers to perform a certain task
    D. illustrate the hazards involved in performing routine everyday tasks

    22.____

23. Which of the following is information *missing* from the above passage but which *should* be included in a report of the incident? The
    A. name of the Laborer's immediate supervisor
    B. contents of the boxes
    C. time at which the accident occurred
    D. object or action that caused the injury to Ortiz' foot

    23.____

24. According to the description of the incident, the accident occurred because
    A. Ortiz attempted to help Harper who resisted his help
    B. Harper failed to follow instructions given him by Meehan
    C. Meehan was not supervising his men as closely as he should have
    D. Harper was not strong enough to carry the box once he lifted it

    24.____

25. Which of the following is MOST important for a foreman to avoid when writing up an official accident report?
    A. Using technical language to describe equipment involved in the accident
    B. Putting in details which might later be judged unnecessary
    C. Giving an opinion as to conditions that contributed to the accident
    D. Recommending discipline for employees who, in his opinion, caused the accident

KEY (CORRECT ANSWERS)

1.	B	11.	B
2.	C	12.	B
3.	A	13.	A
4.	B	14.	A
5.	B	15.	C
6.	D	16.	D
7.	C	17.	A
8.	D	18.	B
9.	A	19.	B
10.	C	20.	D

21.	C
22.	A
23.	C
24.	B
25.	D

TEST 2

DIRECTIONS: Each question or incomplete statement is followed by several suggested answers or completions. Select the one that BEST answers the question or completes the statement. *PRINT THE LETTER OF THE CORRECT ANSWER IN THE SPACE AT THE RIGHT.*

1. Lieutenant X is preparing a report to submit to his commanding officer in order to get approval of a plan of operation he has developed.
   The report starts off with the statement of the problem and continues with the details of the problem. It contains factual information gathered with the help of field and operational personnel. It contains a final conclusion and recommendation for action. The recommendation is supplemented by comments from other precinct staff members on how the recommendations will affect their areas of responsibility. The report also includes directives and general orders ready for the commanding officer's signature. In addition, it has two statements of objections presented by two precinct staff members.
   Which one of the following, if any, is either an item that Lieutenant X should have included in his report and which is not mentioned above, or is an item which Lieutenant X improperly did include in his report?
   A. Considerations of alternative courses of action and their consequences should have been covered in the report.
   B. The additions containing undocumented objections to the recommended course of action should not have been included as part of the report.
   C. A statement on the qualifications of Lieutenant X, which would support his expertness in the field under consideration, should have been included in the report.
   D. The directives and general orders should not have been prepared and included in the report until the commanding officer had approved the recommendations.
   E. None of the above, since Lieutenant X's report was both proper and complete.

2. During a visit to a section, the district supervisor criticizes the method being used by the assistant foreman to prepare a certain report and orders him to modify the method. This change ordered by the district supervisor is in direct conflict with the specific orders of the foreman.
   In this situation, it would be BEST for the assistant foreman to
   A. change the method and tell the foreman about the change at the first opportunity
   B. change the method and rely on the district supervisor to notify the foreman
   C. report the matter to the foreman and delay the preparation of the report
   D. ask the district supervisor to discuss the matter with the foreman but use the old method for the time being

143

3. A department officer should realize that the MOST usual reason for writing a report is to
   A. give orders and follow up their execution
   B. establish a permanent record
   C. raise questions
   D. supply information

4. A very important report which is being prepared by a department officer will soon be due on the desk of the district supervisor. No typing help is available at this time for the officer.
   For the officer to write out this report in longhand in such a situation would be
   A. *bad*; such a report would not make the impression a typed report would
   B. *good*; it is important to get the report in on time
   C. *bad*; the district supervisor should not be required to read longhand reports
   D. *good*; it would call attention to the difficult conditions under which this section must work

5. In a well-written report, the length of each paragraph in the report should be
   A. varied according to the content
   B. not over 300 words
   C. pretty nearly the same
   D. gradually longer as the report is developed and written

6. A clerk in the headquarters office complains to you about the way in which you are filing out a certain report.
   It would be BEST for you to
   A. tell the clerk that you are following official procedures in filling out the report
   B. ask to be referred to the clerk's superior
   C. ask the clerk exactly what is wrong with the way in which you are filling out the report
   D. tell the clerk that you are following the directions of the district supervisor

7. The use of an outline to help in writing a report is
   A. *desirable*, in order to insure good organization and coverage
   B. *necessary*, so it can be used as an introduction to the report itself
   C. *undesirable*, since it acts as a straightjacket and may result in an unbalanced report
   D. *desirable*, if you know your immediate supervisor reads reports with extreme care and attention

8. It is advisable that a department officer do his paper work and report writing as soon as he has completed an inspection MAINLY because
   A. there are usually deadlines to be met
   B. it insures a steady work-flow
   C. he may not have time for this later
   D. the facts are then freshest in his mind

9. Before you turn in a report you have written of an investigation that you have made, you discover some additional information you didn't know about before. Whether or not you re-write the report to include this additional information should depend MAINLY on the
    A. amount of time remaining before the report is due
    B. established policy of the department covering the subject matter of the report
    C. bearing this information will have on the conclusions of the report
    D. number of people who will eventually review the report

10. When a supervisory officer submits a periodic report to the district supervisor, he should realize that the CHIEF importance of such a report is that it
    A. is the principal method of checking on the efficiency of the supervisor and his subordinates
    B. is something to which frequent reference will be made
    C. eliminates the need for any personal follow-up or inspection by higher echelons
    D. permits the district supervisor to exercise his functions of direction, supervision, and control better

11. Conclusions and recommendations are usually placed at the end rather than at the beginning of a report because
    A. the person preparing the report may decide to change some of the conclusions and recommendations before he reaches the end of the report
    B. they are the most important part of the report
    C. they can be judged better by the person to whom the report is sent after he reads the facts and investigators which come earlier in the report
    D. they can be referred to quickly when needed without reading the rest of the report

12. The use of the same method of record-keeping and reporting by all agency sections is
    A. *desirable*, MAINLY because it saves time in section operations
    B. *undesirable*, MAINLY because it kills the initiative of the individual section foreman
    C. *desirable*, MAINLY because it will be easier for the administrator to evaluate and compare section operations
    D. *undesirable*, MAINLY because operations vary from section to section and uniform record-keeping and reporting is not appropriate

13. The GREATEST benefit the section officer will have from keeping complete and accurate records and reports of section operations is that
    A. he will find it easier to run his section efficiently
    B. he will need less equipment
    C. he will need less manpower
    D. the section will run smoothly when he is out

14. You have prepared a report to your superior and are ready to send it forward. But on re-reading it, you think some parts are not clearly expressed and your superior ay have difficulty getting your point.
    Of the following, it would be BEST for you to
    A. give the report to one of your men to read, and if he has no trouble understanding it send it through
    B. forward the report and call your superior the next day to ask whether it was all right
    C. forward the report as is; higher echelons should be able to understand any report prepared by a section officer
    D. do the report over, re-writing the sections you are in doubt about

15. The BEST of the following statements concerning reports is that
    A. a carelessly written report may give the reader an impression of inaccuracy
    B. correct grammar and English are unimportant if the main facts are given
    C. every man should be required to submit a daily work report
    D. the longer and more wordy a report is, the better it will read

16. In writing a report, the question of whether or not to include certain material could be determined BEST by considering the
    A. amount of space the material will occupy in the report
    B. amount of time to be spent in gathering the material
    C. date of the material
    D. value of the material to the superior who will read the report

17. Suppose you are submitting a fairly long report to your superior.
    The one of the following sections that should come FIRST in this report is a
    A. description of how you gathered material
    B. discussion of possible objections to your recommendations
    C. plan of how your recommendations can be put into practice
    D. statement of the problem dealt with

Questions 18-20.

DIRECTIONS: A foreman is asked to write a report on the incident described in the following passage. Answer Questions 18 through 20 based on the following information.

On March 10, Henry Moore, a laborer, was in the process of transferring some equipment from the machine shop to the third floor. He was using a dolly to perform this task and, as he was wheeling the material through the machine shop, laborer Bob Greene called to him. As Henry turned to respond to Bob, he jammed the dolly into Larry Mantell's leg, knocking Larry down in the process and causing the heavy drill that Larry was holding to fall on Larry's foot. Larry started rubbing his foot and then, infuriated, jumped up and punched Henry in the jaw. The force of the blow drove Henry's head back against the wall. Henry did not fight back; he appeared to be dazed. An ambulance was called to take Henry to the hospital, and the ambulance attendant told the foreman that it appeared likely that Henry had suffered a concussion. Larry's injuries consisted of some bruises, but he refused medical attention.

18. An adequate report of the above incident should give as minimum information the names of the persons involved, the names of the witnesses, the date and the time that each event took place, and the

18.____

    A. names of the ambulance attendants
    B. names of all the employees working in the machine shop
    C. location where the accident occurred
    D. nature of the previous safety training each employee had been given

19. The only one of the following which is NOT a fact is

19.____

    A. Bob called to Henry
    B. Larry suffered a concussion
    C. Larry rubbed his foot
    D. the incident took place in the machine shop

20. Which of the following would be the MOST accurate summary of the incident for the foreman to put in his report of the accident?

20.____

    A. Larry Mantell punched Henry Moore because a drill fell on his foot and he was angry. Then Henry fell and suffered a concussion.
    B. Henry Moore accidentally jammed a dolly into Larry Mantell's foot, knocking Larry down. Larry punched Henry, pushing him into the wall and causing him to bang his head against the wall.
    C. Bob Greene called Henry Moore. A dolly than jammed into Larry Mantell and knocked him down. Larry punched Henry who tripped and suffered some bruises. An ambulance was called.
    D. A drill fell on Larry Mantell's foot. Larry jumped up suddenly and punched Henry Moore and pushed him into the wall. Henry may have suffered a concussion as a result of falling.

Questions 21-25.

DIRECTIONS: Questions 21 through 25 are to be answered ONLY on the basis of the information provided in the following passage.

    A written report is a communication of information from one person to another. It is an account of some matter especially investigated, however routine that matter may be. The ultimate basis of any good written report is facts, which become known through observation and verification. Good written reports may seem to be no more than general ideas and opinions. However, in such cases, the facts leading to these opinions were gathered, verified, and reported earlier, and the opinions are dependent upon these facts. Good style, proper form, and emphasis cannot make a good written report out of unreliable information and bad judgment; but, on the other hand, solid investigation and brilliant thinking are not likely to become very useful until they are effectively communicated to others. If a person's work calls for written reports, then his work is often no better than his written reports.

21. Based on the information in the above passage, it can be concluded that opinions expressed in a report should be
    A. based on facts which are gathered and reported
    B. emphasized repeatedly when they result from a special investigation
    C. kept to a minimum
    D. separated from the body of the report

22. In the above passage, the one of the following which is mentioned as a way of establishing facts is
    A. authority
    B. communication
    C. reporting
    D. verification

23. According to the above passage, the characteristic shared by ALL written reports is that they are
    A. accounts of routine matters
    B. transmissions of information
    C. reliable and logical
    D. written in proper form

24. Which of the following conclusions can logically be drawn from the information given in the above passage?
    A. Brilliant thinking can make up for unreliable information in a report.
    B. One method of judging an individual's work is the quality of the written reports he is required to submit.
    C. Proper form and emphasis can make a good report out of unreliable information.
    D. Good written reports that seem to be no more than general ideas should be rewritten.

25. Which of the following suggested titles would be MOST appropriate for this passage?
    A. Gathering and Organizing Facts
    B. Techniques of Observation
    C. Nature and Purpose of Reports
    D. Reports and Opinions: Differences and Similarities

KEY (CORRECT ANSWERS)

1. A
2. A
3. D
4. B
5. A

6. C
7. A
8. D
9. C
10. D

11. C
12. C
13. A
14. D
15. A

16. D
17. D
18. C
19. B
20. B

21. A
22. D
23. B
24. B
25. C

TEST 3

DIRECTIONS: Each question or incomplete statement is followed by several suggested answers or completions. Select the one that BEST answers the question or completes the statement. *PRINT THE LETTER OF THE CORRECT ANSWER IN THE SPACE AT THE RIGHT.*

Questions 1-5.

DIRECTIONS: The following is an accident report similar to those used in departments for reporting accidents. Questions 1 through 5 are be answered using ONLY the information given in this report.

ACCIDENT REPORT

FROM: John Doe	DATE OF REPORT: June 23	
TITLE: Sanitation Worker		
DATE OF ACCIDENT: June 22 time 3 AM PM	CITY: Metropolitan	
PLACE: 1489 Third Avenue		
VEHICLE NO. 1	VEHICLE NO. 2	
OPERATOR: John Doe, Sanitation Worker Title	OPERATOR: Richard Roe	
VEHICLE CODE NO: 14-238	ADDRESS: 498 High Street	
LICENSE NO.: 0123456	OWNER: Henry Roe ADDRESS:786 E.83 St.	LIC. NO.: 5N1492
DESCRIPTION OF ACCIDENT: Light green Chevrolet sedan while trying to pass drove in to rear side of sanitation truck which had stopped to collect garbage. No one was injured but there was property damage.		
NATURE OF DAMAGE TO PRIVATE VEHICLE: Right front fender crushed, bumper bent		
DAMAGE TO CITY VEHICLE: Front of left rear fender pushed in. Paint scraped.		
NAME OF WITNESS: Frank Brown	ADDRESS: 48 Kingsway	
SIGNATURE OF PERSON MAKING THIS REPORT *John Doe*	BADGE NO.: 428	

1. Of the following, the one which has been omitted from this accident report is the
   A. location of the accident
   B. drivers of the vehicles involved
   C. traffic situation at the time of the accident
   D. owners of the vehicles involved

2. The address of the driver of Vehicle No. 1 is not required because he
   A. is employed by the department
   B. is not the owner of the vehicle
   C. reported the accident
   D. was injured in the accident

3. The report indicates that the driver of Vehicle No. 2 was PROBABLY
   A. passing on the wrong side of the truck
   B. not wearing his glasses
   C. not injured in the accident
   D. driving while intoxicated

4. The number of people *specifically* referred to in this report is 4.____
 A. 3 B. 4 C. 5 D. 6

5. The license number of Vehicle No. 1 is 5.____
 A. 428 B. 5N1492 C. 14-238 D. 0123456

6. In a report of unlawful entry into department premises, it is LEAST important to include the 6.____
 A. estimated value of the property missing
 B. general description of the premises
 C. means used to get into the premises
 D. time and date of entry

7. In a report of an accident, it is LEAST important to include the 7.____
 A. name of the insurance company of the person injured in the accident
 B. probable cause of the accident
 C. time and place of the accident
 D. names and addresses of all witnesses of the accident

8. Of the following, the one which is NOT required in the preparation of a weekly functional expense report is the 8.____
 A. hourly distribution of the time by proper heading in accordance with the actual work performed
 B. signatures of officers not involved in the preparation of the report
 C. time records of the men who appear on the payroll of the respective locations
 D. time records of men working in other districts assigned to this location

KEY (CORRECT ANSWERS)

1.	C	5.	D
2.	A	6.	B
3.	C	7.	A
4.	B	8.	B

BASIC FUNDAMENTALS OF DRAWINGS AND SPECIFICATIONS

A building project may be broadly divided into two major phases: (1) the DESIGN phase, and (2) the CONSTRUCTION phase. In accordance with a number of considerations, of which the function and desired appearance of the building are perhaps the most important, the architect first conceives the building in his mind's eye, as it were, and then sets his concept down on paper in the form of PRESENTATION drawings. Presentation drawings are usually done in PERSPECTIVE, by employing the PICTORIAL drawing techniques.

Next the architect and the engineer, working together, decide upon the materials to be used in the structure and the construction methods which are to be followed. The engineer determines the loads which supporting members will carry and the strength qualities the members must have to bear the loads. He also designs the mechanical systems of the structure, such as the lighting, heating, and plumbing systems. The end-result of all this is the preparation of architectural and engineering DESIGN SKETCHES. The purpose of these sketches is to guide draftsmen in the preparation of CONSTRUCTION DRAWINGS.

The construction drawings, plus the SPECIFICATIONS to be described later, are the chief sources of information for the supervisors and craftsman responsible for the actual work of construction. Construction drawings consist mostly of ORTHOGRAPHIC views, prepared by draftsmen who employ the standard technical drawing techniques, and who use the symbols and other designations

You should make a thorough study of symbols before proceeding further with this chapter. Figure 1 illustrates the conventional symbols for the more common types of material used on structures. Figure 2 shows the more common symbols used for doors and windows.

Before you can interpret construction drawings correctly, you must also have some knowledge of the structure and of the terminology for common structural members.

I. STRUCTURES

The main parts of a structure are the LOAD-BEARING STRUCTURAL MEMBERS, which support and transfer the loads on the structure while remaining in equilibrium with each other. The places where members are connected to other members are called JOINTS. The sum total of the load supported by the structural members at a particular instant is equal to the total DEAD LOAD plus the total LIVE LOAD.

The total dead load is the total weight of the structure, which gradually increases, of course, as the structure rises, and remains constant once it is completed. The total live load is the total weight of movable objects (such as people, furniture, bridge traffic or the like) which the structure happens to be supporting at a particular instant.

The live loads in a structure are transmitted through the various load-bearing structural members to the ultimate support of the earth as follows. Immediate or direct support for the live loads is provided by HORIZTONAL members; these are in turn supported by VERTICAL members; which in turn are supported by FOUNDATIONS and/or FOOTINGS; and these are, finally, supported by the earth.

The ability of the earth to support a load is called the SOIL BEARING CAPACITY; it is determined by test and measured in pounds per square foot. Soil bearing capacity varies considerably with different types of soil, and a soil of given bearing capacity will bear a heavier load on a wide foundation or footing than it will on a narrow one.

VERTICAL STRUCTURAL MEMBERS

Vertical structural members are high-strength columns; they are sometimes called PILLARS in buildings. Outside wall columns and inside bottom-floor columns, usually rest directly on footings. Outside-wall columns usually extend from the footing or foundation to the roof line. Inside bottom-floor columns extend upward from footings or foundations to horizontal members which in turn support the

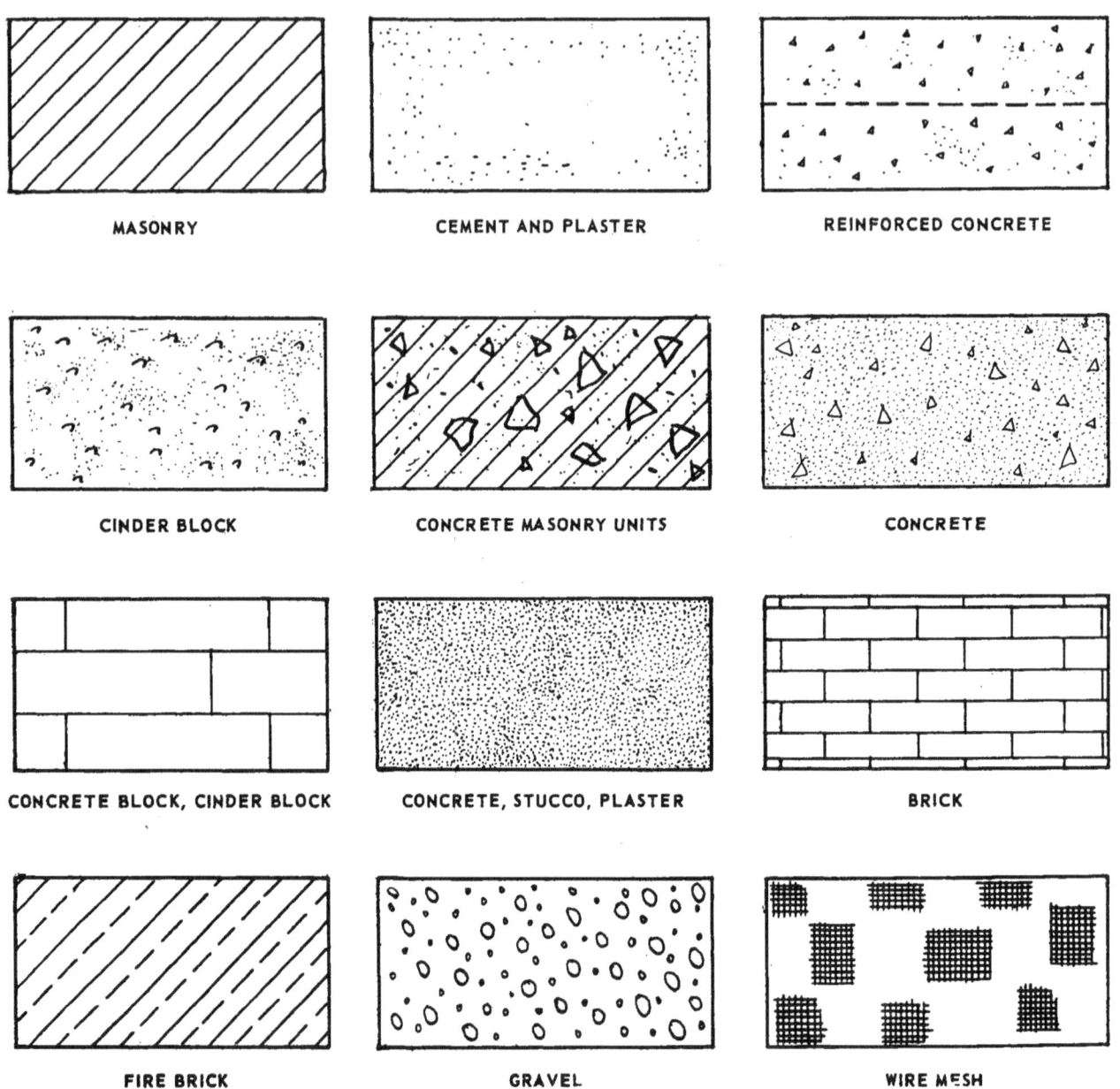

Figure 1.—Material symbols.

first floor. Upper floor columns usually are located directly over lower floor columns.

A PIER in building construction might be called a short column. It may rest directly on a footing, or it may be simply set or driven in the ground. Building piers usually support the lowermost horizontal structural members.

In bridge construction a pier is a vertical member which provides intermediate support for the bridge superstructure.

The chief vertical structural members in light frame construction are called STUDS. They are supported on horizontal members called SILLS or SOLE PLATES, and are topped by horizontal members called TOP PLATES or RAFTER PLATES. CORNER POSTS are enlarged studs, as it were, located at the building corners. In early FULL-FRAME construction a corner post was usually a solid piece of larger timber. In most modern construction BUILT-UP

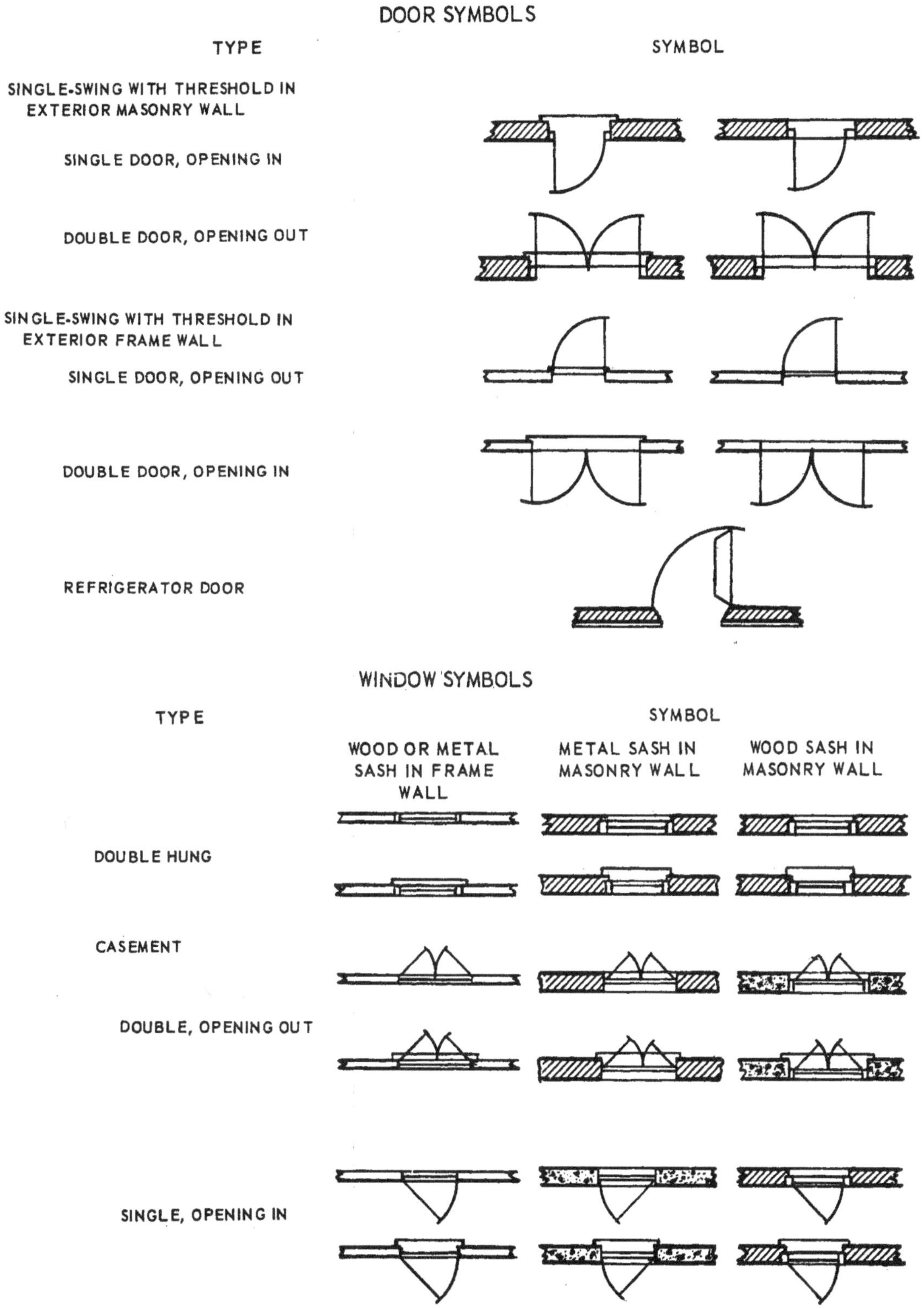

DOOR SYMBOLS

TYPE	SYMBOL
SINGLE-SWING WITH THRESHOLD IN EXTERIOR MASONRY WALL	
SINGLE DOOR, OPENING IN	
DOUBLE DOOR, OPENING OUT	
SINGLE-SWING WITH THRESHOLD IN EXTERIOR FRAME WALL	
SINGLE DOOR, OPENING OUT	
DOUBLE DOOR, OPENING IN	
REFRIGERATOR DOOR	

WINDOW SYMBOLS

TYPE	SYMBOL		
	WOOD OR METAL SASH IN FRAME WALL	METAL SASH IN MASONRY WALL	WOOD SASH IN MASONRY WALL
DOUBLE HUNG			
CASEMENT			
DOUBLE, OPENING OUT			
SINGLE, OPENING IN			

Figure 2 —Architectural symbols (door and windows).

corner posts are used, consisting of various numbers of ordinary studs, nailed together in various ways.

HORIZONTAL STRUCTURAL MEMBERS

In technical terminology, a horizontal load-bearing structural member which spans a space, and which is supported at both ends, is called a BEAM. A member which is FIXED at one end only is called a CANTILEVER. Steel members which consist of solid pieces of the regular structural steel shapes are called beams, but a type of steel member which is actually a light truss is called an OPEN-WEB STEEL JOIST or a BAR STEEL JOIST.

Horizontal structural members which support the ends of floor beams or joists in wood frame construction are called SILLS, GIRTS, or GIRDERS, depending on the type of framing being done and the location of the member in the structure. Horizontal members which support studs are called SILL or SOLE PLATES. Horizontal members which support the wall-ends of rafters are called RAFTER PLATES. Horizontal members which assume the weight of concrete or masonry walls above door and window openings are called LINTELS.

TRUSSES

A beam of given strength, without intermediate supports below, can support a given load over only a certain maximum span. If the span is wider than this maximum, intermediate supports, such as a column must be provided for the beam. Sometimes it is not feasible or possible to install intermediate supports. When such is the case, a TRUSS may be used instead of a beam.

A beam consists of a single horizontal member. A truss, however, is a framework, consisting of two horizontal (or nearly horizontal) members, joined together by a number of vertical and/or inclined members. The horizontal members are called the UPPER and LOWER CHORDS; the vertical and/or inclined members are called the WEB MEMBERS.

ROOF MEMBERS

The horizontal or inclined members which provide support to a roof are called RAFTERS. The lengthwise (right angle to the rafters) member which support the peak ends of the rafters in a roof is called the RIDGE. (The ridge may be called the Ridge board, the Ridge PIECE, or the Ridge pole.) Lengthwise members other than ridges are called PURLINS. In wood frame construction the wall ends of rafters are supported on horizontal members called RAFTER PLATES, which are in turn supported by the outside wall studs. In concrete or masonry wall construction, the wall ends of rafters may be anchored directly on the walls, or on plates bolted to the walls.

II. CONSTRUCTION DRAWINGS

Construction drawings are drawings in which as much construction information as possible is presented GRAPHICALLY, or by means of pictures. Most construction drawings consist of ORTHOGRAPHIC views. GENERAL drawings consist of PLANS AND ELEVATIONS, drawn on a relatively small scale. DETAIL drawings consist of SECTIONS and DETAILS, drawn on a relatively large scale.

PLANS

A PLAN view is, as you know, a view of an object or area as it would appear if projected onto a horizontal plane passed through or held above the object or area. The most common construction plans are PLOT PLANS (also called SITE PLANS), FOUNDATION PLANS, FLOOR PLANS, and FRAMING PLANS.

A PLOT PLAN shows the contours, boundaries, roads, utilities, trees, structures, and any other significant physical features pertaining to or located on the site. The locations of proposed structures are indicated by appropriate outlines or floor plans. By locating the corners of a proposed structure at given distances from a REFERENCE or BASE line (which is shown on the plan and which can be located on the site), the plot plan provides essential data for those who will lay out the building lines. By indicating the elevations of existing and proposed earth surfaces (by means of CONTOUR lines), the plot plan provides essential data for the graders and excavators.

A FOUNDATION PLAN (fig. 3) is a plan view of a structure projected on a horizontal plane passed through (in imagination, of course) at the level of the tops of the foundations. The plan shown in figure 3 tells you that the main foundation of this structure will consist of a rectangular 12-in. concrete block wall, 22 ft

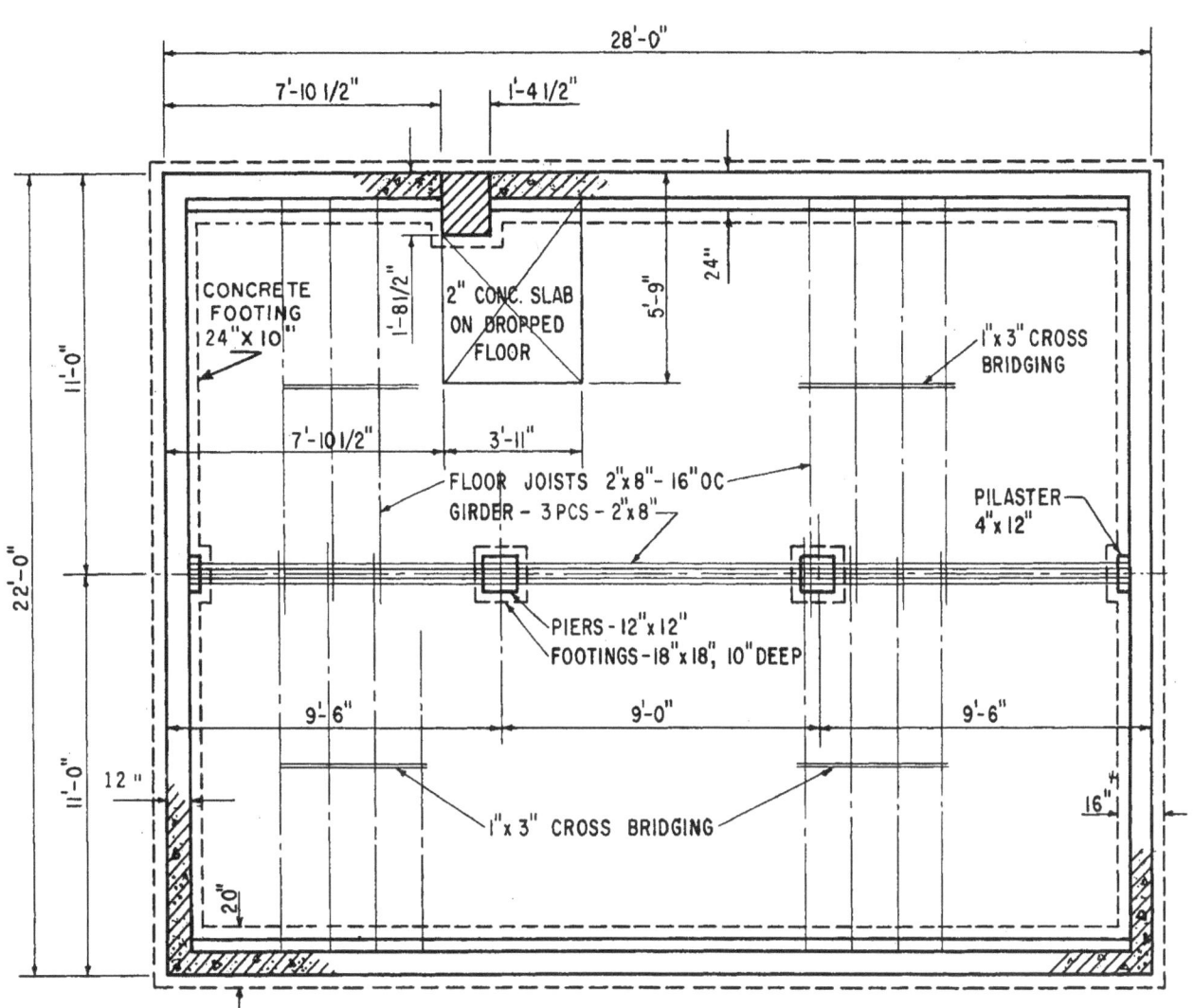

Figure 3.—Foundation plan.

wide by 28 ft long, centered on a concrete footing 24 in. wide. Besides the outside wall and footing, there will be two 12-in. square piers, centered on 18-in. square footings, and located on center 9 ft 6 in. from the end wall building lines. These piers will support a ground floor center-line girder.

A FLOOR PLAN (also called a BUILDING PLAN) is developed as shown in figure 4. Information on a floor plan includes the lengths, thicknesses, and character of the building walls at that particular floor, the widths and locations of door and window openings, the lengths and character of partitions, the number and arrangement of rooms, and the types and locations of utility installations. A typical floor plan is shown in figure 5.

FRAMING PLANS show the dimensions, numbers, and arrangement of structural members in wood frame construction. A simple FLOOR FRAMING PLAN is superimposed on the foundation plan shown in figure 3. From this foundation plan you learn that the ground-floor joists in this structure will consist of 2 x 8's, lapped at the girder, and spaced 16 in. O. C. The plan also shows that each row of joists is to be braced by a row of 1 x 3 cross bridging. For a more complicated floor framing problem, a framing plan like the one shown in figure 2-6 would be required. This plan

  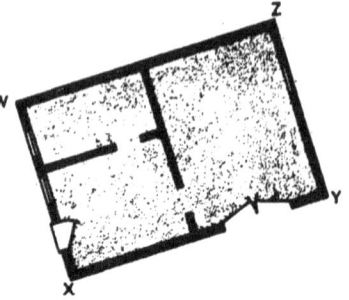

PERSPECTIVE VIEW OF A BUILDING SHOWING CUTTING PLANE WXY

PREVIOUS PERSPECTIVE VIEW AT CUTTING PLANE WXYZ, TOP REMOVED

DEVELOPED FLOOR PLAN WXYZ

Figure 4.—Floor plan development.

shows, among other things, the arrangement of joists and other members around stair wells and other floor openings.

A WALL FRAMING PLAN gives similar information with regard to the studs, corner posts, bracing, sills, plates, and other structural members in the walls. Since it is a view on a vertical plane, a wall framing plan is not a plan in the strict technical sense. However, the practice of calling it a plan has become a general custom. A ROOF FRAMING PLAN gives similar information with regard to the rafters, ridge, purlins, and other structural members in the roof.

A UTILITY PLAN is a floor plan which shows the layout of a heating, electrical, plumbing, or other utility system. Utility plans are used primarily by the ratings responsible for the utilities, but they are important to the Builder as well. Most utility installations require the leaving of openings in walls, floors, and roofs for the admission or installation of utility features. The Builder who is placing a concrete foundation wall must study the utility plans to determine the number, sizes, and locations of the openings he must leave for utilities.

Figure 7 shows a heating plan. Figure 8 shows an electrical plan.

ELEVATIONS

ELEVATIONS show the front, rear, and sides of a structure projected on vertical planes parallel to the planes of the sides. Front, rear, right side, and left side elevations of a small building are shown in figure 9.

As you can see, the elevations give you a number of important vertical dimensions, such as the perpendicular distance from the finish floor to the top of the rafter plate and from the finish floor to the tops of door and window finished openings. They also show the locations and characters of doors and windows. Dimensions of window sash and dimensions and character of lintels, however, are usually set forth in a WINDOW SCHEDULE.

A SECTION view is a view of a cross-section, developed as indicated in figure 10. By general custom, the term is confined to views of cross-sections cut by vertical planes. A floor plan or foundation plan, cut by a horizontal plane, is, technically speaking, a section view as well as a plan view, but it is seldom called a section.

The most important sections are the WALL sections. Figure 11 shows three wall sections for three alternate types of construction for the building shown in figures 3, 5, 7 and 8. The angled arrows marked "A" in figure 5 indicate the location of the cutting plane for the sections.

The wall sections are of primary importance to the supervisors of construction and to the craftsmen who will do the actual building. Take the first wall section, marked "masonry construction," for example. Starting at the bottom, you learn that the footing will be concrete, 2 ft wide and 10 in. high. The vertical distance of the bottom of the footing below FINISHED GRADE (level of the finished earth surface around the house) "varies"—meaning that it will depend on the soil-bearing capacity at the particular site. The foundation wall will consist of

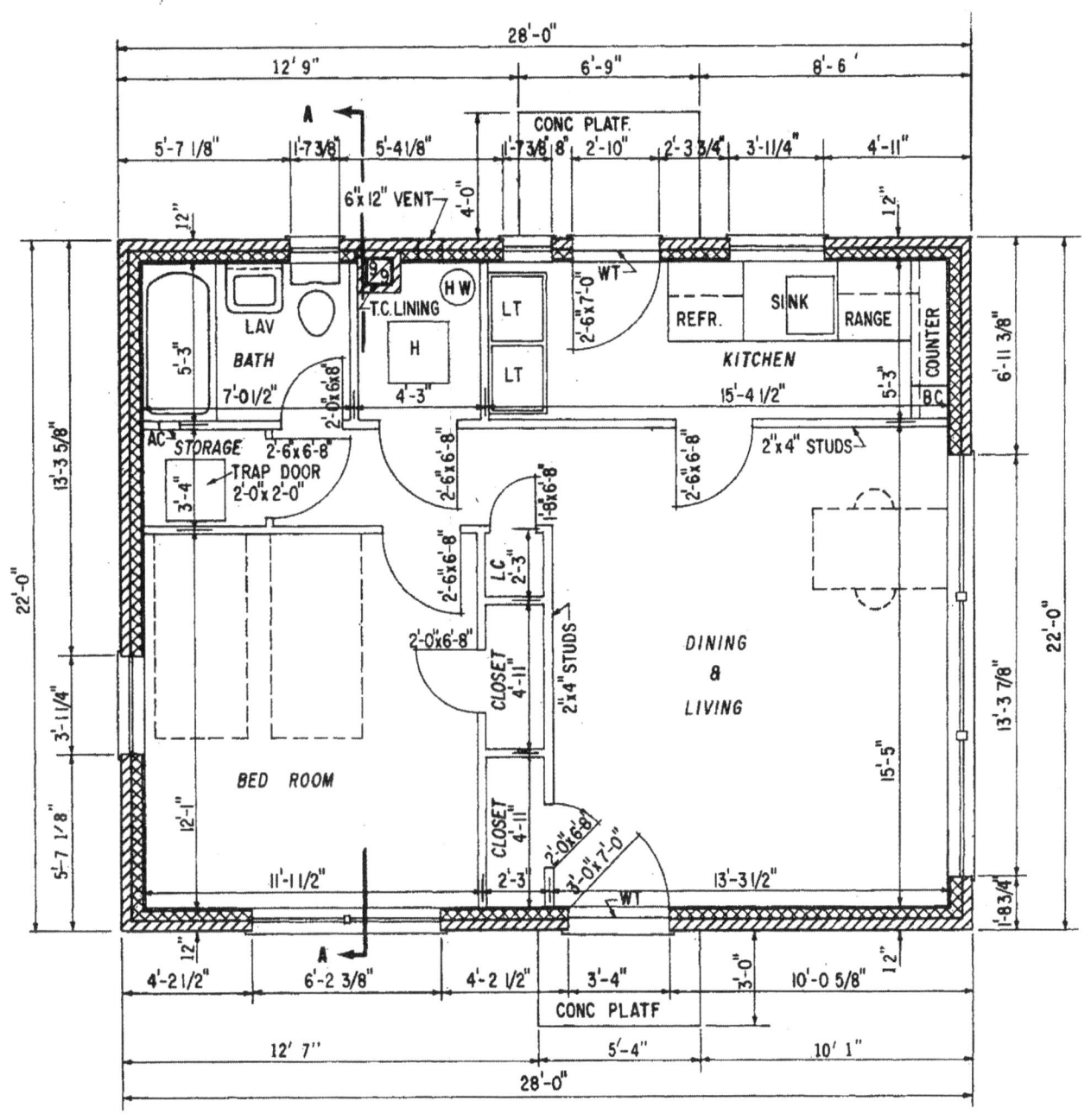

Figure 5.—Floor plan.

12-in. CMU, centered on the footing. Twelve-inch blocks will extend up to an unspecified distance below grade, where a 4-in. brick FACING (dimension indicated in the middle wall section) begins. Above the line of the bottom of the facing, it is obvious that 8-in. instead of 12-in. blocks will be used in the foundation wall.

The building wall above grade will consist of a 4-in. brick FACING TIER, backed by a BACKING TIER of 4-in. cinder blocks. The floor joists, consisting of 2 x 8's placed 16 in. O.C., will be anchored on 2 x 4 sills bolted to the top of the foundation wall. Every third joist will be additionally secured by a 2 x 1/4 STRAP ANCHOR embedded in the cinder block backing tier of the building wall.

The window (window B in the plan front elevation, fig. 9) will have a finished opening

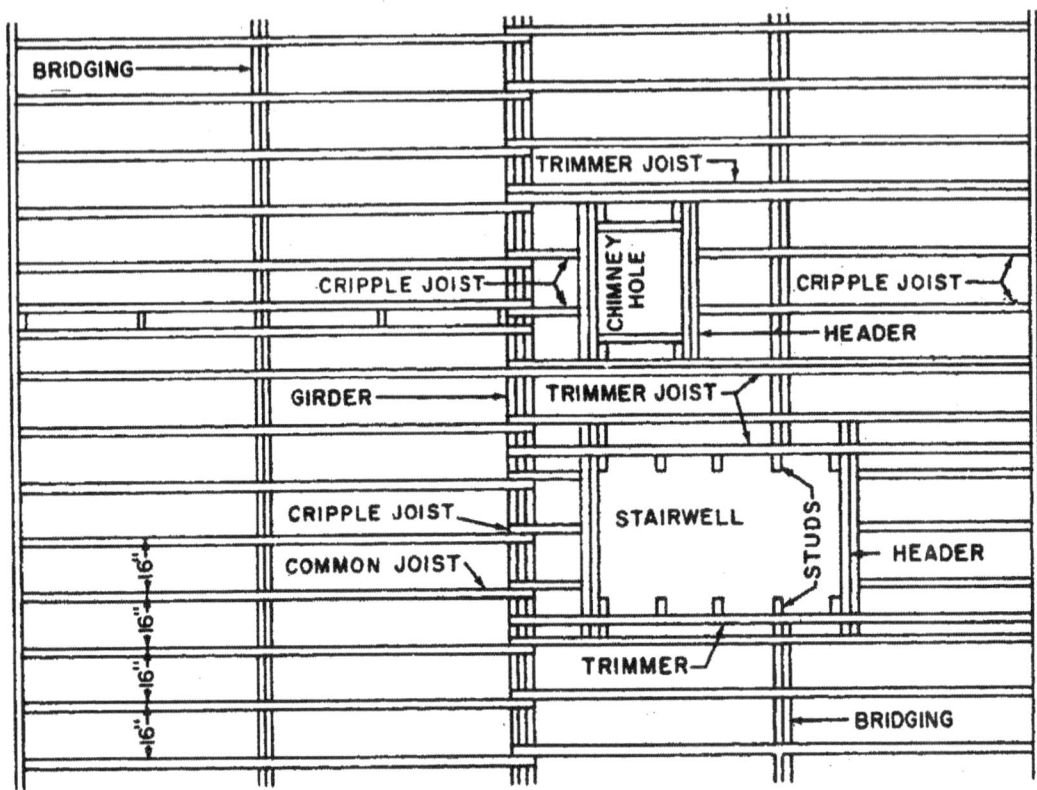

Figure 6.—Floor framing plan.

4 ft 2-5/8 in. high. The bottom of the opening will come 2 ft 11-3/4 in. above the line of the finished floor. As indicated in the wall section, (fig. 11) 13 masonry COURSES (layers of masonry units) above the finished floor line will amount to a vertical distance of 2 ft 11-3/4 in. As also indicated, another 19 courses will amount to the prescribed vertical dimension of the finished window opening.

Window framing details, including the placement and cross-sectional character of the lintel, are shown. The building wall will be carried 10-1/4 in., less the thickness of a 2 x 8 RAFTER PLATE, above the top of the window finished opening. The total vertical distance from the top of the finished floor to the top of the rafter plate will be 8 ft 2-1/4 in. Ceiling joists and rafters will consist of 2 x 6's, and the roof covering will consist of composition shingles laid on wood sheathing.

Flooring will consist of a wood finisher floor laid on a wood subfloor. Inside walls will be finished with plaster on lath (except on masonry wall which would be with or without lath as directed). A minimum of 2 vertical feet of crawl space will extend below the bottoms of the floor joists.

The middle wall section in figure 2-11 gives you similar information for a similar building constructed with wood frame walls and a DOUBLE-HUNG window. The third wall section shown in the figure gives you similar information for a similar building constructed with a steel frame, a casement window, and a concrete floor finished with asphalt tile.

DETAILS

DETAIL drawings are drawings which are done on a larger scale than that of the general drawings, and which show features not appearing at all, or appearing on too small a scale, on the general drawings. The wall sections just described are details as well as sections, since

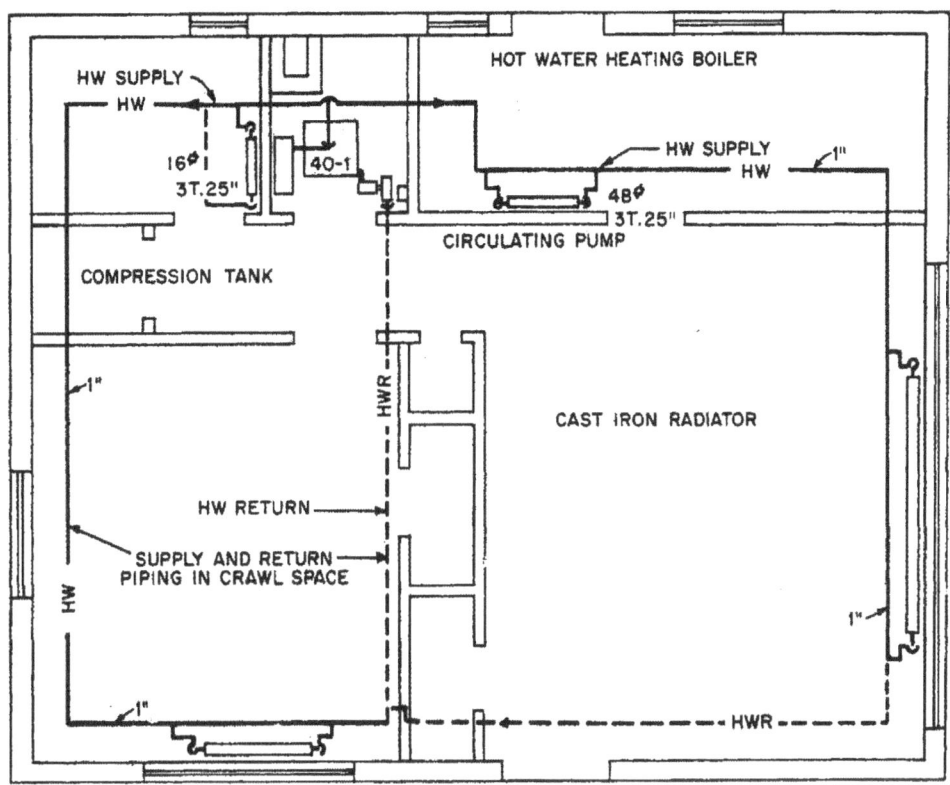

Figure 7.—Heating plan.

they are drawn on a considerable larger scale than the plans and elevations. Framing details at doors, windows, and cornices, which are the most common types of details, are practically always sections.

Details are included whenever the information given in the plans, elevations, and wall sections is not sufficiently "detailed" to guide the craftsmen on the job. Figure 12 shows some typical door and window wood framing details, and an eave detail for a very simple type of CORNICE. You should study these details closely to learn the terminology of framing members.

III. SPECIFICATIONS

The construction drawings contain much of the information about a structure which can be presented GRAPHICALLY (that is, in drawings). A very considerable amount of information can be presented this way, but there is more information which the construction supervisors and artisans must have and which is not adaptable to the graphic form of presentation. Information of this kind includes quality criteria for materials (maximum amounts of aggregate per sack of cement, for example), specified standards of workmanship, prescribed construction methods, and the like.

Information of this kind is presented in a list of written SPECIFICATIONS, familiarly known as the "SPECS." A list of specifications usually begins with a section on GENERAL CONDITIONS. This section starts with a GENERAL DESCRIPTION of the building, including the type of foundation, type or types of windows, character of framing, utilities to be installed, and the like. Next comes a list of DEFINITIONS of terms used in the specs, and next certain routine declarations of responsibility and certain conditions to be maintained on the job.

SPECIFIC CONDITIONS are grouped in sections under headings which describe each of the major construction phases of the job. Separate specifications are written for each phase, and the phases are then combined to more or less follow the usual order of construction sequences on the job. A typical list of sections under "Specific Conditions" follows:

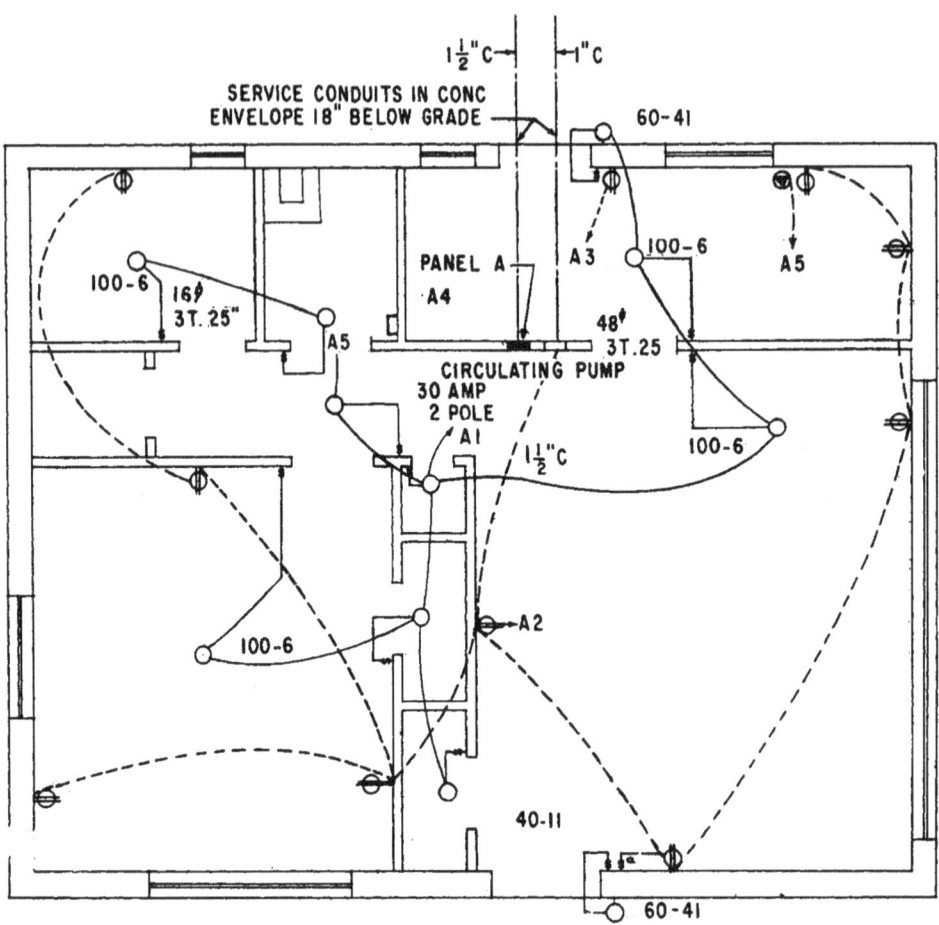

Figure 8.—Electrical plan.

2.—EARTHWORK 3.—CONCRETE 4.—MASONRY 5.—MISCELLANEOUS STEEL AND IRON 6.—CARPENTRY AND JOINERY 7.—LATHING AND PLASTERING 8.—TILE WORK 9.—FINISH FLOORING 10.—GLAZING 11.—FINISHING HARDWARE 12.—PLUMBING 13.—HEATING 14.—ELECTRICAL WORK 15.—FIELD PAINTING.

A section under "Specific Conditions" usually begins with a subsection of GENERAL REQUIREMENTS which apply to the phase of construction being considered. Under Section 6, CARPENTRY AND JOINERY, for example, the first section might go as follows:

6-01. GENERAL REQUIREMENTS. All framing, rough carpentry, and finishing woodwork required for the proper completion of the building shall be provided. All woodwork shall be protected from the weather, and the building shall be thoroughly dry before the finish is placed. All finish shall be dressed, smoothed, and sandpapered at the mill, and in addition shall be hand smoothed and sandpapered at the building where necessary to produce proper finish. Nailing shall be done, as far as practicable, in concealed places, and all nails in finishing work shall be set. All lumber shall be S4S (meaning, "surfaced on 4 sides"); all materials for millwork and finish shall be kiln-dried; all rough and framing lumber shall be air- or kiln-dried. Any cutting, fitting, framing, and blocking necessary for the accommodation of other work shall be provided. All nails, spikes, screws, bolts, plates, clips, and other fastenings and rough hardware necessary for the proper completion of the building shall be provided.

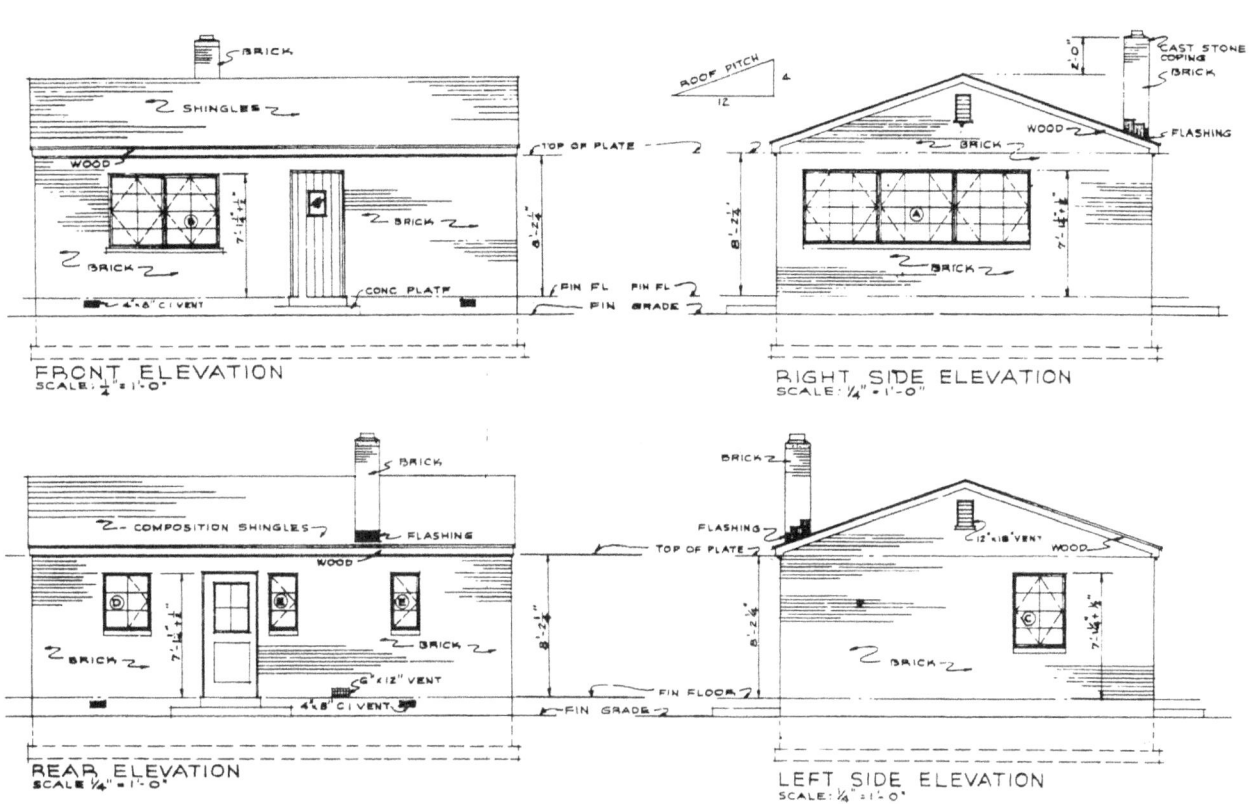

Figure 2-9.—Elevations.

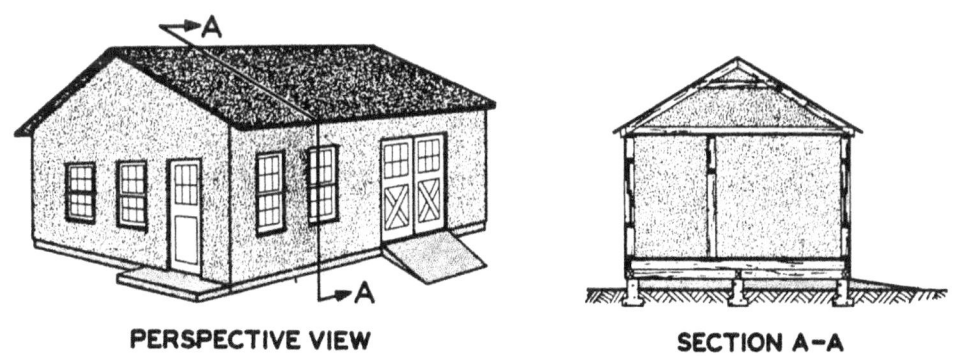

Figure 10.—Development of a section view.

All finishing hardware shall be installed in accordance with the manufacturers' directions. Calking and flashing shall be provided where indicated, or where necessary to provide weathertight construction.

Next after the General Requirements for Carpentry and Joinery, there is generally a subsection on "Grading," in which the kinds and grades of the various woods to be used in the structure are specified. Subsequent subsections

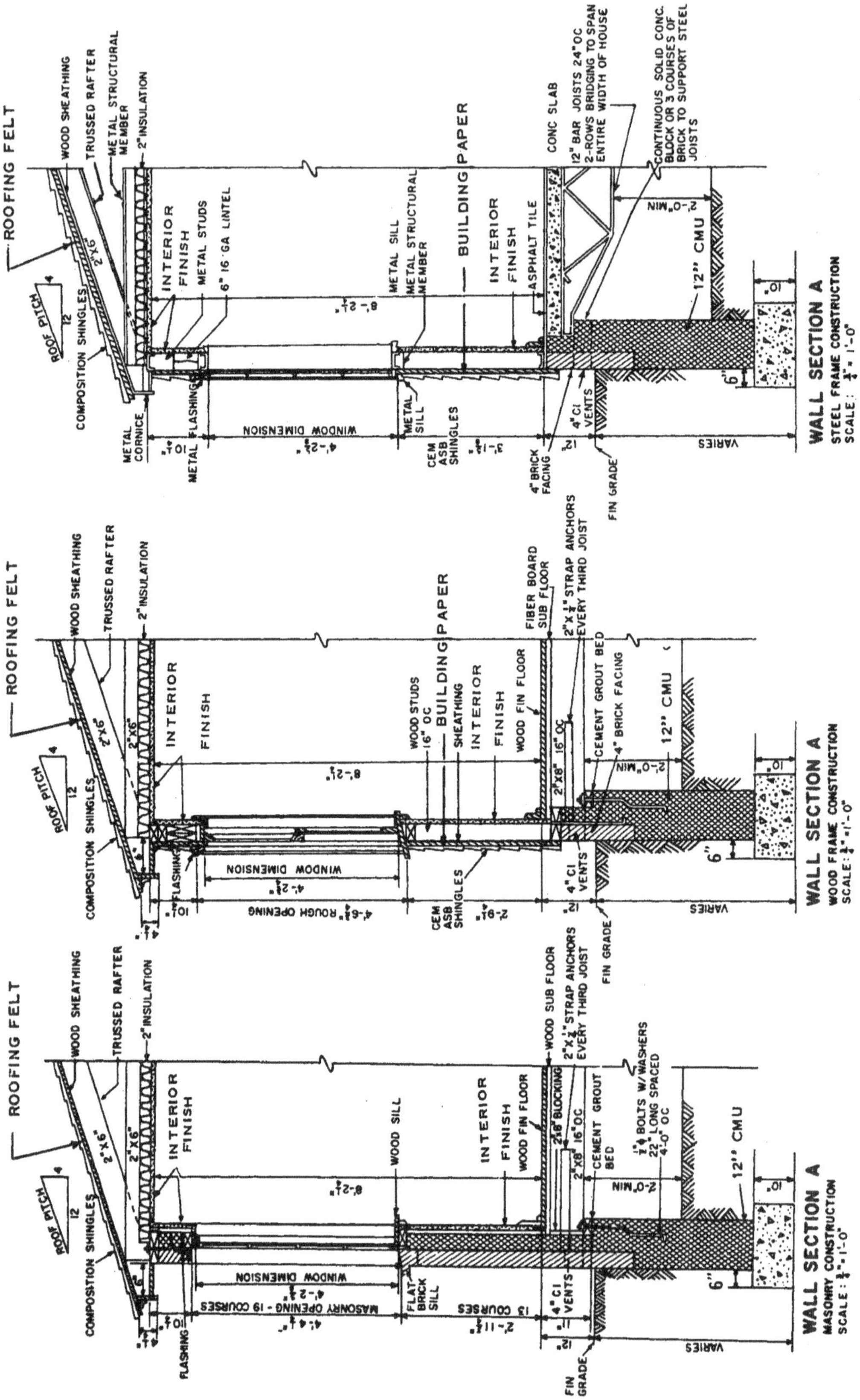

DRAWINGS AND SPECIFICATIONS

Figure 11.—Wall sections

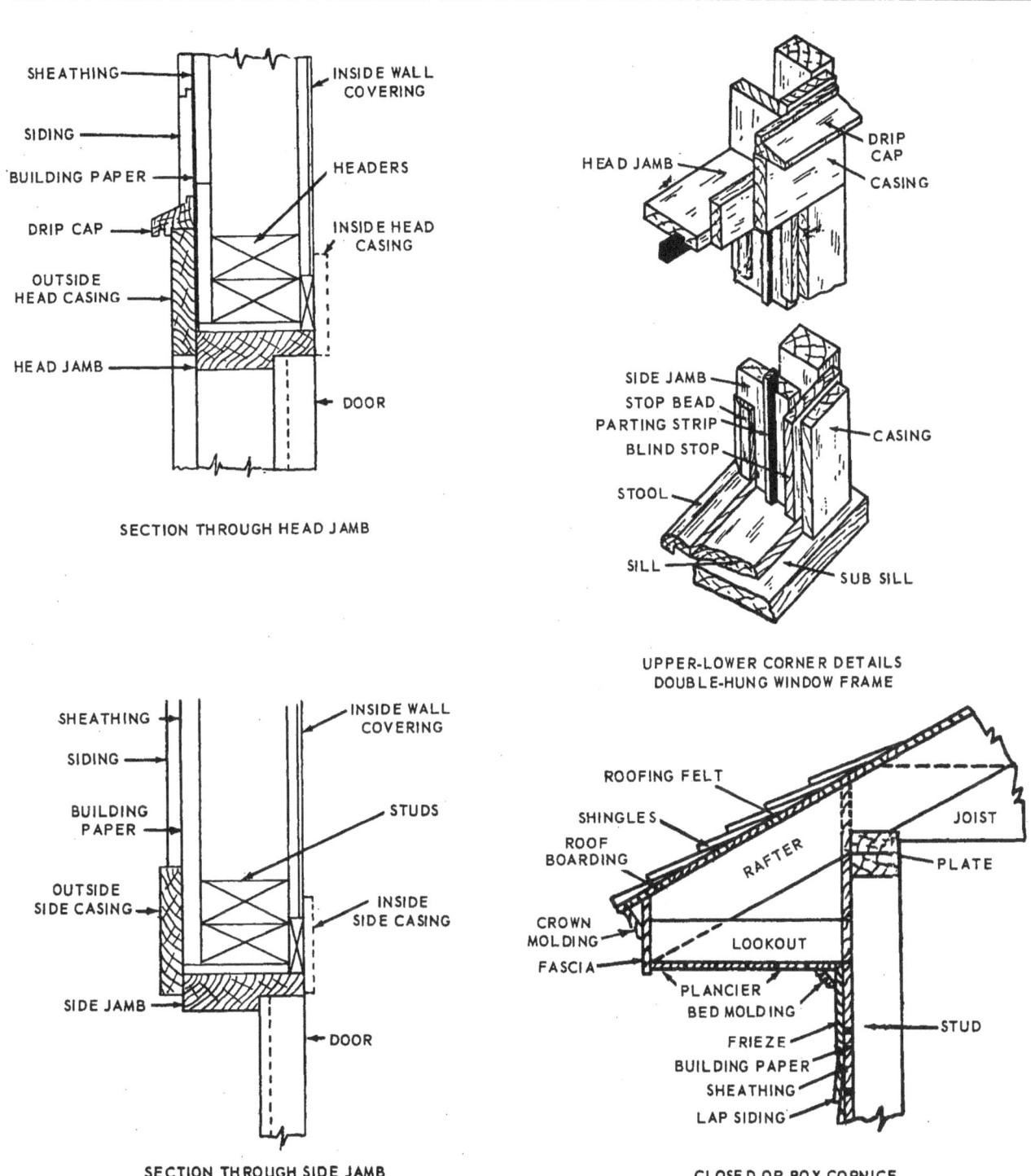

Figure 12.—Door, window and eave details.

specify various quality criteria and standards of workmanship for the various aspects of the rough and finish carpentry work, under such headings as FRAMING; SILLS, PLATES, AND GIRDERS; FLOOR JOISTS AND ROOF RAFTERS; STUDDING; and so on. An example of one of these subsections follows:

> STUDDING for walls and partitions shall have doubled plates and doubled stud caps. Studs shall be set plumb and not to exceed 16-in. centers and in true alignment; they shall be bridged with one row of 2 x 4 pieces, set flatwise, fitted tightly, and nailed securely to each stud. Studding shall be doubled around openings and the heads of openings shall rest on the inner studs. Openings in partitions having widths of 4 ft and over shall be trussed. In wood frame construction, studs shall be trebled at corners to form posts.

From the above samples, you can see that a knowledge of the relevant specifications is as essential to the construction supervisor and the construction artisan as a knowledge of the construction drawings.

It is very important that the proper spec be used to cover the material requested. In cases in which the material is not covered by a Government spec, the ASTM (American Society for Testing Materials) spec or some other approved commercial spec may be used. It is EXTREMELY IMPORTANT in using specifications to cite all amendments, including the latest changes.

As a rule, the specs are provided for each project by the A/E (ARCHITECT-ENGINEERS). These are the OFFICIAL guidelines approved by the chief engineer or his representative for use during construction. These requirements should NOT be deviated from without prior approval from proper authority. This approval is usually obtained by means of a change order. When there is disagreement between the specifications and drawings, the specifications should normally be followed; however, check with higher authority in each case.

IV. BUILDER'S MATHEMATICS

The Builder has many occasions for the employment of the processes of ordinary arithmetic, and he must be thoroughly familiar with the methods of determining the areas and volumes of the various plane and solid geometrical figures. Only a few practical applications and a few practical suggestions, will be given here.

RATIO AND PROPORTION

There are a great many practical applications of ratio and proportion in the construction field. A few examples are as follows:

Some dimensions on construction drawings (such as, for example, distances from base lines and elevations of surfaces) are given in ENGINEER'S instead of CARPENTER's measure. Engineer's measure is measure in feet and decimal parts of a foot, or in inches and decimal parts of an inch, such as 100.15 ft or 11.14 in. Carpenter's measure is measure in yards, feet, inches, and even-denominator fractions of an inch, such as 1/2 in., 1/4 in., 1/16 in., 1/32 in., and 1/64 in.

You must know how to convert an engineer's measure given on a construction drawing to a carpenter's measure. Besides this, it will often happen that calculations you make yourself may produce a result in feet and decimal parts of a foot, which result you will have to convert to carpenter's measure. To convert engineer's to carpenter's measure you can use ratio and proportion as follows:

Let's say that you want to convert 100.14 ft to feet and inches to the nearest 1/16 in. The 100 you don't need to convert, since it is already in feet. What you need to do, first, is to find out how many twelfths of a foot (that is, how many inches) there are in 14/100 ft. Set this up as a proportional equation as follows: x:12::14:100.

You know that in a proportional equation the product of the means equals the product of the extremes. Consequently, $100x = (12 \times 14)$, or 168. Then $x = 168/100$, or 1.68 in. Next question is, how many 16ths of an in. are there in 68/100 in.? Set this up, too, as a proportional equation, thus: x:16::68:100. Then $100x = 1088$, and $x = 10\ 88/100$ sixteenths. Since 88/100 of a sixteenth is more than one-half of a sixteenth, you ROUND OFF by calling it 11/16. In 100.14 ft, then, there are 100 ft 1 11/16 in. For example:

A. $\underbrace{\text{means}}_{\text{Extremes}}$
$$x:12::14:100$$

Product of extremes = product of means:

$$100\,x = 168$$
$$x = 1.68 \text{ IN.}$$

B. $x:16::68:100$

$$100\,x = 1088$$
$$x = 10.88$$
$$x = 10\,\frac{88}{100}\text{ sixteenths}$$

Rounded off to 11/16

Another way to convert engineer's measurements to carpenter's measurements is to multiply the decimal portion of a foot by 12 to get inches; multiply the decimal by 16 to get the fraction of an inch.

There are many other practical applications of ratio and proportion in the construction field. Suppose, for example, that a table tells you that, for the size and type of brick wall you happen to be laying, 12,321 bricks and 195 cu ft of mortar are required per every 1000 sq ft of wall. How many bricks and how much mortar will be needed for 750 sq ft of the same wall? You simply set up equations as follows; for example:

Brick: $x:750::12,321:1000$
Mortar: $x:750::195:1000$

Brick: $\dfrac{X}{750} = \dfrac{12,321}{1000}$ Cross multiply

$$1000\,X = 9,240,750 \quad \text{Divide}$$
$$X = 9,240.75 = 9241 \text{ Brick.}$$

Mortar: $\dfrac{X}{750} = \dfrac{195}{1000}$ Cross multiply

$$1000\,X = 146,250 \quad \text{Divide}$$
$$X = 146.25 = 146\,1/4 \text{ cu ft}$$

Suppose, for another example, that the ingredient proportions by volume for the type of concrete you are making are 1 cu ft cement to 1.7 cu ft sand to 2.8 cu ft coarse aggregate. Suppose you know as well, by reference to a table, that ingredients combined in the amounts indicated will produce 4.07 cu ft of concrete. How much of each ingredient will be required to make a cu yd of concrete?

Remember here, first, that there are not 9, but 27 (3 ft x 3 ft x 3 ft) cu ft in a cu yd. Your proportional equations will be as follows:

Cement: $x:27::1:4.07$

Sand: $x:27::1.7:4.07$

Coarse aggregate: $x:27::2.8:4.07$

Cement: $x:27::1:4.07$

$$\frac{x}{27} = \frac{1}{4.07}$$
$$4.07\,x = 27$$
$$x = 6.63 \text{ cu ft Cement}$$

Sand: $x:27::1.7:4.07$

$$\frac{x}{27} = \frac{1.7}{4.07}$$
$$4.07\,x = 45.9$$
$$x = 11.28 \text{ cu ft Sand}$$

Coarse aggregate: $x:27::2.8:407$

$$\frac{x}{27} = \frac{2.8}{4.07}$$
$$4.07\,x = 75.6$$
$$x = 18.57 \text{ cu ft Coarse aggregate}$$

ARITHMETICAL OPERATIONS

The formulas for finding the area and volume of geometric figures are expressed in algebraic equations which are called formulas. A few of the more important formulas and their mathematical solutions will be discussed in this section.

To get an area, you multiply 2 linear measures together, and to get a volume you multiply 3 linear measures together. The linear measures you multiply together must all be expressed in the SAME UNITS; you cannot, for example, multiply a length in feet by a width in inches to get a result in square feet or in square inches.

Dimensions of a feature on a construction drawing are not always given in the same units. For a concrete wall, for example, the length and height are usually given in feet and the thickness in inches. Furthermore, you may want to get a result in units which are different from any shown on the drawing. Concrete volume, for example, is usually expressed in cubic yards, while the dimensions of concrete work are given on the drawings in feet and inches.

You can save yourself a good many steps in calculating by using fractions to convert the original dimension units into the desired end-result units. Take 1 in., for example. To express 1 in. in feet, you simply put it over 12, thus: 1/12 ft. To express 1 in. in yards, you simply put it over 36, thus: 1/36 yd. In the same manner, to express 1 ft in yards you simply put it over 3, thus 1/3 yd.

Suppose now that you want to calculate the number of cu yd of concrete in a wall 32 ft long by 14 ft high by 8 in. thick. You can express all these in yards and set up your problem thus:

$$\frac{32}{3} \times \frac{14}{3} \times \frac{8}{36}$$

Next you can cancel out, thus:

$$\frac{\overset{16}{\cancel{32}}}{3} \times \frac{\cancel{14}}{3} \times \frac{8}{\underset{9}{\cancel{\underset{18}{\cancel{36}}}}} = \frac{896}{81}$$

Dividing 896 by 81, you get 11.06 cu yds of concrete in the wall.

The right triangle is a triangle which contains one right (90°) angle. The following letters will denote the parts of the triangle indicated in figure 2-13—a = altitude, b = base, c = hypotenuse.

In solving a right triangle, the length of any side may be found if the lengths of the other two sides are given. The combinations of 3-4-5 (lengths of sides) or any multiple of these combinations will come out to a whole number. The following examples show the formula for finding

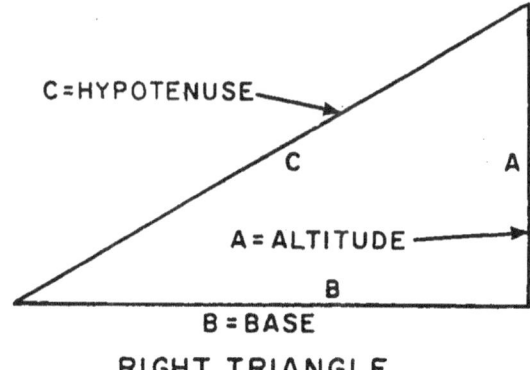

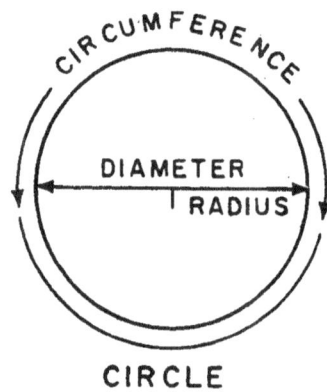

Figure 13.—Right triangle and circle.

each side. Each of these formulas is derived from the master formula $c^2 = a^2 + b^2$.

(1) Find c when a = 3, and b = 4.
$$c = \sqrt{a^2 + b^2} = \sqrt{3^2 + 4^2} = \sqrt{9 + 16} = \sqrt{25} = 5$$

(2) Find a when b = 8, and c = 10.
$$a = \sqrt{c^2 - b^2} = \sqrt{10^2 - 8^2} = \sqrt{100 - 64} = \sqrt{36} = 6$$

(3) Find b when a = 9, and c = 15.
$$b = \sqrt{c^2 - a^2} = \sqrt{15^2 - 9^2} = \sqrt{225 - 81} = \sqrt{144} = 12.$$

There are tables from which the square roots of numbers may be found; otherwise, they may be found arithmetically as explained later in this chapter.

Areas And Volumes Of
Geometric Figures

This section on areas and volumes of geometric figures will be limited to the most commonly used geometric figures. Reference books, such as Mathematics, Vol. 1, are available for additional information if needed. Areas are expressed in square units and volumes in cubic units.

1. A circle is a plane figure bounded by a curved line every point of which is the same distance from the center.
    a. The curved line is called the circumference.
    b. A straight line drawn from the center to any point on the circumference is called a radius. (r = 1/2 the diameter.)
    c. A straight line drawn from one point of the circumference through the center and terminating on the opposite point of the circumference is called a diameter. (d = 2 times the radius.) See figure 2-13.
    d. The area of a circle is found by the following formulas: $A = \pi r^2$ or $A = .7854 d^2$. (π is pronounced pie = 3.1416 or 3 1/7, .7854 is 1/4 of π.) Example: Find the area of a circle whose radius is 7". $A = \pi r^2 = 3\ 1/7 \times 7^2 = 22/7 \times 49 = 154$ sq in. If you use the second formula you obtain the same results.
    e. The circumference of a circle is found by multiplying π times the diameter or 2 times π times the radius. Example: Find the circumference of a circle whose diameter is 56 inches. $C = \pi d = 3.1415 \times 56 = 175.9296$ inches.

2. The area of a right triangle is equal to one-half the product of the base by the altitude. (Area = 1/2 base x altitude.) Example: Find the area of a triangle whose base is 16" and altitude 6". Solution:

$$A = 1/2\ bh = 1/2 \times 16 \times 6 = 48 \text{ sq in.}$$

3. The volume of a cylinder is found by multiplying the area of the base times the height. ($V = 3.1416 \times r^2 \times h$). Example: Find the volume of a cylinder which has a radius of 8 in. and a height of 4 ft. Solution:

$$8 \text{ in} = \frac{2}{3} \text{ ft and } \left(\frac{2}{3}\right)2 = \frac{4}{9} \text{ sq ft.}$$

$$V = 3.1416 \times \frac{4}{9} \times 4 = \frac{50.2656}{9} = 5.59 \text{ cu ft.}$$

4. The volume of a rectangular solid equals the length x width x height. (V = lwh.) Example: Find the volume of a rectangular solid which has a length of 6 ft, a width of 3 ft, and a height of 2 ft. Solution:

$$V = lwh = 6 \times 3 \times 2 = 36 \text{ cu ft.}$$

5. The volume of a cone may be found by multiplying one-third times the area of the base times the height.

$$\left(V = \frac{1}{3} \pi r^2 h\right)$$

Example: Find the volume of a cone when the radius of its base is 2 ft and its height is 9 ft. Solution:

$$\pi = 3.1416, r = 2, 2^2 = 4$$

$$V = \frac{1}{3} r^2 h = \frac{1}{3} \times 3.1416 \times 4 \times 9 = 37.70 \text{ cu ft.}$$

Powers And Roots

1. Powers—When we multiply several numbers together, as $2 \times 3 \times 4 = 24$, the numbers 2, 3, and 4 are factors and 24 the product. The operation of raising a number to a power is a special case of multiplication in which the factors are all equal. The power of a number is the number of times the number itself is to be taken as a factor. Example: 2^4 is 16. The second power is called the square of the number, as 3^2. The third power of a number is called the cube of the number, as 5^3. The exponent of a number is a number placed to the right and above a base to show how many times the base is used as a factor. Example:

$$4^3 \leftarrow \text{exponent} = \\ \leftarrow \text{base}$$

$$4 \times 4 \times 4 = 64.$$

2. Roots—To indicate a root, use the sign $\sqrt{\ }$, which is called the radical sign. A small figure, called the index of the root, is placed in the opening of the sign to show which root is to be taken. The square root of a number is one of the two equal factors into which a number is

divided. Example: $\sqrt{81} = \sqrt{9 \times 9} = 9$. The cube root is one of the three equal factors into which a number is divided. Example: $\sqrt[3]{125} = \sqrt[3]{5 \times 5 \times 5} = 5$.

Square Root

1. The square root of any number is that number which, when multiplied by itself, will produce the first number. For example; the square root of 121 is 11 because 11 times 11 equals 121.

2. How to extract the square root arithmetically:

```
                      95.
     √9025       √90'25.
                   : -81
                   ─────
         180  :   925
          +5  :  -925
         ───     ─────
         185  :   000
```

a. Begin at the decimal point and divide the given number into groups of 2 digits each (as far as possible), going from right to left and/or left to right.

b. Find the greatest number (9) whose square is contained in the first or left hand group (90). Square this number (9) and place it under the first pair of digits (90), then subtract.

c. Bring down the next pair of digits (25) and add it to the remainder (9).

d. Multiply the first digit in the root by 20 and use it as a trial divisor (180). This trial divisor (180) will go into the new dividend (925) five times. This number, 5 (second digit in the root), is added back to the trial divisor, obtaining the true divisor (185).

e. The true divisor (185) is multiplied by the second digit (5) and placed under the remainder (925). Subtract and the problem is solved.

f. If there is still a remainder and you want to carry the problem further, add zeros (in pairs) and continue the above process.

Coverage Calculations

You will frequently have occasion to estimate the number of linear feet of boards of a given size, or the number of tiles, asbestos shingles, and the like, required to cover a given area. Let's take the matter of linear feet of boards first.

What you do here is calculate, first, the number of linear feet of board required to cover 1 sq ft. For boards laid edge-to-edge, you base your calculations on the total width of a board. For boards which will lap each other, you base your calculations on the width laid TO THE WEATHER, meaning the total width minus the width of the lap.

Since there are 144 sq in. in a sq ft, linear footage to cover a given area can be calculated as follows. Suppose your boards are to be laid 8 in. to the weather. If you divide 8 in. into 144 sq in., the result (which is 18 in., or 1.5 ft) will be the linear footage required to cover a sq ft. If you have, say, 100 sq ft to cover, the linear footage required will be 100 x 1.5, or 150 ft.

To estimate the number of tiles, asbestos shingles, and the like required to cover a given area, you first calculate the number of units required to cover a sq ft. Suppose, for example, you are dealing with 9 in. x 9 in. asphalt tiles. The area of one of these is 9 in. x 9 in. or 81 sq in. In a sq ft there are 144 sq in. If it takes 1 to cover 81 sq in., how many will it take to cover 144 sq in.? Just set up a proportional equation, as follows.

$$1:81::x:144$$

When you work this out, you will find that it takes 1.77 tiles to cover a sq ft. To find the number of tiles required to cover 100 sq ft, simply multiply by 100. How do you multiply anything by 100? Just move the decimal point 2 places to the right. Consequently, it takes 177 9 x 9 asphalt tiles to cover 100 sq ft of area.

Board Measure

BOARD MEASURE is a method of measuring lumber in which the basic unit is an abstract volume 1 ft long by 1 ft wide by 1 in. thick. This abstract volume or unit is called a BOARD FOOT.

There are several formulas for calculating the number of board feet in a piece of given dimensions. Since lumber dimensions are most frequently indicated by width and thickness in inches and length in feet, the following formula is probably the most practical.

$$\frac{\text{Thickness in in.} \times \text{width in in.} \times \text{length in ft}}{12}$$

= board feet

Suppose you are calculating the number of board feet in a 14-ft length of 2 x 4. Applying the formula, you get:

$$\frac{\overset{1}{\cancel{2}} \times \overset{2}{\cancel{4}} \times 14}{\underset{3}{\cancel{\underset{\cancel{6}}{\cancel{12}}}}} = \frac{28}{3} = 9\ 1/3 \text{ bd ft}$$

The chief practical use of board measure is in cost calculations, since lumber is bought and sold by the board foot. Any lumber less than 1 in. thick is presumed to be 1 in. thick for board measure purposes. Board measure is calculated on the basis of the NOMINAL, not the ACTUAL, dimensions of lumber.

The actual size of a piece of dimension lumber (such as a 2 x 4, for example) is usually less than the nominal size.

GLOSSARY OF HOUSING TERMS

TABLE OF CONTENTS

	Page
Airway ... Beam	1
Bearing Partition ... Butt Joint	2
Cabinet ... Coped Joint	3
Corner Bead ... Doorjamb, Interior	4
Dormer ... Flat Paint	5
Flue ... Gable	6
Gloss (Paint or Enamel) ... Insulation Board, Rigid	7
Insulation, Thermal ... Lintel	8
Lookout ... Millwork	9
Miter Joint ... Preservative	10
Primer ... Riser	11
Roll Roofing ... Shingles	12
Shingles, Siding ... Square	13
Stain, Shingle ... Termites	14
Termite Shield ... Varnish	15
Vent ... Weatherstrip	16

Glossary of Housing Terms

A

AIRWAY
A space between roof insulation and roof boards for movement of air.

APRON
The flat member of the inside trim of a window placed against the wall immediately beneath the stool.

ASPHALT
Most native asphalt is a residue from evaporated petroleum. It is insoluble in water but soluble in gasoline and melts when heated. Used widely in building for such items as waterproof roof coverings of many types, exterior wall coverings, and flooring tile.

ATTIC VENTILATORS
In houses, screened openings provided to ventilate an attic space. They are located in the soffit area as inlet ventilators and in the gable end or along the ridge as outlet ventilators. They can also consist of powerdriven fans used as an exhaust system. (See also LOUVER.)

B

BACK-FILL
The replacement of excavated earth into a trench or pier excavation around and against a basement foundation.

BALUSTERS
Usually small vertical members in a railing used between a top rail and the stair treads or a bottom rail.

BASE OR BASEBOARD
A board placed around a room against the wall next to the floor to finish properly between floor and plaster or dry wall.

BASE MOLDING
Molding used to trim the upper edge of interior baseboard.

BASE SHOE
Molding used next to the floor on interior baseboard. Sometimes called a carpet strip.

BATTEN
Narrow strips of wood used to cover joints or as decorative vertical members over plywood or wide boards.

BEAM
A structural member transversely supporting a load.

BEARING PARTITION
A partition that supports any vertical load in addition to its own weight.

BEARING WALL
A wall that supports any vertical load in addition to its own weight.

BED MOLDING
A molding in an angle, as between the overhanging cornice, or eaves, of a building and the sidewalks.

BLIND-NAILING
Nailing in such a way that the nailheads are not visible on the face of the work. Usually at the tongue of matched boards.

BLIND STOP
A rectangular molding, usually 3/4 by 1 3/8 inches or more in width used in the assembly of a window frame. Serves as a stop for storm and screen or combination windows and to resist air infiltration.

BOILED LINSEED OIL
Linseed oil in which enough lead, manganese, or cobalt salts have been incorporated to make the oil harden more rapidly when spread in thin coatings.

BOLTS, ANCHOR
Bolts to secure a wooden sill plate to concrete or masonry floor or wall or pier.

BOSTON RIDGE
A method of applying asphalt to wood shingles at the ridge or at the hips of a roof as a finish.

BRACE
An inclined piece of framing lumber applied to wall or floor to stiffen the structure. Often used on walls as temporary bracing until framing has been completed.

BUCK
Often used in reference to rough frame opening members. Door bucks used in reference to metal door frame.

BUILT-UP ROOF
A roofing composed of three to five layers of asphalt felt laminated with coal tar, pitch, or asphalt. The top is finished with crushed slag or gravel. Generally used on flat or low-pitched roofs.

BUTT JOINT
The junction where the ends of two timbers or other members meet in a square-cut joint.

C

CABINET
A shop- or job-built unit for kitchens or other rooms. Often includes combinations of drawers, doors, and the like.

CASING
Molding of various widths and thicknesses used to trim door and window openings at the jambs.

CASEMENT FRAMES AND SASH
Frames of wood or metal enclosing part or all of the sash, which may be opened by means of hinges affixed to the vertical edges.

COLLAR BEAM
Nominal 1- or 2-inch-thick members connecting opposite roof rafters. They serve to stiffen the roof structure.

COMBINATION DOORS OR WINDOWS
Combination doors or windows used over regular openings. They provide winter insulation and summer protection. They often have self-storing or removable glass and screen inserts. This eliminates the need for handling a different unit each season.

CONCRETE, PLAIN
Concrete without reinforcement, or reinforced only for shrinkage or temperature changes.

CONDENSATION
Beads or drops of water, and frequently frost in extremely cold weather, that accumulates on the inside of the exterior covering of a building when warm, moisture-laden air from the interior reaches a point where the temperature no longer permits the air to sustain the moisture it holds. Use of louvers or attic ventilators will reduce moisture condensation in attics. A vapor barrier under the gypsum lath or dry wall on exposed walls will reduce condensation in walls.

CONDUIT, ELECTRICAL
A pipe, usually metal, in which wire is installed.

CONSTRUCTION, DRY-WALL
A type of construction in which the interior wall finish is applied in a dry condition, generally in the form of sheet materials or wood paneling, as contrasted to plaster.

CONSTRUCTION, FRAME
A type of construction in which the structural parts are of wood or depend upon a wood frame for support. In building codes, if masonry veneer is applied to the exterior walls, the classification of this type of construction is usually unchanged.

COPED JOINT
Fitting woodwork to an irregular surface. In moldings, cutting the end of one piece to fit the molded face of the other at an interior angle to replace a miter joint.

CORNER BEAD
A strip of formed sheet metal, sometimes combined with a strip of metal lath, placed on corners before plastering to reinforce them. Also, a strip of wood finish three-quarters round or angular placed over a plastered corner for protection.

CORNER BOARDS
Used as trim for the external corners of a house or other frame structures against which the ends of the siding are finished.

CORNER BRACES
Diagonal braces at the corners of frame structure to stiffen and strengthen the wall.

CORNICE
Overhang of a pitched roof at the eave line, usually consisting of a facia board, a soffit for a closed cornice, and appropriate moldings.

COUNTERFLASHING
A flashing usually used on chimneys at the roofline to cover shingle flashing and to prevent moisture entry.

COVE MOLDING
A molding with a concave face used as trim or to finish interior corners.

CRAWL SPACE
A shallow space below the living quarters of a basementless house sometimes enclosed.

D

d
See PENNY.

DADO
A rectangular groove across the width of a board or plank. In interior decoration, a special type of wall treament.

DECK PAINT
An enamel with a high degree of resistance to mechanical wear, designed for use on such surfaces as porch floors.

DENSITY
The mass of substance in a unit volume. When expressed in the metric system (in g. per cc.), it is numerically equal to the specific gravity of the same substance.

DIMENSION
See LUMBER, DIMENSION.

DOORJAMB, INTERIOR
The surrounding case into and out of which a door closes and opens. It consists of two upright pieces, called side jambs, and a horizontal head jamb.

DORMER
A projection in a sloping roof, the framing of which forms a vertical wall suitable for windows or other openings.

DOWNSPOUT
A pipe, usually metal, for carrying rainwater from roof gutters

DRESSED AND MATCHED (TONGUED AND GROOVED)
Boards or plans machined in such a manner that there is a groove on one edge and a corresponding tongue on the other.

DRIER, PAINT
Usually oil-soluble soaps of such metals as lead, manganese, or cobalt, which, in small proportions, hasten the oxidation and hardening (drying) of the drying oils in paints.

DRIP CAP
A molding placed on the exterior top side of a door or window frame to cause water to drip beyond the outside of the frame.

DRY-WALL
See CONSTRUCTION, DRY WALL.

DUCTS
In a house, usually round or rectangular metal pipes for distributing warm air from the heating plant to rooms, or air from a conditioning device, or as cold air returns. Ducts are also made of asbestos and composition materials.

E

EAVES
The overhang of a roof projecting over the walls.

F

FACE NAILING
To nail perpendicular to the initial surface or to the junction of the pieces joined.

FACIA OR FASCIA
A flat board, band, or face, used sometimes by itself but usually in combination with moldings, often located at the outer face of the cornice.

FLASHING
Sheet metal or other material used in roof and wall construction to protect a building from seepage of water.

FLAT PAINT
An interior paint that contains a high proportion of pigment, and dries to a flat or lusterless finish.

FLUE
The space or passage in a chimney through which smoke, gas, or fumes ascend. Each passage is called a flue, which, together with any others and the surrounding masonry, make up the chimney.

FLUE LINING
Fire clay or terracotta pipe, round or square, usually made in all of the ordinary flue sizes and in 2-foot lengths, used for the inner lining of chimneys with a brick or masonry work around the outside. Flue lining in chimneys runs from about a foot below the flue connection to the top of the chimney.

FLY RAFTER
End rafters of the gable overhang supported by roof sheathing and lookouts.

FOOTING
A masonry section, usually concrete in a rectangular form wider than the bottom of the foundation wall or pier it supports.

FOUNDATION
The supporting portion of a structure below the first floor construction, or below grade, including the footings.

FRAMING, BALLOON
A system of framing a building in which all vertical structural elements of the bearing walls and partitions consist of single pieces extending from the top of the foundation sill plate to the roofplate and to which all floor joists are fastened.

FRAMING, PLATFORM
A system of framing a building in which floor joists of each story rest on the top plates of the story below or on the foundation sill for the first story, and the bearing walls and partitions rest on the subfloor of each story.

FRIEZE
In house construction, a horizontal member connecting the top of the siding with the soffit of the cornice or roof sheathing.

FROSTLINE
The depth of frost penetration in soil. This depth varies in different parts of the country. Footings should be placed below this depth to prevent movement.

FURRING
Strips of wood or metal applied to a wall or other surface to even it and usually to serve as a fastening base for finish material.

G

GABLE
The triangular vertical end of a building formed by the eaves and ridge of a sloped roof.

GLOSS (PAINT OR ENAMEL)
A paint or enamel that contains a relatively low proportion of pigment and dries to a sheen or luster.

GIRDER
A large or principal beam of wood or steel used to support concentrated loads at isolated points along its length.

GRAIN
The direction, size, arrangement, appearance, or quality of the fibers in wood.

GRAIN, EDGE (VERTICAL)
Edge-grain lumber has been sawed parallel to the pith of the log and approximately at right angles to the growth rings, i.e., the rings form an angle of 45 or more with the surface of the piece.

GUSSET
A flat wood, plywood, or similar type member used to provide a connection at the intersection of wood members. Most commonly used at joints of wood trusses. They are fastened by nails, screws, bolts, or adhesives.

GUTTER OR EAVE TROUGH
A shallow channel or conduit of metal or wood set below and along the eaves of a house to catch and carry off rainwater from the roof.

H

HEADER
(a) A beam place perpendicular to joists and to which joists are nailed in framing for chimney, stairway, or other opening.
(b) A wood lintel.

HEARTWOOD
The wood extending from the pith to the sapwood, the cells of which no longer participate in the life processes of the tree.

HIP
The external angle formed by the meeting of two sloping sides of a roof.

HIP ROOF
A roof that rises by inclined planes from all four sides of a building.

I

INSULATION BOARD, RIGID
A structural building board made of wood or cane fiber in and 25/32" thicknesses. It can be obtained in various size sheets, in various densities, and with several treatments.

INSULATION, THERMAL
Any material high in resistance to heat transmission that, when place in the walls, ceiling, or floors of a structure, will reduce the rate of heat flow.

J

JACK RAFTER
A rafter that spans the distance from the wallplate to a hip, or from a valley to a ridge.

JAMB
The side and head lining of a doorway, window, or other opening.

JOINT
The space between the adjacent surfaces of two members or components joined and held together by nails, glue, cement, mortar, or other means.

JOINT CEMENT
A powder that is usually mixed with water and used for joint treatment in gypsum-wallboard finish. Often called "spackle."

JOIST
One of a series of parallel beams, usually 2 inches thick, used to support floor and ceiling loads, and supported in turn by larger beams, girders, or bearing walls.

K

KNOT
In lumber, the portion of a branch or limb of a tree that appears on the edge or face of the piece.

L

LANDING
A platform between flights of stairs or at the termination of a flight of stairs.

LATH
A building material of wood, metal, gypsum, or insulating board that is fastened to the frame of a building to act as a plaster base.

LEDGER STRIP
A strip of lumber nailed along the bottom of the side of a girder on which joists rest.

LIGHT
Space in a window sash for a single pane of glass. Also, a pane of glass.

LINTEL
A horizontal structural member that supports the load over an opening such as a door or window.

LOOKOUT
A short wood bracket or cantilever to support an overhanging portion of a roof or the like, usually concealed from view.

LOUVER
An opening with a series of horizontal slats so arranged as to permit ventilation but to exclude rain, sunlight, or vision. See also ATTIC VENTILATORS.

LUMBER
Lumber is the product of the sawmill and planning mill not further manufactured other than by sawing, resawing, and passing lengthwise through a standard planing machine, cross cutting to length, and matching.

LUMBER, BOARDS
Yard lumber less than 2 inches thick and 2 or more inches wide.

LUMBER, DIMENSION
Yard lumber from 2 inches to, but including, 5 inches thick, and 2 or more inches wide. Includes joists, rafters, studs, plank and small timbers. The actual size dimension of such lumber after shrinking from green dimension and after machining to size or pattern is called the dress size.

LUMBER, MATCHED
Lumber that is dressed and shaped on one edge in a grooved pattern and on the other in a tongued pattern.

LUMBER, SHIPLAP
Lumber that is edge-dressed to make a close rabbeted or lapped joint.

LUMBER, YARD
Lumber of those grades, sizes, and patterns which are generally intended for ordinary construction, such as framework and rough coverage of houses.

M

MASONRY
Stone, brick, concrete, hollow-tile, concrete-block, gypsum-block, or other similar building units or materials or a combination of the same, bonded together with mortar to form a wall, pier, buttress, or similar mass.

MEETING RAILS
Rails sufficiently thicker than a window to fill the opening between the top and bottom sash made by the parting stop in the frame of double-hung windows. They are usually beveled.

MILLWORK
Generally all building materials made of finished wood and manufactured in millwork plants and planing mills are included under the term "millwork." It includes such items as inside and outside doors, window and doorframes, blinds, porchwork, mantels, panelwork, stairways, moldings, and interior trim. It normally does not include flooring, ceiling, or siding.

MITER JOINT
The joint of two pieces at an angle that bisects the joining angle. For example, the miter joint at the side and head casing at a door opening is made at a 45 angle.

MOISTURE CONTENT OF WOOD
Weight of the water contained in the wood, usually expressed as a percentage of the weight of the ovendry wood.

MOLDING
A wood strip having a curved or projecting surface used for decorative purposes.

MORTISE
A slot cut into a board, plank, or timber, usually edgewise, to receive tenon of another board, plank, or timber to form a joint.

N

NATURAL FINISH
A transparent finish which does not seriously alter the original color or grain of the natural wood. Natural finishes are usually provided by sealers, oils, varnishes, water-repellent, preservatives, and other similar materials.

NONLOADBEARING WALL
A wall supporting no load other than its own weight.

NOTCH
A crosswise rabbet at the end of a board.

O

O.C. ON CENTER
The measurement of spacing for studs, rafters, joists, and the like in a building from center of one member to the center of the next.

P

PLYWOOD
A piece of wood made of three or more layers of veneer joined with glue and usually laid with the grain of adjoining plies at right angles. Almost always an odd number of plies are used to provide balanced construction.

PLUMB
Exactly perpendiular; vertical.

PORCH
A roofed area extending beyond the main house. May be open or enclosed and with concrete or wood frame floor system.

PRESERVATIVE
Any substance that, for a reasonable length of time, will prevent the action of wood-destroying fungi, borers of various kinds, and similar destructive life when the wood has been properly coated or impregnated with it.

PRIMER
The first coat of paint in a paint job that consists of two or more coats; also the paint used for such a first coat.

PUTTY
A type of cement usually made of whiting and boiled linseed oil, beaten or kneaded to the consistency of dough, and used in sealing glass in sash, filling small holes and crevices in wood, and for similar purposes.

Q

QUARTER ROUND
A small molding that has the cross-section of a quarter circle.

R

RAFTER
One of a series of structural members of a roof designed to support roof loads. The rafters of a flat roof are sometimes called roof joists.

RAFTER, HIP
A rafter that forms the intersection of an external roof angle.

RAFTER, VALLEY
A rafter that forms the intersection of an internal roof angle. The valley rafter is normally made of doubled 2-inch-thick members.

RAIL
Cross members of panel doors or of a sash. Also the upper and lower members of a balustrade or staircase extending from one vertical support, such as a post, to another.

RAKE
The inclined edge of a gable roof (the trim member is a rake molding).

RIDGE
The horizontal line at the junction of the top edges of two sloping roof surfaces.

RIDGE BOARD
The board placed on edge at the ridge of the roof into which the upper ends of the rafters are fastened.

RISE
In stairs, the vertical height of a step or flight of stairs.

RISER
Each of the vertical boards closing the spaces between the treads of stairways.

ROLL ROOFING
Roofing material, composed of fiber and saturated with asphalt, that is supplied in rolls containing 108 square feet in 36-inch widths. It is generally furnished in weights of 45 to 90 pounds per roll.

ROOF SHEATHING
The boards or sheet material fastened to the roof rafters on which the shingle or other roof covering is laid.

ROUTED
See MORTISED.

RUN
In stairs, the net width of a step or the horizontal distance covered by a flight of stairs.

S

SASH
A single light frame containing one or more lights of glass.

SATURATED FELT
A felt which is impregnated with tar or asphalt.

SCAB
A short piece of wood or plywood fastened to two abutting timbers to splice them together.

SEALER
A finishing material, either clear or pigmented, that is usually applied directly over uncoated wood for the purpose of sealing the surface.

SEMIGLOSS PAINT OR ENAMEL
A paint or enamel made with a slight insufficiency of nonvolatile vehicle so that its coating when dry, has some luster but is not very glossy.

SHAKE
A thick handsplit shingle, resawed to form two shakes; usually edge grained.

SHEATHING
The structural covering, usually wood boards or plywood, used over studs or rafters of a structure. Structural building board is normally used only as wall sheathing.

SHEATHING PAPER
See PAPER, SHEATHING

SHINGLES
Roof covering of asphalt, asbestos, wood, tile, slate, or other material cut to stock lengths, widths, and thicknesses.

SHINGLES, SIDING
Various kinds of shingles, such as wood shingles or shakes and nonwood shingles, that are used over sheathing for exterior sidewall covering of a structure.

SHIPLAP
See LUMBER, SHIPLAP.

SIDING
The finish covering of the outside wall of a frame building, whether made of horizontal weatherboards, vertical boards with battens, shingles, or other material.

SIDING, BEVEL (LAP SIDING)
Wedge-shaped boards used as horizontal siding in a lapped pattern. This siding varies in butt thickness from 1/2 to 3/4" and in widths up to 12 inches. Normally used over some type of sheathing.

SIDING, DROP
Usually 3/4" thick and 6 and 8" in width with tongued-and-grooved or shiplap edges. Often used as siding without sheathing in secondary buildings.

SIDING, PANEL
Large sheets of plywood or hardboard which serve as both sheathing and siding.

SILL
The lowest member of the frame of a structure, resting on the foundation and supporting the floor joists or the uprights of the wall. The member forming the lower side of an opening, as a door sill, window sill, etc.

SOFFIT
Usually the underside covering of an overhanging cornice.

SOIL COVER (GROUND COVER)
A light covering of plastic film, roll roofing, or similar material used over the soil in crawl spaces of buildings to minimize moisture permeation of the area.

SOIL STACK
A general term for the vertical main of a system of soil, waste, or vent piping.

SOLE OR SOLE PLATE
See PLATE.

SPAN
The distance between structural supports such as walls, columns, piers, beams, girders, and trusses.

SQUARE
A unit of measure - 100 square feet - usually applied to roofing material. Sidewall coverings are sometimes packed to cover 100 square feet and are sold on that basis.

STAIN, SHINGLE

A form of oil paint, very thin in consistency, intended for coloring wood with rough surfaces, like shingles, without forming a coating of significant thickness or gloss.

STAIR CARRIAGE

Supporting member for stair treads. Usually a 2-inch plank notched to receive the treads; sometimes termed a "rough horse."

STOOL

A flat molding fitted over the window will between jambs and contacting the bottom rail of the lower sash.

STORM SASH OR STORM WINDOW

An extra window usually placed on the outside of an existing window as additional protection against cold weather.

STORY

That part of a building between any floor and the floor or roof next above.

STRING, STRINGER

A timber or other support for cross members in floors or ceilings. In stairs, the support on which the stair treads rest, also stringboard.

STUD

One of a series of slender wood or metal vertical structural members placed as supporting elements in walls and partitions. (Plural: studs or studding.)

SUBFLOOR

Boards or plywood laid on joists over which a finish floor is to be laid.

T

TAIL BEAM

A relatively short beam or joist supported in a wall on one end and by a header at the other.

TERMITES

Insects that superficially resemble ants in size, general appearance, and habit of living in colonies, hence, frequently called "white ants." Subterranean termites do not establish themselves in buildings by being carried in with lumber, but by entering from ground nests after the building has been constructed. If unmolested they eat out the woodwork, leaving a shell of sound wood to conceal their activities, and damage may proceed so far so to cause collapse of parts of a structure before discovery. There are about 56 species of termites known in the United States; but the two main species, classified from the manner in which they attack wood, subterranean (ground-inhabiting) termites, the most common, and drywood termites, found almost exclusively along the extreme southern border and the Gulf of Mexico in the United States.

TERMITE SHIELD
A shield, usually of noncorrodible metal, placed in or on a foundation wall or other mass of masonry or around pipes to prevent passage of termites.

THRESHOLD
A strip of wood or metal with beveled edges used over the finished floor and the sill of exterior doors.

TOENAILING
To drive a nail at a slant with the initial surface in order to permit it to penetrate into a second member.

TREAD
The horizontal board in a stairway on which the foot is placed.

TRIM
The finish materials in a building, such as moldings, applied around openings (window trims, door trim) or at the floor and ceiling of rooms (baseboard, cornice, picture molding).

TRIMMER
A beam or joist to which a header is nailed in framing for a chimney, stairway, or other opening.

TRUSS
A frame or jointed structure designed to act as a beam of long span, while each member is usually subjected to longitudinal stress only, either tension or compression.

TURPENTINE
A volatile oil used as a thinner in paints, and as a solvent in varnishes. Chemically, it is a mixture of terpenes.

U

UNDERCOAT
A coating applied prior to the finishing or top coats of a paint job. It may be the first of two or the second of three coats. In some usage of the word, it may become synonymous with priming coat.

V

VAPOR BARRIER
Material used to retard the movement of water vapor into walls and prevent condensation in them. Usually considered as having a perm value of less than 1.0. Applied separately over the warm side of exposed walls or as a part of batt or blanket insulation.

VARNISH
A thickened preparation of drying oil or drying oil and resin suitable for spreading on surfaces to form continuous, transparent coatings, or for mixing with pigments to make enamels.

VENT
A pipe or duct which allows flow of air as an inlet or outlet.

VERMICULITE
A mineral closely related to mica, with the faculty of expanding on heating to form lightweight material with insulation quality. Used as bulk insulation and as aggregate in insulating and acoustical plaster and in insulating concrete floors.

W

WATER-REPELLENT PRESERVATIVE
A liquid designed to penetrate into wood and impart water repellency and a moderate preservative protection. It is used for millwork, such as sash and frames, and is usually applied by dipping.

WEATHERSTRIP
Narrow or jamb-width sections of thin metal or other material to prevent infiltration of air and moisture around windows and doors.

www.ingramcontent.com/pod-product-compliance
Lightning Source LLC
Chambersburg PA
CBHW081813300426
44116CB00014B/2345